The Knowledge Translation Toolkit

Thank you for choosing a SAGE product! If you have any comment, observation or feedback, I would like to personally hear from you. Please write to me at contactceo@sagepub.in

—Vivek Mehra, Managing Director and CEO,
SAGE Publications India Pvt Ltd, New Delhi

Bulk Sales

SAGE India offers special discounts for purchase of books in bulk. We also make available special imprints and excerpts from our books on demand.

For orders and enquiries, write to us at

Marketing Department
SAGE Publications India Pvt Ltd
B1/I-1, Mohan Cooperative Industrial Area
Mathura Road, Post Bag 7
New Delhi 110044, India
E-mail us at marketing@sagepub.in

Get to know more about SAGE, be invited to SAGE events, get on our mailing list. Write today to marketing@sagepub.in

This book is also available as an e-book.

The Knowledge Translation Toolkit

Bridging the Know-Do Gap: A Resource for Researchers

Edited by

Gavin Bennett
and
Nasreen Jessani

International Development Research Centre
Ottawa • Cairo • Dakar • Montevideo • Nairobi • New Delhi • Singapore

SAGE www.sagepublications.com
Los Angeles • London • New Delhi • Singapore • Washington DC

Jointly published in 2011 by

SAGE Publications India Pvt Ltd
B1/I-1 Mohan Cooperative Industrial Area
Mathura Road, New Delhi 110 044, India
www.sagepub.in

SAGE Publications Inc
2455 Teller Road
Thousand Oaks, California 91320, USA

SAGE Publications Ltd
1 Oliver's Yard
55 City Road
London EC1Y 1SP, United Kingdom

SAGE Publications Asia-Pacific Pte Ltd
33 Pekin Street
#02-01 Far East Square
Singapore 048763

and

International Development Research Centre
P.O. Box 8500
Ottawa, ON
Canada K1G 3H9
www.idrc.ca
info@idrc.ca
IDRC (e-book) 978-1-55250-508-3

Published by Vivek Mehra for SAGE Publications India Pvt Ltd, typeset in 11/14 Adobe Garamond Pro by Tantla Composition Pvt Ltd, Chandigarh and printed at Chaman Enterprises, New Delhi.

Library of Congress Cataloging-in-Publication Data

Bennett, Gavin.
The knowledge translation toolkit: bridging the know-do gap: a resource for researchers/Gavin Bennett, Nasreen Jessani.
p. cm.
Summary: "The Knowledge Translation Toolkit provides a thorough overview of what knowledge translation (KT) is and how to use it most effectively to bridge the 'know-do' gap between research, policy, practice, and people. It presents the theories, tools, and strategies required to encourage and enable evidence-informed decision-making. This toolkit builds upon extensive research into the principles and skills of KT: its theory and literature, its evolution, strategies, and challenges. The book covers an array of crucial KTenablers—from context mapping to evaluative thinking—supported by practical examples, implementation guides, and references. Drawing from the experience of specialists in relevant disciplines around the world, The Knowledge Translation Toolkit aims to enhance the capacity and motivation of researchers to use KT and to use it well"—Provided by publisher.
Includes bibliographical references and index.
1. Research—Methodology. 2. Knowledge management. 3. Evaluation. 4. Communication in science. 5. Research—Social aspects. I. Jessani, Nasreen. II. Title.
Q180.55.M4B4135 001.4—dc22 2011 2011000949

ISBN: 978-81-321-0585-5 (PB)

The SAGE Team: Rekha Natarajan, Swati Sengupta, Nand Kumar Jha and Deepti Saxena

Contents

SECTION III The Message

SECTION IV The Medium—Print, Multimedia, and Social Media

SECTION V The Toolbox—Examples, Templates, and Guides

List of Tables

List of Figures

List of Boxes

List of Abbreviations

AAR	After Action Reviews
ACTs	Artemisinin-based Combination Therapies
AI	Appreciative Inquiry
AIDS	Acquired Immune Deficiency Syndrome
ARV	Antiretroviral Drug
CD-ROM	Compact Disc, Read-Only-Memory
CHSRF	Canadian Health Services Research Foundation
CMO	Chief Medical Officer
CoP	Community of Practice
DFID	Department for International Development
DVD	Digital Video Disc
ET	Evaluative Thinking
EVIPNet	Evidence Informed Policy Network
FCTC	Framework Convention on Tobacco Control
FOAF	Friend-of-a-Friend
HE	Horizontal Evaluation
HIV	Human Immunodeficiency Virus
HRCS	Health Research Capacity Strengthening
IDRC	International Research Development Center
IGM	Inform, Guide, and Motivate
IMF	International Monetary Fund
ITNs	Insecticide-treated Nets
JAMA	Journal of the American Medical Association
KM	Knowledge Management

KT	Knowledge Translation
KTP	Knowledge Translation Platform
LFA	Logical Framework Approach
LMIC	Low and Middle Income Countries
M&E	Monitoring and Evaluation
MB	Megabyte
MC	Male Circumcision
MIC	Ministry of Information and Communications
MSC	Most Significant Change
NGO	Non-governmental Organization
NOELs	Nod-off Episodes per Lecture
NPD	National Policy Dialogue
NPI-Africa	Nairobi Peace Initiative-Africa
NRT	Nutritional Research Team
ODI	Overseas Development Institute
OECD	Organization for Economic Cooperation and Development
OM	Outcome Mapping
PS	Permanent Secretary
PV	Participatory Video
REACH	Regional East African Community Health
RM	Research Matters
SADC	Smiss Agency for Development and Cooperation
SMART	Specific, Measurable, Achievable, Realistic, Time-bound
TEHIP	Tanzania Essential Health Interventions Project
THRI	Thailand Health Research Institute
UN	United Nations
UNAIDS	The Joint United Nations Programme on HIV/AIDS
UNICEF	United Nations International Children's Emergency Fund
UQAM	Université du Québec à Montréal
VASS	Vietnam Academy of Social Sciences

VERN	Vietnam Economic Research Network
WHO	World Health Organization
WWF	World Wildlife Fund
ZAMFOHR	Zambia Forum for Health Research
ZHRC	Zonal Health Resource Centers

Foreword

Despite significant increases in investment and some notable successes, infectious diseases continue to exert a heavy toll on many countries, particularly in sub-Saharan Africa. Also, the burden of chronic and non-communicable diseases is rising, including the poorest countries of Africa, Asia, Latin America, and the Caribbean. Climate change and emerging infectious diseases are increasingly recognized as a global threat. Many countries are far from being on track to achieve the Millennium Development Goals. Simultaneously, the world is facing its most serious financial crisis in many decades.

When resources are scarce, it is particularly important to use them wisely: the health problems causing suffering and millions of premature deaths every year cannot afford wasted time or money. Policies and interventions must reflect the best possible current knowledge. New research—in both implementation and basic social and natural science—is needed. In addition, there is a huge "know-do gap" that needs closing, by applying to policy and practice what is already known. Both researchers and decision-makers can do better in helping to make sure that this happens. The Research Matters' *Knowledge Translation Toolkit* is a practical contribution to this effort.

Over several years, the Governance, Equity, and Health (GEH) program at Canada's International Development Research Centre (IDRC) and the Swiss Agency for Development and Cooperation (SDC) have been working together to link research and evidence more closely with policy and practice in health development. GEH supports innovative ideas and practice that encourage political and governance challenges, equity concerns, and health policy and systems questions to be addressed together. It supports research that seeks to better understand and redress health inequities facing people in low and middle-income countries (LMICs). Linking research with action in an ongoing dialogue is crucial to this endeavour. The Research Matters (RM) team, working with researchers and decision-makers to foster the action-oriented dialogue we call "Knowledge Translation", has yielded a wealth of ideas and experience. In this toolkit, the RM team shares some of these concepts and practical tips with you, inviting you to try them, share them, comment, and help achieve the goals of health and social equity.

This Toolkit is offered primarily to researchers on issues related to LMICs and takes its inspirations from the field of health systems research. However, it will be of interest to many other audiences as well. You will see within it stories of effective KT by researchers in all areas of development supported by IDRC. It is not a book of recipes—it aims to open new understanding, provoke debate, and build skills in asking and beginning to answer the many new questions that complex development challenges force us to address. Readers will not become experts in KT, nor is success guaranteed. However, readers will come away with new ideas and methods to get started right now, along with thoughts about whom else to include, how to learn more, and renewed commitment and confidence to try something challenging, new, and important.

The Research Matters KT Toolkit is a unique contribution for researchers and to the KT field more broadly. It is shaped by direct, on-the-ground work and ongoing dialogue with researchers and reflects their creativity, courage, and commitment—many of whom work under difficult and risky conditions. We hope this contribution will make them stronger and more effective champions of social equity by truly "making research matter."

Dr Christina Zarowsky
Director, HIV and AIDS Research Centre,
University of the Western Cape
Program Leader for IDRC's Governance,
Equity and Health Program (2003–07)

Acknowledgements

Research Matters (RM), a collaboration of the International Development Research Centre (IDRC) and Swiss Agency for Development and Cooperation (SDC), wishes to express its sincere thanks to all those who contributed towards the success of this book. First and foremost we wish to thank all contributors for their valuable technical input and their collegiality during the development of this guide. The current version of the Knowledge Translation Toolkit has benefited from continuous and dedicated input from Sandy Campbell, the original champion of this publication. IDRC/SDC Research Matters is particularly indebted to him. Significant contributors to this current version include Sandy Campbell, Anne-Marie Schryer-Roy, Nasreen Jessani, Andrew Hubbertz, Gavin Bennett and Anna Seifried.

Technical inputs on earlier drafts of select chapters came from: Christina Zarowsky, Kevin Kelpin, Amy Etherington, Sarah Earl, John Lavis, Graham Reid, Rosemary Kennedy, Alastair Ager, Dominique Rychen, Adrian Gnagi, Claudia Kessler, Harriet Nabudere, Ritz Kakuma, Joel Lehmann, TJ Ngulube, and many other members and partners of IDRC's Research for Health Equity program. Several chapters were presented, distributed, and discussed at various workshops in 2007, 2008, 2009, and 2010 in Kenya, Tanzania, Uganda, Cameroon, Ethiopia, Zambia, USA, Lebanon, and Canada.

All reasonable precautions have been taken to verify the information contained in this publication, and the opinions of the contributors are written and published in good faith. However, the published material is distributed without warranty of any kind, either expressed or implied. Responsibility for the interpretation and use of the material lies with the reader.

Introduction

The Difference Between a Paper and a Purpose

The primary audience for this book is researchers in systems and policy research, seeking to strengthen their capacity at the individual and at the organizational level, from particular research projects to larger issues of organizational development. This book emphasizes that successful publication on the part of researchers is not "job finished." It is "job started." And then sets out what more must be done—and how—to drive the research findings to wherever they need to be to provide real and maximum benefit to policy, to practice, to people.

In the context of evidence-to-policy, there can be only four reasons for the "know-do" gap. People with the ability and authority to use good information to design their action either:

1. **Don't know** – that the information exists, or what action to take, or
2. **Don't understand** – the information, what it means, why it is important, or
3. **Don't care** – see the information as irrelevant, not beneficial to their agenda, or
4. **Don't agree** – think the information is misguided or false.

The tools in this book will help researchers ensure that their good science reaches more people, is more clearly understood, and is more likely to lead to positive action. In sum, that their work becomes more useful, and therefore more valuable.

That demands better "communication"—the transmission of information that is relevant and in a form that is meaningful to all those who might benefit from it. It therefore informs, guides, and motivates. Only when that is achieved does latent information become active knowledge. Knowledge Translation (KT) is the process which delivers that change.

KT helps ensure the answers leave the target in no doubt that:

I must stop and look at this – it's interesting

This is for my agenda – it's relevant

I understand – it's clear and credible

I must do something about it – it's compelling

This toolkit therefore comprises:

The Concept (Section I) – closing the know-do gap: turning knowledge into action.

The Audience (Section II) – identifying who has the power to take action (policy/practice).

The Message (Section III) – packaging the knowledge appropriately for that audience.

The Medium (Section IV) – delivering the message, closing the gap, triggering the action.

The Tools (Section V) – a few more thoughts about the methods of doing all those things.

This is Knowledge Translation. It makes research matter.

STORIES

Demonstrative examples of successful, innovative, and daring KT techniques by research teams all over the world are sprinkled throughout the book. Here are snippets of those stories.

Kenya—From Tobacco to Bamboo

A research project on "alternative livelihoods" for former tobacco growers is so relevant to policy that instead of researchers promoting their idea to government, the government is running TV documentaries to promote the research to the public!

South Africa—Radio as Part of a Multipronged Approach

Strong KT through publications, the web, conferences, radio spots, and a seminar has changed the image of a research team working on health equity from "radical" to "key advisors." The team itself—EQUINET—is a collaboration between professionals, researchers, civil society organizations, and policy makers.

Kenya and Malawi—Evaluative Thinking

The "Health Research Capacity Strengthening" initiatives in Kenya and Malawi are harnessing the dynamism of ET not only to change research capacity, but also to design themselves. This KT tool is working equally on the "know" and the "do" sides.

Beirut—The Power of a Pamphlet

Effective KT often requires numerous tools in a complex communication programme, but sometimes just the right one tool, in the right place, at the right time, can move mountains. Research on the hazards of the narghile (smoking) pipe achieved global impact with a single pamphlet at a WHO conference.

Brazil—Mercury Research

Research on the source of mercury contamination in the Amazon had two unexpected and major outcomes. It successfully traced a source of mercury contamination; but then used its findings and KT processes, in the wider context, to do much more—it helped prevent illness, save lives, improve diets, address environmental damage, and tapped into the influential role of women in these communities to build social networks that are bringing profound long-term benefits to the way villagers communicate and partner with the local authorities.

Malawi—Seek and Solve at the Same Time

A research team assessing the linkage between soil fertility, nutrition, and health among poor rural communities used KT and a participatory ecosystems approach to involve farmers and communities so closely with their study that the means of identifying the problem became the means of solving it—simultaneously!

South Africa—Homes Versus Housing

Slum dwellers who moved to new housing estates were neither happier nor healthier. Research identified the disconnect between city planners, managers, and communities; KT brought them together, and not only did the dialogue bring an investment shift toward improving rather than replacing low-quality homes, but also spawned networks and institutional collaborations that are now addressing a wide range of other urban issues.

Benin—The Power of One Meeting

A single and simple symposium in Benin—about mothers and babies—was such a powerful demonstration of collaboration between researchers, civil society, and decision-makers that it is influencing health policy-making throughout West Africa.

Jamaica—Tobacco Myths

In a fine example of "pull" research, scientists identified "fear of revenue loss" as a major obstacle to policy on tobacco control through pricing. By study, they found the tax level that would deter smokers and increase revenue. Price-driven Control policies were immediately implemented.

Tanzania—Affecting Policy and Practice

Attempts at national scale-up of successful health interventions are few. The TEHIP "Legacy" initiative describes the pivotal role of Zonal Health Resource Centers in relieving Tanzania of its staggering burden of disease and realizing the county's Millennium Development Goal for health by 2015. PowerPoint presentations and media articles led to an upsurge in interest and change.

Guatemala—Second-Hand Smoke

Research-backed efforts to ban smoking in restaurants and bars got nowhere for many years until the research team launched a combined mass-media and policy brief campaign. A few months later, the ban was legislated and enforced.

Senegal—Medical Services

Petty corruption bedevilled the health system for many years, until Transparency International used focus groups, interviews, and observation to get the facts, and then hit the public psyche with research findings through a report, a national forum, a media campaign, and the political bombshell of cartoons. Reform has begun.

South Africa—Water

Privatization of essential services was already a major policy thrust with national momentum, so when researchers identified a health downside they had to sell their message against a strong countercurrent. They had to use every KT tool in the book to succeed; but succeed they did and are now policy advisors to the process!

Global KT—Women's Rights

KT techniques and values are not only engaged by specific research projects; Canada's IDRC have used them to test colloquial evidence and simultaneously formed networks, spread concepts, developed tools, and promoted positive global impacts—for example, on women's rights.

Senegal—From Waste Sorters to Policy Stokers

The power of stakeholder consultations and platforms was demonstrated by a municipality in Dakar, with such success that it gave a "World Urban Forum" voice to waste-pickers who were both living off and suffering from the offerings of a massive dumpsite.

Jakarta—Participatory Planning

A slum community in Jakarta that was forcibly evicted as an urban hazard, is coming back with plans for a "dream development" of the space—thanks to a participatory planning exercises and partnerships with the other stakeholders.

Vietnam—Economic Restructuring

By engaging policy-makers from the outset, a research team in Vietnam has had its work guided by policy dilemmas and questions, and has been appointed as an official advisor to government. The relationship is facilitated by a website, policy and economic briefs, and a policy workshop.

Kenya—The Truth Behind Truth Commissions

By using KT methods to share insights on Truth and Reconciliation Commissions, work in one city is informing a whole continent and making a major contribution to global peace-building.

Zambia—Equity Gauge

A health equity project using theatre and video to engage communities, to get them to think through and express their key issues, then used a competition between dramatic performances to deliver a powerful message direct from the grassroots to a national audience that included senior policy-makers. The effects were as dramatic as the show!

Bolivia—Waste Management

By informing the public and policy-makers about their anti-pollution and pro-recycling strategies, municipal authorities achieved maximum compliance when they asked residents to assist with solid waste management. Multiple forms of involvement and knowledge sharing from researchers earned immense cooperation from the community and decision-makers alike.

SECTION

I

The Concept

Knowledge Translation and Management

Knowledge is like fine wine. The researcher brews it, the scientific paper bottles it, the peer review tastes it, the journal sticks a label on it, and archive systems store it carefully in a cellar. Splendid! Just one small problem: wine is only useful when somebody drinks it. Wine in a bottle does not quench thirst. Knowledge Translation (KT) opens the bottle, pours the wine into a glass, and serves it.

The researcher might reasonably leave that part of the work to a broker, but must surely never leave it to pure chance. As a perspective on what those chances are, there are 24,000 journals and several million scientific papers in the system. What are the odds of the right person finding yours…even by search, less still by luck?

It follows that the effective researcher must ensure that knowledge goes beyond publication. The researcher must also know *what, how, where, when*, and to *who* else the information should be communicated. Section I shows what must be done to ensure that evidence reaches policy—that between knowing and doing there is no gap. That way, and only that way, can research claim to do more than produce a paper. It can achieve a purpose.

The greatest wisdom or discovery in the world will go unheeded if it is unheard. For research to matter, it must be heard—and understood—by people in a position to bring about change. The way to make it heard, understood, and acted on, is effective KT.

1

Knowledge Translation

An Introduction

Knowledge Translation (KT) is the meeting ground between two fundamentally different processes: research and action. It knits them with communicative relationships. KT relies upon partnerships, collaborations, and personal contact between researchers and research-users. In connecting the purity of science with the pragmatism of policy, the intangibles of trust, rapport, and even friendship can be more potent than logic and more compelling than evidence.

Though the concept of KT has existed for decades, the Mexico City Ministerial Summit of Health Ministers in 2004 put the first real focus on the world's "know-do gap."[1] In an age where we know much, why are we applying so little of it?

The Summit made this problem a priority and called for increased involvement of the demand side in the research process, emphasizing knowledge brokering to "involve potential users of research in setting research priorities", and insisting on "evidence-based" health policy. The declaration was made with enthusiasm but without guidance on how, in practice, to connect all these pivotal actors.

Exploration of this question has led to three core KT principles:

1. **Knowledge:** KT efforts at any level depend upon a robust, accessible, and contextualized knowledge base.
2. **Dialogue:** The relationships at the heart of KT can only be sustained through regular dialogue and exchange.
3. **Capacity:** Researchers, decision-makers, and other research-users require a strengthened skill-base to create and respond to KT opportunities.

THE FOUR MODELS OF KT

Lavis et al. offer "push, pull, exchange, and integrated"[2] models of KT.

In the push model, the researcher's knowledge is the principal catalyst for change, through attractively-packaged tools (e.g., syntheses, policy briefs, videos) that make findings more accessible. These techniques recognize policy contexts and pressures, but decision-makers are receivers of information. "Push" efforts provide decision-makers with information on a particular topic.

The pull model makes research-users the main driver of action. Decision-makers ask for the information, evidence, and research-appraisal skills they think they need.

The (linkage and) exchange model rests on partnerships, with researchers and research-users collaborating for mutual benefit. Such partnerships may be short- or long-term, may occur at any point in the research or policy process, and may include priority-setting exercises, collaborative research projects, and create knowledge systems (e.g., databases). Knowledge brokers can play a crucial role in establishing these strategies.

The integrated model adopts the emerging Knowledge Translation Platform (KTP), a national- or regional-level institution which fosters linkage and exchange across a (health) system. KTP is the institutional equivalent of a knowledge broker, working to connect the needs of the policy process with the tools of research, and to

FIGURE 1.1
Models of Knowledge Translation

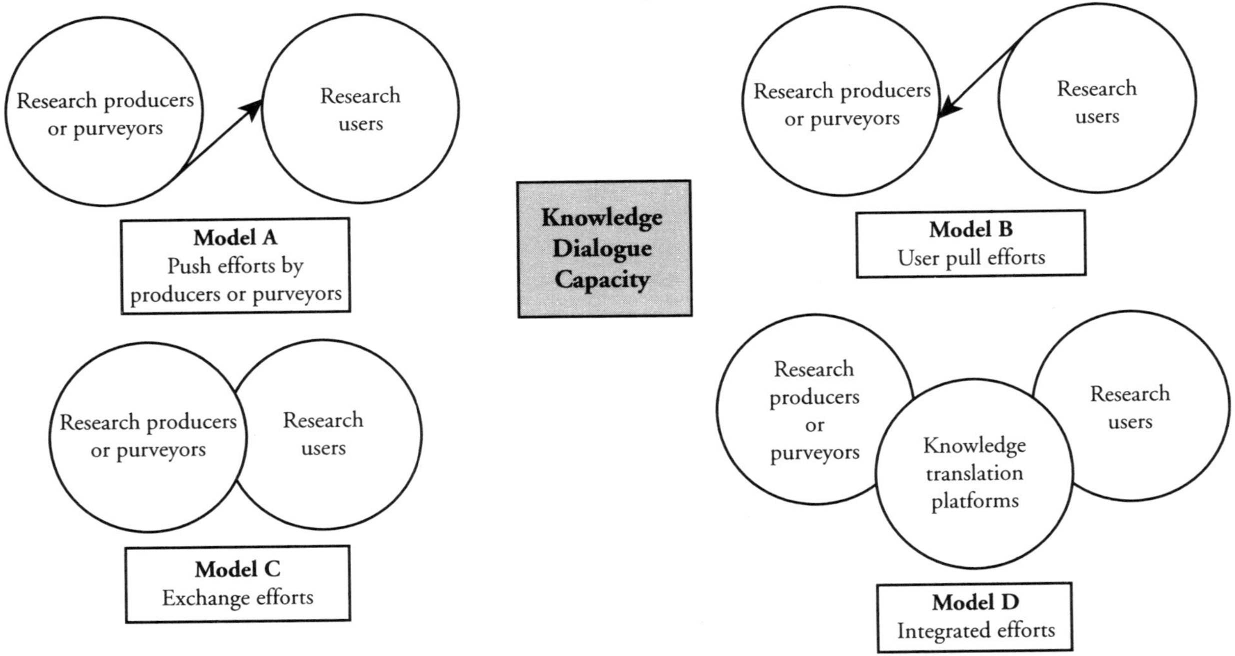

Source: Adapted from Lavis, J., J. Lomas, M. Hamid and N. Sewankambo. 2006. "Assessing Country-level Efforts to Link Research to Action." *Bulletin of the World Health Organisation,* 84: 620–628.

infuse public dialogue with an understanding of research processes and evidence. KTPs may contribute to the creation of a user-friendly knowledge base, convene dialogues and meetings, and offer routine capacity building courses.

While this book explores all four models throughout, its main focus is the "push" side, inspired by researchers who want to improve their ability to inform, influence, and engage with policy and practice. This book draws from both academic sources (for concepts), and practical examples to make them operational.

KNOWLEDGE TRANSLATION AT WORK: BRINGING RESEARCH ALIVE

Different contexts require different strategies. Every researcher, project, and organization is different; so the choice of "push" tools will differ, as will the opportunities for facilitating pull and creating linkage and exchange partnerships. A study on competing health financing modalities in rural Tanzania may be better served by a "national policy dialogue." A study on Antiretroviral Drugs (ARVs) in South Africa may become a cutting-edge "best practice" model packaged for decision-makers, the media, communities, practitioners, and researchers.

Researchers are not agents of change only in their own contexts; every researcher is an audience as well. Linkage and exchange between researchers can be some of the strongest KT strategies.

RESOURCES

1. Canadian Institutes of Health Research Online Tutorial. "Introduction to Evidence-Informed Decision Making." Available online at http://www.learning.cihr-irsc.gc.ca/course/view.php?id=10 (accessed on September 26, 2010).
2. National Collaborating Centre for Methods and Tools (NCCMT). 2010. "Introduction to Evidence-Informed Decision Making." Available online at http://learning.nccmt.ca/en/ (accessed on September 26, 2010).
3. Straus, S., J. Tetroe and I.D. Graham. 2009. *Knowledge Translation in Health Care: Moving from Evidence to Practice.* Hoboken: Wiley-Blackwell.

The book explains how to use research findings to improve health care in real life everyday situations. It defines and describes knowledge translation, and outlines strategies for successful knowledge translation in practice, and policy-making. The book is full of examples of how knowledge translation models work in closing the gap between evidence and action.

REFERENCES

1. WHO Executive Board. 2005. "Ministerial Summit on Health Research", Mexico City, 16-20 November 2004. Report by the Secretariat. Available online at http://www.who.int/gb/ebwha/pdf_files/EB115/B115_30-en.pdf (accessed October 14, 2010).
2. J. Lavis, J. Lomas, M. Hamid and N. Sewankambo. "Assessing Country-level Efforts to Link Research to Action," *Bulletin of the World Health Organisation,* 84 (2006): 620–28.

2

Knowledge Management

The scaling up of knowledge management efforts in public health will be important for translating research and evidence into policy, practice, and social transformation.[1]

A quick web search on Knowledge Management (KM) brings up a tangle of interlocking notions, descriptions, and definitions that are more likely to confuse than clarify.

Fortunately, scholarship and practice has reduced KM into digestible bits. Knowledge is information we can write down (explicitly) and what we know in our heads (tacitly). Successful KM is developing ways to knit together both tacit and explicit knowledge. To do that, we must ask basic questions: Do we know what we "do" know and where that information is? Do we know what we "do not" know, and need to know, and where we might get that information?

KM is about creating, identifying, capturing, and sharing knowledge. It is about getting "the right knowledge, in the right place, at the right time" to influence an action or a decision.[2]

Researchers must recognize that the right knowledge is the most valuable resource of any society, organization, or individual. It determines what they do, how they do it, and the probable results of their action—in every context, always. It is also important to recognize that knowledge renders this value only when it is translated, transmitted, and used.

This chapter examines tacit and explicit knowledge, and ways to understand, capture, and maximize the impact of both. It looks at formulating a KM strategy, and offers a suite of tools, including after-action reviews, knowledge audits, identifying and sharing best practice, knowledge harvesting, storytelling, communities of practice, and the peer assist.

BOX 2.1
Organic Knowledge Management

KM is "a more organic and holistic way of understanding and exploiting the role of knowledge in the processes of managing and doing work, and an authentic guide for individuals and organizations in coping with the increasingly complex and shifting environment of the modern economy."

Source: Denning, S. "What is Knowledge Management? Definitions." Available online at http://www.stevedenning.com/Knowledge-Management/what-is-knowledge-management.aspx

TOWARDS A KNOWLEDGE MANAGEMENT STRATEGY

Tacit versus Explicit: What do We Mean by Knowledge?

Information is "data arranged in meaningful patterns," but it becomes knowledge only when it is interpreted in a context.[3] As Davenport and Prusak explain, transforming information into knowledge involves making comparisons, thinking about consequences and connections, and engaging in conversations with others.[4]

According to Wikipedia, "knowledge" can be defined as "awareness or familiarity gained by experience of a fact or situation;" Plato formulated it as "justified true belief."[5] Put differently, we might best describe knowledge as "know-how" or "applied action."[6]

Explicit knowledge can be recorded and easily organized (e.g., on computers). This includes research findings, lessons learned, toolkits, and so on. Tacit knowledge is subconscious—we are generally not even aware that we possess it. It is context-specific and includes, among other things, insights, intuitions, and experiences.[7]

Capturing this is more difficult and involves time and personal interaction.

BOX 2.2
Knowledge

"Each of us is a personal store of knowledge with training, experiences, and informal networks of friends and colleagues whom we seek out when we want to solve a problem or explore an opportunity. Essentially, we get things done and succeed by knowing an answer or knowing someone who does."

Source: National Library for Health (NHS). 2005. "ABC of Knowledge Management." Available online at www.library.nhs.uk/knowledgemanagement/ (accessed September 26, 2010).

Imagine receiving a Call for Proposals from an established funding organization. Explicit knowledge would be used to set out a proposal—presenting research findings, highlighting relevant publications, an external review. Tacit knowledge would help shape the application for a particular audience, recalling that a previous collaborator is now on the organization's board, that they tend to favour proposals in certain formats, prefer Log Frame Analyses, and identifying a colleague who has "inside track" information on what the funding organization is really looking for. The effective use of both types of knowledge would likely lead to a more informed, and therefore successful, proposal.

What is a KM Strategy?

There is no "one size fits all" or "ready to use" prescription for KM. The starting point for any sound strategy is a self-audit of assets, needs, mandate, mission and goals, values, and ways of working. In essence, the three main questions are:[8]

- **Where are we now?** What kinds of knowledge do we produce (or gather/store)? What outputs have we created? How do our culture and systems either serve or hinder sound KM practices?

- **Where do we want to be?** In five years' time, how will a sound KM strategy change our organization? How will we know when we have a sound KM system? How will we measure the value of our efforts?
- **How do we get there?** An action plan outlining the three resources of people, processes, and technology. What specific tools and practices will we use? How will we motivate people to change their practices?

In a slightly different formulation, Denning advises that a KM strategy should ask: What knowledge do we want to share (type and quality)? With whom do we want to share it (audience)? How will our knowledge actually be shared (channels)? And why will this knowledge be shared (motivations and objectives)?[9]

FIGURE 2.1
The KM Strategy: Legs, Flows, Processes

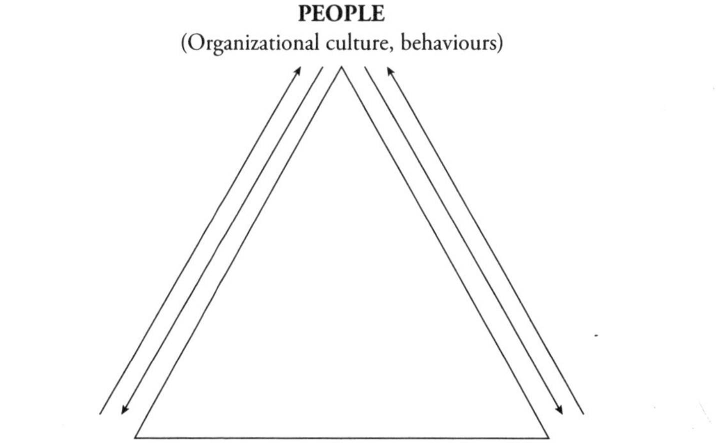

Note: Technology is an enabler and a method, not a saviour nor a strategy. The right technological tools can help us organize, store, and access our explicit knowledge as well as helping to connect people and furthering their abilities to share their tacit knowledge.[11] However, technology alone cannot be the beginning and end of a KM strategy.

People, processes, and technology are like a three-legged stool—"if one is missing the stool will collapse."[10] While there is some argument as to which leg is the most important, consensus is emerging in favour of the first—people. After all, it is people—human resources—who are the ones that create, share, and use knowledge.

It follows that a successful KM strategy requires a change in an organization's culture and behaviour. At the heart of this change would be recognizing the centrality of knowledge, and how the organization must improve the way it creates, captures, shares, and uses it.

THE COMPONENTS OF A KM STRATEGY

In designing a KM strategy, there are several approaches and tools that can be employed. These would depend on the resources (human, financial, technological) at hand and the type of knowledge being captured and shared.

The Knowledge Audit

A knowledge audit assesses and lists an organization's knowledge resources, assets, and flows. If we do not know what knowledge we already have, what our knowledge gaps are, and how that knowledge flows within our organization, how can we even assess, never mind improve, current practices? Knowledge audits "reveal the organization's knowledge management needs, strengths, weaknesses, opportunities, threats, and risks."[12]

BOX 2.3

Why Conduct a Knowledge Audit?

Knowledge audits can help identify a number of things, including:

Information glut or scarcity;

Lack of awareness of information elsewhere in the organization;

Inability to keep abreast of relevant information;

(Box 2.3 contd.)

(Box 2.3 contd.)

Continual "reinvention" of the wheel;

Quality and quantity of in-house knowledge and information;

Common use of out-of-date information;

Not knowing where to go for expertise in a specific area.

Source: Wiig, K. 1993. *Knowledge Management Methods.* Arlington, TX: Schema Press.

What does a knowledge audit involve?[13]

1. **Identify knowledge needs**: Questionnaires, interviews, and/or facilitated group discussions can answer the central question: to be successful, what knowledge does our organization need?
2. **Conduct a knowledge inventory**: Knowledge assets—tacit and explicit—must be identified and located. For tacit knowledge, that means people, where they are located, what they do, what they know, and what they may be learning. For explicit knowledge, it means quantifying in-house knowledge (papers, reports, databases, etc.) by locating it, understanding how it is organized and accessed, analyzing how appropriate it is, and determining whether available resources are being used. This inventory will reveal critical knowledge gaps.
3. **Analyze knowledge flows**: Understanding how knowledge moves within an organization—"from where it is to where it is needed"—is crucial.[14] How do people find the knowledge they need to execute their tasks? This analysis will cover both tacit and explicit knowledge, and include people, processes, and technologies.
4. **Create a knowledge map**: A visual representation of knowledge resources and assets, with added details of how it flows from one point to the next, is helpful.

An audit should lead to important conclusions and trigger recommendations for addressing knowledge gaps, in terms of both content and flow.

BOX 2.4
A Selection of KM Tools and Techniques

Knowledge Audits: A systematic process to identify an organization's knowledge needs, resources and flows, as a basis for understanding where and how better knowledge management can add value, also called "Knowledge Inventories."

Knowledge Harvesting: A tool used to capture the knowledge of "experts," making it widely available to others.

Best Practices: Approaches to capturing best practices discovered in one part of the organization and sharing them for the benefit of all.

Communities of Practice: Widely regarded as "the killer KM application," communities of practice link people together to develop and share knowledge around specific themes.

Peer Assists: A tool to learn from the experiences of others, especially within an organization, before embarking on an activity or project.

Storytelling: Using the ancient art of storytelling to share knowledge in a more meaningful and interesting way. (For more information on storytelling, see Chapter 9: popular media)

After Action Reviews (AAR): A tool now widely used by many organizations to capture lessons learned both during and after an activity or project. (For more information on AARs, see Chapter 3: evaluative thinking)

Exit Interviews: A tool used to capture the knowledge of departing employees.

Knowledge Centers: Similar to libraries but with a broader remit including connecting people with each other as well as with information in documents and databases.

Social Network Analysis: Mapping relationships between people, groups and organizations to understand how these relationships either facilitate or impede knowledge flows.

White Pages: A step-up from the usual staff directory, this is an online resource that allows people to find colleagues with specific knowledge and expertise.

Source: National Library for Health (NHS). 2005. "ABC of Knowledge Management." Available online at www.library.nhs.uk/knowledgemanagement/ (accessed September 26, 2010); and Swiss Agency for Development and Cooperation. 2009. *Knowledge Management Toolkit.* Berne: SDC. Available online at http://www.daretoshare.ch/en/Dare_To_Share/Knowledge_Management_Methods_and_Tools/Knowledge_Management_Toolkit (accessed January 24, 2011).

Knowledge Harvesting

How can we truly capitalize on the knowledge of our organization's experts? How do we capture what is in their heads and then share it with others in an accessible and understandable format? This process aims to make tacit knowledge explicit. As Eisenhart (2001) explains, "the ultimate goal of knowledge harvesting is to capture an individual's decision-making process with enough clarity that someone else guided by it could repeat the steps of the process and achieve the same result."[15]

What does knowledge harvesting involve?[16]

1. **Focus:** What specific knowledge and expertise are we looking for? The answer to this question will affect the strategy for capturing that information.
2. **Find:** Locate the experts whose knowledge is wanted—a staff directory, authors of key documents, or simply "ask around."[17]
3. **Elicit:** Harvesters, or interviewers, can get experts to talk about their knowledge—even when they are not aware that they possess it. Skilled harvesters must get the dialogue started.
4. **Organize:** Once the knowledge has been gathered, it must be arranged in a coherent and systematic form that is easy to access.
5. **Package:** The format should be designed to best serve the audience it is aimed at.
6. **Share:** What is the ultimate purpose of sharing this knowledge? Why and for whom have we packaged what we know? We might start with an online repository, but then what?
7. **Apply:** This will be done by members of an organization in their every-day work. It is important to keep track of whether, and how, that knowledge is being applied and to record any feedback.

8. **Evaluate and adapt:** Based on the feedback of users, the effectiveness of efforts must be evaluated and adapted to the changing needs of an organization.

Best Practice

The term "best practice" need not be too literal. It indicates a strong or useful case study or approach that might helpfully inform future activities. Identifying, capturing, and sharing best practice generally involves explicit knowledge captured in such "sharing" tools as databases, and tacit knowledge disseminated via, for instance, communities of practice.[18]

One useful way of identifying and sharing best practice has been developed by Skyrme:[19]

1. **Identify user requirements:** Is a database of best practices needed, or should selected aspects be shared through storytelling and face-to-face interactions?
2. **Discover best practices**: Tools include identifying individuals who are performing well and understanding how they work, communities of practice, after action reviews, knowledge harvesting, and exit interviews.
3. **Create a dossier of good practices**: Databases are typically used, with title, profile, context, resources, description, improvement measures, lessons learned, and links to resources.
4. **Validate best practices**: Review identified best practices to reaffirm their validity, using a panel of subject experts and peers.
5. **Disseminate and apply:** Even if there is a database, face-to-face dissemination of best practices is essential through communities of practice, peer assists, improvement groups or quality circles, visits to other departments or organizations

with good performance, organized learning events, job secondments or exchanges, etc.

Communities of Practice

Face-to-face discussions are not only effective ways to share existing knowledge, but can also create more. Communities of practice (CoPs)—"groups of practitioners who share a common interest or passion in an area of competence and are willing to share the experiences of their practice"—are ways of formalizing such exchanges.[20] They are based on the assumption that acquisition of knowledge is a social process, and that knowledge and information can best be shared and learned within communities.[21] CoPs are not formed around a specific assignment and are not bound by time or geography. They exist "indefinitely for the promotion of the issue around which the community is formed."[22] Membership of a CoP is voluntary and the group's composition and mission are fluid, flexible, and informal. Their mandate can include stimulating interaction, fostering learning, creating new knowledge, and identifying and sharing best practices.[23]

How do we get started?

A CoP—of any demarcation or size—must focus on a single issue or area of expertise around which people are willing to share ideas, find solutions, and innovate. Their exact format and modes of operation will depend upon what kind of knowledge people need to share, how tightly bonded the community is, and how closely new knowledge needs to be linked with people's everyday work.[24] The first few questions when setting up a CoP include: What is the knowledge focus? Who can contribute? What are the common needs and interests of the group? And what is the group's ultimate purpose?[25] In this CoP start-up kit, Nickols[26] provides a step-by-step view of the process:

FIGURE 2.2
Steps in Starting Up a Community of Practice

Preliminaries ⇨	⇨	**Behaviours and Activities**
• Indentify the champion and sponsor • Pick a focal point: - Problem - Practice - Process • Prepare a business case • Present a proposal (where resources or support will be needed): - Value/benefits - Sponsorship/support - Interactions - Outcomes • Select/enlist members • Get organized	• Set the agenda: - Issues/interests - Problems - Goals/outcomes • Devise interaction modes: - Email - Face-to-face meetings (scheduled/ unscheduled) - Virtual meetings Telephone/conference call - Videoconferencing • Confirm and secure support requirements: - Technology - Resources • Get underway	• Share experience and know-how • Discuss common issues and interests • Collaborate in solving problems • Analyze causes and contributing factors • Experiment with new ideas and novel approaches • Capture/codify new know-how • Evaluate actions and effects • Learning

Source: Nickols, F. 2003. *Communities of Practice: A Start-Up Kit.* Mount Vernon. Ohio: Distance Consulting.

Peer Assist

We often struggle to find solutions to what we think are new problems. But in most cases, somebody, somewhere—even within our own organization—has had to deal with similar issues in the past. By turning to them, we can often find solutions, or at least good starting points. Pioneered by BP Amoco in 1994, the Peer Assist technique—tapping into our peers' experience and expertise—saw the company save US$750 million over its first three years of use.[17]

BOX 2.5
When is Peer Assist Useful?

You are starting a new assignment. You want to benefit from the advice of more experienced people.

You face a problem that another group has faced in the past.

You have not had to deal with a given situation for a long time. You are no longer sure what procedures to follow.

You are planning a project that is similar to a project another group has completed.

Source: CIDA. 2003. *Knowledge Sharing: Methods, Meetings and Tools*. Ottava, Canada: CIDA.

What does a Peer Assist Involve?

A Peer Assist is a meeting, before (and sometimes during a project) in which a group of peers discuss a particular problem. The meeting is usually convened by project leaders, selecting the participants whose advice and knowledge is particularly sought. The project leaders must manage the entire meeting (or set of meetings) which typically last from half-a-day to two days.[28]

BOX 2.6
Steps in Conducting a Peer Assist

1. **Purpose:** Clearly define the problem we are seeking assistance with and ensure that our aim is to learn something.
2. **Background research:** Find out whether others have previously tackled a similar problem.
3. **Facilitator:** Getting someone from outside the team often helps ensure that the process runs smoothly.
4. **Timing:** Make sure the results of the Peer Assist will be available in time and on time.
5. **Participants:** Invite four to eight people who have the relevant knowledge, skills, and experience. Avoid hierarchies and ensure people feel free to share their views.
6. **Deliverables:** Know what is wanted and plan accordingly. Deliverables should be options and insights as opposed to "answers".

(Box 2.6 contd.)

(Box 2.6 contd.)

7. **Socializing:** People will work better together if there is time to get to know each other before and during the meeting.
8. **Ground rules:** At the start of the meeting, make sure that everyone is on the same footing and is clear about the purpose and individual roles.
9. **Context:** The host team should present the context, history and future plans with regard to the problem being presented.
10. **Questions and feedback:** At this point, the host team should take a back seat and allow the visitors to discuss what they have heard and share ideas.
11. **Analysis:** The visiting team should now analyze and reflect on what they have learned and look at different options.
12. **Actions:** The visitors present their feedback to the host team. Time should be allowed for questions and clarifications. The host team should agree on a timeline for implementation.

Source: Adapted from National Library for Health (NHS). 2005. "ABC of Knowledge Management." Available online at www.library.nhs.uk/knowledgemanagement/ (accessed September 26, 2010).

Resources

1. Canadian International Development Agency. 2003. "Knowledge Sharing: Methods, Meetings and Tools." Available online at http://www.km4dev.org/?module=articles&func=view&catid=172 (accessed September 26, 2010).
2. Davenport, T.H. and L. Prusak. 1998. *Working Knowledge, How Organisations Manage What They Know*. Boston, MA: Harvard Business School Press.
3. Dixon N. 2000. "Peer Assist: Guidelines for Practice." Available online at http://www.commonknowledge.org/userimages/resources_peer_assist_guidellines+.pdf (accessed September 26, 2010).
4. Eisenhart, M. 2001. "Gathering Knowledge While it's Ripe," *Knowledge Management Magazine*. Available online at http://www.knowledgeharvesting.org/documents/Knowledge%20Management%20Magazine%20Feature%20Article.pdf (accessed August 23, 2008).
5. Knowledge Sharing Toolkit. Available online at: http://www.kstoolkit.org/ (accessed September 26, 2010).
6. Lave, J. and E. Wenger 1991. *Situated Learning—Legitimate Peripheral Participation*. Cambridge: Cambridge University Press.
7. McDermott, R. 1998. "Learning Across Teams: The role of communities of practice in team organizations," *Knowledge Management Review*. Available online at http://home.att.net/~discon/KM/Learning.pdf (accessed February 29, 2008).

8. McDermott, R. 1999. "Nurturing Three Dimensional Communities of Practice: How to get the most out of human networks." *Knowledge Management Review*. Available online at http://www.impactalliance.org/ev_en.php?ID=1931_201&ID2=DO_TOPIC (accessed January 24, 2011).
9. Mission-Centered Solutions, Inc. 2008. "Guidelines for the AAR." Available online at Mission-Centered Solutions, Inc. 2008. www.fireleadership.gov/toolbox/after_action_review/aar.pdf (accessed September 26, 2010).
10. National Library for Health (NHS). 2005. "ABC of Knowledge Management." Available online at www.library.nhs.uk/knowledgemanagement/A comprehensive resource for anyone interested in KM issues. The place to start. (accessed September 26, 2010).
11. Nepal, R.B. "Knowledge Management: Concept, Elements and Process." Available online at http://www.km4dev.org/forum/topics/knowledge-management-concept (accessed September 26, 2010).
12. Nickols, F. 2003. "Communities of Practice: An Overview." *Distance Consulting*. Available online at http://home.att.net/~discon/KM/CoPTypes.htm (accessed September 26, 2010).
13. Ramalingam, B. 2006. *Tools for Knowledge and Learning: A Guide for Development and Humanitarian Organisations*. London: ODI. Also available at http://www.odi.org.uk/rapid/publications/Tools_KM.html (accessed September 26, 2010).
14. Skyrme, D. "Best Practices in Best Practices: Guide on Developing a Sharing Best Practices Programme." Available online at www.skyrme.com/kshop/kguides.htm (accessed September 26, 2010).
15. Swiss Agency for Development and Cooperation. 2009. *Knowledge Management Toolkit*. Berne: SDC. Also available online at http://www.daretoshare.ch/en/Dare_To_Share/Knowledge_Management_Methods_and_Tools/Knowledge_Management_Toolkit (accessed January 24, 2011).
16. Wallace, Susan. USAID. 2006. "After Action Review: Technical Guidance." Available online at http://www.docstoc.com/docs/673425/The-After-Action-Review-Technical-Guidance (accessed on December 14, 2010).
17. Welch, N. "Peer Assist Overview." Available online at www.welch-consulting.com/PeerAssist.htm (accessed October 19, 2009).
18. Wiig, K. 1993. *Knowledge Management Methods*. Arlington, TX: Schema Press.
19. www.creatingthe21stcentury.org (accessed September 26, 2010).
20. *KM4Dev*. Available online at www.km4dev.org/?module=articles&func=display&ptid=1&aid=725 (accessed February 11, 2011).
21. *Knowledge Harvesting*. Available online at www.knowledgeharvesting.com (accessed February 11, 2011).
22. *Steve Denning*. Available online at www.stevedenning.com (accessed February 11, 2011).

REFERENCES

1. World Health Organisation. 2004. "Strengthening Health Research Systems," in *World Report on Knowledge for Better Health*. Geneva.
2. National Library for Health (NHS). 2005. "ABC of Knowledge Management." Available online at www.library.nhs.uk/knowledgemanagement/(accessed September 26, 2010).
3. Denning, S. *What is Knowledge? Definitions of Knowledge*. Available online at www.stevedenning.com (accessed September 26, 2010).
4. Davenport, T.H. and L. Prusak. 1998. *Working Knowledge, How Organisations Manage What They Know*. Boston, MA: Harvard Business School Press.
5. "Knowledge." Available online at http://en.wikipedia.org/wiki/Knowledge (accessed June, 2007).
6. National Library of Health, "ABC of Knowledge Management."
7. Nepal, R.B. "Knowledge Management: Concept, Elements and Process." Available online at http://www.km4dev.org/forum/topics/knowledge-management-concept (accessed September 26, 2010).
8. National Library of Health, "ABC of Knowledge Management."
9. Denning, S. 2002. *The Springboard: How Storytelling Ignites Action in Knowledge-Era Organisations*. Boston, MA: Butterworth Heinemann.
10. National Library of Health, "ABC of Knowledge Management."
11. National Library of Health, "ABC of Knowledge Management."
12. National Library of Health, "ABC of Knowledge Management."
13. National Library of Health, "ABC of Knowledge Management." Also *see* Ramalingam, B. 2005. Implementing Knowledge Strategies: From Policy to Practice in Development Agencies, ODI Working Paper 244. London: ODI.
14. National Library of Health, "ABC of Knowledge Management."
15. Eisenhart, M. 2001. Available online at http://www.knowledgeharvesting.org/documents/Knowledge%20Management%20Magazine%20Feature%20Article.pdf (accessed August 23, 2008).
16. *Approach*. Knowledge Harvesting. Available online at http://www.knowledgeharvesting.com/approach.htm (accessed September 26, 2010).
17. National Library of Health, "ABC of Knowledge Management."
18. National Library of Health, "ABC of Knowledge Management."
19. Skyrme, D. "Best Practices in Best Practices: Guide on Developing a Sharing Best Practices Programme." Available online at www.skyrme.com/kshop/kguides.htm (accessed September 26, 2010).
20. Denning, S. "Communities for Knowledge Management." Available online at www.stevedenning.com (accessed September 26, 2010).

21. Lave, J. and E. Wenger. 1991. *Situated Learning—Legitimate Peripheral Participation.* Cambridge: Cambridge University Press.
22. Denning, "Communities for Knowledge Management."
23. Nickols, F. 2003. *Communities of Practice: An Overview.* Distance Consulting.
24. McDermott, R. 1999. "Nurturing Three Dimensional Communities of Practice: How to Get the Most out of Human Networks." *Knowledge Management Review.* Available online at http://www.co-i-l.com/coil/knowledge-garden/cop/dimensional.shtml (accessed September 26, 2010).
25. Ramalingam, B. 2006. *Tools for Knowledge and Learning: A Guide for Development and Humanitarian Organisations.* London: ODI. Also available online at http://www.odi.org.uk/rapid/publications/Tools_KM.html (accessed September 26, 2010).
26. Nickols, *Communities of Practice.*
27. Welch, N. "Peer Assist Overview." Available online at www.welch-consulting.com/PeerAssist.htm (accessed October 19, 2009).
28. Dixon, N. 2000. "Peer Assist: Guidelines for Practice." Available online at www.commonknowledge.org/userimages/resources_peer_assist_guidelines+.pdf (accessed September 26, 2010).

3

Evaluative Thinking

Monitoring and Evaluation (M&E) is integral to any operation. It is usually conducted at the end of a project or term. It assesses performance in order to reward, correct, or improve. It is as useful to the concluded project itself as a post-mortem is to a corpse.

Evaluative Thinking (ET) is an equivalent of questioning, reflecting, learning, and modifying but it is conducted all the time. It is a constant state-of-mind within an organization's culture and all its systems. So it is not a forensic mortician; it is a doctor—checking the pulse, diagnosing condition, prescribing for prevention, remedy, and enhanced performance.

The difference is dramatic. With M&E a project is fired like a cannonball, and not until it has landed can its accuracy or effect be assessed. With ET, the project is like a guided missile, able to constantly adapt and steer to ensure maximum accuracy and impact.

ET is an inherently reflective process, a means of resolving the "creative tension" between our current and desired levels of performance.[1] By going beyond the more time- and activity-bound processes of M&E, ET is learning for change. It is learning to inform and shape action.[2]

A full annex to this chapter can be found in Section V (chapter 15: Frequently Asked Questions).

KEY CONCEPTS

In Roper and Pettit's useful conception, learning—particularly at an organizational level—can be divided into three different types of loops. "Single-loop learning" works to identify and correct inefficiencies, while "double-loop learning" involves a routine testing of assumptions and a re-imagining of core strategy. "Triple-loop learning," on the other hand, asks individuals to question and probe the organization's very core, casting an introspective eye on its vision, mission, and guiding fictions.[3] ET demonstrates the very essence of the triple-loop.

FIGURE 3.1
The Feedback Loop

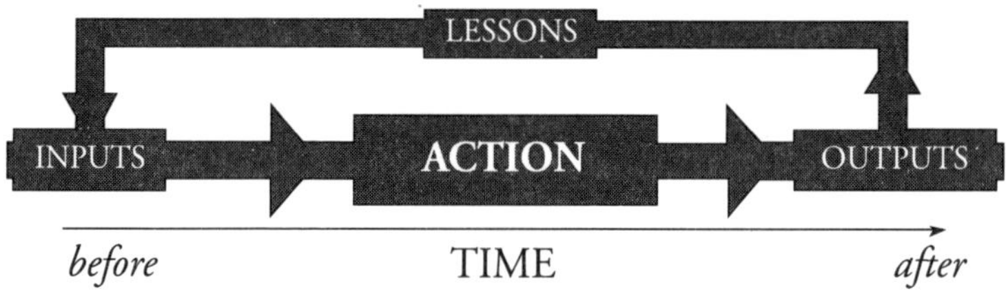

Source: Adapted from Principia Cybernetica Web, "Feedback" http://pespmcl.vub.ac.be/feedback.html

ET, like Patton's concept of "developmental evaluation,"[4] aims to create context-specific knowledge to shape our work. Each stage within the triangles on the next page demonstrates that learning is at both the heart of the digram and our every activity: an ability to recognize failure and success allows us to take steps to correct, modify, or amplify our actions. Learning allows for mid-course correction, in the understanding that goals will shift as activities progress and knowledge deepens: for any individual or organization, the only failure is not to learn.[5]

THE LEARNING ORGANIZATION

The "learning organization" is any organization dedicated to generating lessons and then using these new insights to modify core operations.[6] Senge adds that learning organizations nurture new ways of thinking "where people are continually learning to see the whole together."[7] It creates and supports robust learning systems that align core with evolving goals. To Agarwal, the five key activities of a learning organization include:[8]

- **Systematic:** Insisting on data over assumptions.
- **Adventurous:** Willing to try different approaches.
- **Confident:** Of the values of productive failure instead of unproductive success.
- **Open-minded:** Borrowing enthusiastically from best practice.
- **Dynamic:** Sharing knowledge and rotating and training its people.

FIGURE 3.2
Evaluative Thinking Processes

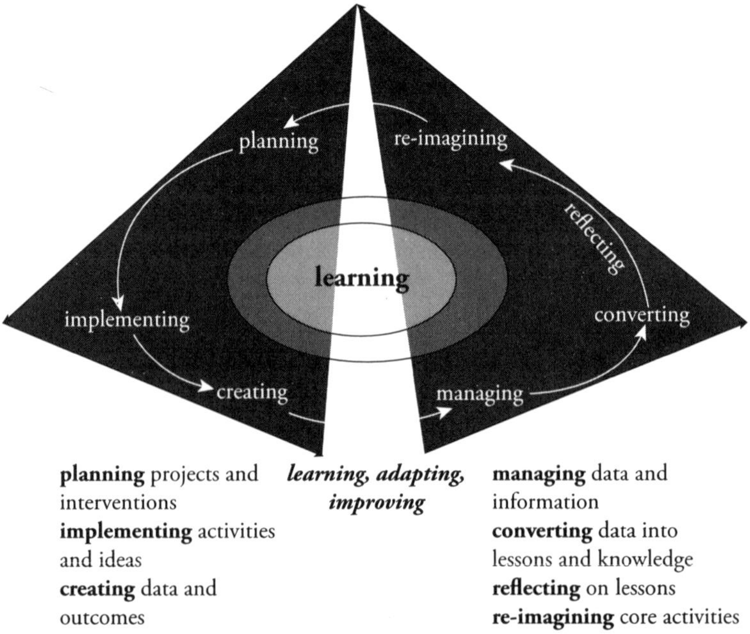

In sum, learning organizations encourage intellectual risks, inspired by their ability to exploit bright ideas while still safe in the knowledge that that they have the reflexes to rectify mistakes: i.e., embrace Davidson's spirit of "creative tension."[9] This ethos not only allows but also nurtures a spirit of reflection and on-going learning. Instead of fear of not knowing, it engenders an enthusiasm to find out and know more.

As with all KT processes, the participatory nature of ET tends to create "flatter" organizational structures—it allows the leadership qualities of every person to emerge, it drives more interaction between individuals at all levels, and it builds teamwork.[10]

> *How many of us work in organizations where we are rewarded for reflecting on our work, for reading and listening to what others have to say, for systematizing and sharing our experiences so others can critique our work, both within our institutions and in the broader development community?*
>
> **L. Roper and J. Pettit**

RESOURCES

1. Armstrong, A. and P. Foley P. 2003. "Foundations for a Learning Organisation: Organisational Learning Mechanisms". *The Learning Organisation*, 10(2).
2. Chawla, S. and John Renesch (eds). 1995. *Learning Organisations: Developing Cultures for Tomorrow's Workplace*. Portland, OR: Productivity Press.
3. Senge, P.M. 2006. *The Fifth Discipline: The Art and Practice of the Learning Organization*. New York, NY: Doubleday.
4. Simonin, B. 1997. "The Importance of Collaborative Know-How: An Empirical Test of the Learning Organisation." *The Academy of Management Journal*. 40(5).

EVALUATIVE THINKING TOOLS

ET uses eight familiar tools to gather and assess information and opinion on a rolling basis, before it establishes a mindset (culture) which is: How do we become evaluative thinkers? How do we make the Evaluative Thinking abstract a reality?

This section reviews and discusses:

1. Most Significant Change.
2. Appreciative Inquiry.
3. After Action Review.
4. Horizontal Evaluation.
5. Impact Logs.
6. Formal Surveys.
7. Rapid Appraisal Methods.
8. Performance Indicators.

Most Significant Change

This process asks stakeholders to reflect on the past and describe the strongest aspects of change—"who did what, when, and why—and the reasons why the event was important."[11] Stakeholders read these stories aloud, and discuss the value of the reported changes; an expert "panel" can also select the most significant stories for group discussion.

As Davies and Dart explain, Most Significant Change (MSC) is especially useful at capturing ever-changing trends and shows concrete changes in specific time-frames. While MSC stories can certainly be used as a public relations tool—positive testimonials, for instance—they are particularly useful at giving an organization's staff a fuller sense of the impact and influence their work has had, and often in the words of non-professionals.[12] A "full" implementation of MSC typically involves 10 steps[13] and requires no special skills.

1. As a result of your work over the past year, what was the most significant change you observed?
2. As we look at all these stories of most significant change, which do we think is the most significant of all?

By focusing on learning—as opposed to accountability—MSC allows a superb snapshot of actions, their effect, and their potential.

Resources

1. Davies, R. and J. Dart. 2005. "The Most Significant Change (MSC) Technique: A Guide to its Use." Available online at www.mande.co.uk/docs/MSCGuide.htm (accessed September 26, 2010). This is the definitive place to start.
2. For more on storytelling as a knowledge management tool, please *see* chapter 9.
3. The News Group website. Available online at http://groups.yahoo.com/group/MostSignificantChanges/ (accessed September 26, 2010). It has an excellent repository of groups around the world that have implemented MSC approaches.

Appreciative Inquiry

Appreciative Inquiry (AI) looks to past performance (and/or an ideal vision of the future) and uses story-telling to capture and deliver key ingredients. AI asks stakeholders to remember a time when the project, programme or organization was at its best. When were people most proud of the work? What made that high point possible? What would the organization look like if that high point were an everyday event?[14]

AI is an excellent motivator: if we can understand the conditions and context of a previous excellent performance, not only can we replicate it, we can institutionalize it. With this mindset, an organization can shift from dwelling on problems to chasing excellence. AIs addition to the suite of ET tools is a movement past the maxim that we only learn from studying past failures. AI reveals the conditions, context, and factors crucial to success, and allows stakeholders to imagine how those elements can be further nurtured and implemented.[15]

AI is typically broken into five stages (Definition, Discovery, Dream, Design, and Destiny) and is often done in a combination of small groups and a plenary session.

Resources

1. Acosta, A. and B. Douthwaite. 2005. "Appreciative Inquiry: An Approach for Learning and Change Based on our Own Best." Available online at www.cgiar-ilac.org/downloads/Briefs/Brief6Proof2.pdf (accessed August 23, 2008). It is an excellent place to start.
2. Appreciate Inquiry Commons (AI Central). Available online at http://appreciativeinquiry.cwru.edu (accessed September 29, 2010). It has a number of good stories around implementing the AI technique.
3. Appreciative Inquiry Approach to Community Development. "The World Vision Tanzanian Experience." Available online at http://appreciativeinquiry.case.edu/gem/tanzania.html (accessed September 29, 2010).

After Action Review

Originally designed by the US military, the After Action Review (AAR) is an open and participatory process to understand "what happened, why it happened, and how it can be done better."[16] Group discussion looks at the many technical and human factors at play, resulting in a set of key lessons to improve performance or sustain success.

An AAR brings accountability—by bringing events into an organization's "learning cycle," and by providing evidence and experience for modifying future practice and goals through:

- candid insights into specific strengths and weaknesses from various perspectives;
- feedback and insight critical to improved performance; and
- details often lacking in evaluation reports alone.[17]

AAR can be formal (typically with a facilitator and strong logistical support) or informal (usually on the same day as the event or program under review). Both types tend to answer four different sets of questions: What was planned? What really happened? Why did it happen? And what can we do better next time?[18] Subjects discussed can include technical performance, techniques, communication, lessons learned, roles and responsibilities, organizational issues, stress impacts, and so on.

FIGURE 3.3
The Formal AAR Process

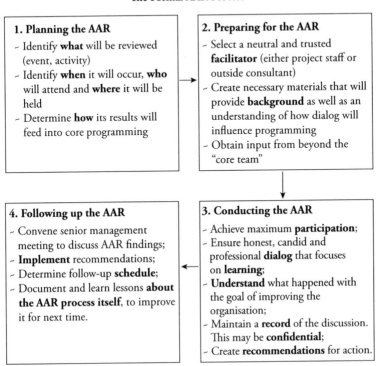

1. Planning the AAR
- Identify **what** will be reviewed (event, activity)
- Identify **when** it will occur, **who** will attend and **where** it will be held
- Determine **how** its results will feed into core programming

→

2. Preparing for the AAR
- Select a neutral and trusted **facilitator** (either project staff or outside consultant)
- Create necessary materials that will provide **background** as well as an understanding of how dialog will influence programming
- Obtain input from beyond the "core team"

↓

3. Conducting the AAR
- Achieve maximum **participation**;
- Ensure honest, candid and professional **dialog** that focuses on **learning**;
- **Understand** what happened with the goal of improving the organisation;
- Maintain a **record** of the discussion. This may be **confidential**;
- Create **recommendations** for action.

←

4. Following up the AAR
- Convene senior management meeting to discuss AAR findings;
- **Implement** recommendations;
- Determine follow-up **schedule**;
- Document and learn lessons **about the AAR process itself**, to improve it for next time.

Source: Wallace, S. 2006. "After Action Review: Technical Guidance." Available online at http://www.docstoc.com/docs/673425/The-After-Action-Review-Technical-Guidance.

Resources

1. For more, *see* Wallace, S. 2006. "After Action Review: Technical Guidance." Available online at http://www.docstoc.com/docs/673425/The-After-Action-Review-Technical-Guidance (accessed September 29, 2010).
2. Also *see* Mission-Centered Solutions, Inc. 2008. "Guidelines for the AAR." Available online at http://www.mcsolutions.com/resources/AAR_Wildland_Fire.pdf (accessed August 24, 2008).

Horizontal Evaluation

This "linkage and exchange" tool is based on a peer visit. Selected colleagues are invited to contribute towards assessment, both as experts and as like-minded peers familiar with the context and terrain. They will have very informed opinions, and additional motivation to take this learning back to their own organization.[19]

Experience shows that a participatory workshop—lasting about three days and with an equal mix of local participants and visitors—is essential to the success of Horizontal Evaluation (HE). The local participants typically present their experience on a particular project, with the visitors providing some critical assessments as well as observations from their own context. As Thiele et al. explain, the workshop should be professionally facilitated, with Day One dedicated to discussing the project's methodology and criteria for evaluating it. Day Two comprises field visits, where visitors can see the methodology in action and discuss its progress with staff and participants. Day Three sees plenary discussion, an identification of strengths and weaknesses, and the creation of a roadmap to implement changes arising from the HE findings.[20]

Critical advantages of HE over more traditional external evaluations include: adaptability; enhanced learning opportunities in a fluid but tightly structured environment; the ability to receive feedback from peers as opposed to external experts; and it can be used with more formal M&E systems.

Resources

1. Thiele, G., A. Devaux, C. Velasco and K. Manrique 2006. "Horizontal Evaluation: Stimulating Social Learning among Peers." ILAC Brief 13, November 2006. Available online at www.cgiar-ilac.org/downloads/Briefs/ILAC_Brief13.pdf (accessed August 24, 2008).
2. Hovland, I. 2007. "Making a Difference: M&E of Policy Research." ODI Working Paper 281. Available online at www.odi.org.uk/rapid/Publications/Documents/WP281.pdf (accessed August 24, 2008) for a good discussion on many of these tools.

Impact Logs

An impact log is a simple and informal record of impacts or influence that a project or organization has had. The log can include stakeholder feedback, a list of media references (articles, internet, TV, emails), anecdotes, speeches citing the work, and so on. This is qualitative and non-systematic, but can be an excellent way to gauge where we are, what we are doing well, and what we might do better. "The cumulative effect," as Hovland states, "can be valuable in assessing where and how the project or programme is triggering the most direct responses, and in informing future choices."[21] For an organization running several different projects, an impact log can be a powerful (yet inexpensive and skill-light) way to chart which of its projects is commanding the most attention, and if other ET tools might be used to better nuance existing perceptions and important lessons.

Much like libraries use citation analyses to determine what they should buy, discontinue or discard, an impact log can use citation analysis to gauge achievement. An "expanded" form of citation measurement can combine academic analysis (e.g., peer-reviewed papers) with new measurements, such as:

- government policy documents;
- operational guidelines issued by government bodies, professional associations or NGOs;
- training manuals and textbooks;
- newspaper articles; and
- websites.

Resources

1. Hovland, I. 2007. "Making a Difference: M&E of Policy Research." ODI Working Paper 281. Available online at www.odi.org.uk/rapid/Publications/Documents/WP281.pdf (accessed August 24, 2008) for how ODI has used Impact Logs.

Formal Surveys

A formal survey is useful for collecting data from a large number of people. This might involve targeting stakeholders directly affected by the project as well as a control group that was not affected. It can be conducted at any point in an activity cycle, provided there is a clear idea of how data will be coded and used.

The questions can be open-ended (analysis can be time consuming but allows gathering of unexpected information) or closed (e.g., multiple-choice which simplifies response analysis).[22]

Resources

1. Clark, M. and R. Sartorius R. 2004. "Monitoring and Evaluation: Some Tools, Methods and Approaches." Washington DC: The World Bank. Available online at http://bit.ly/monitoringevaluation (accessed on December 14, 2010).
2. Survey Monkey website. Available online at www.survey-monkey.com/ (accessed September 26, 2010). It allows anyone to create professional online surveys, both free and, with more features, for a fee.
3. Westat, J. F. 2002. "The 2002 User Friendly Handbook for Project Evaluation." National Science Foundation. Available online at www.nsf.gov/pubs/2002/nsf02057/start.htm (accessed September 26, 2010).
4. Zoomerang website. Available online at www.zoomerang.com (accessed September 26, 2010). It allows users to create online surveys; free and also for a fee.

Rapid Appraisal Methods

These are like surveys but smaller, quicker, cheaper, and less formal. They allow faster feedback and lessons from the unexpected. Examples range from recorded interviews that are later produced as radio-spots and podcasts (*see* chapter 8) or quotations from a synthesis report.

Key Informant Interviews

Key informants are selected for their particular experience and knowledge—especially useful when time, funding, and/or personnel are limited, and in-depth information is required about a small number of topics (which may be sensitive). They only yield qualitative data and are susceptible to bias, on the part of both the informant and the interviewer.

The process involves qualitative, in-depth, and semi-structured interviews—a "conversation"—between the researcher/evaluator and a number of informants (say, 15–35) in which ideas and information are allowed to flow freely. Topic lists or open-ended questions typically guide the interview process.

Resources

1. Kumar, K. 1989. *Conducting Key Informant Interviews in Developing Countries.* A.I.D. Program Design and Evaluation Methodology Report No.13. Agency for International Development. Available online at http://pdf.dec.org/pdf_docs/PNAAX226.pdf (accessed August 23, 2008).
2. USAID Center for Development Information and Evaluation. 1996. "Conducting Key Informant Interviews," *Performance Monitoring and Evaluation TIPS,* Number 2. Available online at http://pdf.usaid.gov/pdf_docs/PNABS541.pdf (accessed August 23, 2008).

Focus Groups

Eight to twelve people with similar backgrounds and characteristics are selected and collectively "interviewed" in a group setting where they are expected to freely exchange ideas, issues, and experiences. A facilitator can be used to keep the dialogue going (and on track) with a prepared discussion guide, and to ensure all voices are heard.[23] As focus groups take place within a social context, "the technique inherently allows observation of group dynamics, discussion, and first-hand insights into the respondents' behaviours, attitudes, language, etc."[24]

Focus groups deliver only qualitative data and are susceptible to bias.

Resources

1. USAID Center for Development Information and Evaluation. 1996. "Conducting Focus Group Interviews," *Performance Monitoring and Evaluation*

TIPS, Number 10. Available online at http://www.usaid.gov/pubs/usaid_eval/ascii/pnaby233.txt (accessed August 23, 2008).

2. Westat, J.F. 2002. *The 2002 User Friendly Handbook for Project Evaluation.* National Science Foundation. Available online at www.nsf.gov/pubs/2002/nsf02057/nsf02057.pdf (accessed August 23, 2008).

Community Group Interviews

These take place in a group setting and use a prepared questionnaire. In addition, the discussion primarily takes place between the participants and the interviewer, as opposed to between the participants themselves. The interview takes place in a public meeting and is typically open to all interested participants. It is particularly useful when gathering data about community needs, concerns and perceptions, and to gauge the project's progress and impact.

Direct Observations

With a detailed check-list in hand, an observer visits a project site to collect (by observing and listening to) information about on-going activities, processes, social interactions, and observable results. This method captures better understanding of the context and allows the observer "to learn about issues the participants or staff may be unaware of or that they are unwilling or unable to discuss candidly in an interview or focus group."[25]

Resources

1. USAID Center for Development Information and Evaluation. 1996. "Using Direct Observation Techniques," *Performance Monitoring and Evaluation TIPS,* Number 4. Available online at http://pdf.dec.org/pdf_docs/PNABY208.pdf (accessed August 23, 2008).
2. Taylor-Powell, E. and S. Steele. 1996. "Program Development and Evaluation, Collecting Evaluation Data: Direct Observation." Madison, WI: Cooperative Extension Publications. Available online at http://learningstore.uwex.edu/pdf/G3658-5.pdf (accessed August 23, 2008).

Mini Surveys

While these serve purposes similar to formal surveys, mini surveys are much shorter in the number of questions being asked, and they use multiple-choice questions. They are usually administered to no more than 50–75 individuals. The major difference between this and other rapid appraisal methods is that it renders quantitative data.

RESOURCE

1. Kumar, K. 1990. *Conducting Mini Surveys in Developing Countries.* A.I.D. Program Design and Evaluation Methodology Report No. 15. (PN-AAX-249). Available online at http://pdf.usaid.gov/pdf_docs/PNAAX249.pdf (accessed August 23, 2008).

Performance Indicators

These measure quantitative performance and focus on tangible results; they can be used to assess progress against predetermined benchmarks. Performance indicators can be framed against objectives that are SMART (Specific, Measurable, Achievable, Realistic, Time-bound), or objectives that are result-oriented, reasonable, and verifiable. For example, if assessing the effectiveness of introducing insecticide-treated nets (ITNs) in a particular community, a "10 percent yearly reduction in under-five mortality rates for the next three years" could be identified as a performance indicator.

In most cases, performance indicators are derived from the targets of the project itself. In some cases, projects "may be assessed against policy-level goals and principles, or they may be evaluated against standards derived from comparisons with similar interventions elsewhere or from models of best practice."[26]

RESOURCES

1. USAID Center for Development Information and Evaluation. 1996. "Selecting Performance Indicators." *Performance Monitoring and Evaluation TIPS,* Number 6. Available online at http://pdf.usaid.gov/pdf_docs/PNABY214.pdf (accessed August 23, 2008).

2. Clark, M. and R. Sartorius. *Monitoring and Evaluation: Some Tools, Methods and Approaches*. Washington: The World Bank. Available at http://bit.ly/monitoringevaluation (accessed on December 14, 2010).

CREATING AN EVALUATIVE THINKING STRATEGY

Strategies will vary according to context, but key principles will hold:

- The purpose of ET is to learn and adapt. Structures and processes must create this "evolving" environment.
- ET must incorporate the voice of the stakeholders. How can they participate in feedback loops?
- If an M&E framework exists, ET practices must borrow from it, add to it, "repurpose" some of the M&E funds, and impose ET inputs and logic.
- Time and resources must be available for ET.
- Organizational policies to create and sustain an ET environment could include staff development (training needs), executing ET and M&E practices, and flexible and responsive technology.
- An ET strategy—a document or report spelling out the approach—should be circulated to stakeholders and donors (if relevant) for comment.

FOUR EVALUATIVE THINKING STRATEGIES

The Self-assessment Survey and Fora

Any attempt to institutionalize ET should ideally start with a self-assessment. One easy method for organizations to self-assess is through the Bruner Foundation's ET Self-Assessment Tool (see Table 3.1). Following the administration of this tool, an organization- or project-wide forum may be convened so as to discuss the results and design practical ways for further incorporating or developing ET tools—both on an internal and a programmatic level. The forum could be a "safe harbour" meeting whereby there will be no attributions given to any comments, and no official record or transcript (for more on safe harbours, see chapter 5).

TABLE 3.1
Excerpts from the Bruner Foundation Evaluative Thinking Self-assessment Tool

	Assessment	*Priority*
1. Organization Mission		
a. The mission statement is reviewed and revised on a scheduled basis with input from key stakeholders as appropriate	0	High
b. The organization regularly assesses compatibility between programmes and mission	1	
c. The organization acts on the findings of compatibility assessments (e.g., if a programme is not compatible with the mission, it is changed or discontinued	0	Low
2. Finance		
a. Financial status of organization is assessed regularly (at least quarterly) by board and leadership	1	
b. The organization has established a plan identifying actions to take in the event of a reduction or loss in funding	1	
3. Leadership		
a. Executive leaders support and value program evaluation and Evaluative Thinking	1	
b. Executive leaders use evaluation findings in decision-making for the organization	1	
c. Executive leaders motivate staff to regularly use specific evaluation strategies	0	High
d. Executive leaders foster use of technology to support evaluation and Evaluative Thinking	1	

(Table 3.1 contd.)

(Table 3.1 contd.)

	Assessment	Priority
4. Human Resources		
a. Organization has an established personnel performance review process	0	High
b. The organization uses results of data collected regarding staff credentials, training and cultural competencies to recruit, hire and train culturally competent staff	0	Medium
c. Results of staff satisfaction surveys are used to inform modification of policies and procedures at the agency	1	

Source: Bruner Foundation. 2007. "Evaluative Thinking Assessment Tool: v2 Sample Report 2007." Available online at http://brunerfoundation.org/ei/docs/sample.report.pdf

Note: "Assessment" = 1 if the indicator is present, 0 if not. A high score indicates strong Evaluative Thinking practice. "Priority" = High, Medium or Low. This is a qualitative measure of the weight placed on select indicators and need not always be filled in.

Resources

1. *See* Bruner Foundation. 2007. "Evaluative Thinking Assessment Tool: v2 Sample Report 2007." Available online at http://brunerfoundation.org/ei/docs/sample.report.pdf (accessed August 23, 2008).
2. Also *see* their spreadsheet version of the Evaluative Thinking Assessment Tool. Available online at http://brunerfoundation.org/ei/docs/evaluativethinking.assessment.v4.xls (accessed August 23, 2008).

Progress Review

There are advantages to hiring an outside expert (more objective, more outspoken, no vested interest)[27] to guide strategy by conducting key-informant interviews (with staff and stakeholders), using some direct observation techniques, reviewing impact logs, reviewing and assessing any previous M&E reports or frameworks, and reading project reports and other documents. The consultant may conduct a Most Significant

Change workshop or an Appreciative Inquiry to get a more nuanced sense of where a project or organization has been and where it wants to go. A consultant may be retained to capture long-term lessons. For instance, if a project has two scheduled "all-stakeholder" meetings per year, a consultant may attend, and then conduct an after-action review, a Most Significant Change analysis, or Key-informant interviews to dissect the key changes since the last meeting. Disadvantages of an external consultant include the potential loss of consultant prior to end of evaluation as well as reports in unusable formats.

Externally driven activity is an opportunity to:

- Create action-oriented learning documents not a final progress report—that details emerging lessons and responses. The emphasis here is on action and thus requires the consultant to become familiar with staff and modus operandi to diagnose how actions might be modified or improved. This is an on going treatment, not a post-mortem.
- Create a synthesis paper outlining progress, lessons, achievements, and shortcomings as a public relations or communication tool, that can be framed by a theoretical analysis and thus peer-reviewed and published, and which can be seen as a "snapshot", that can be collated into a dynamic album that reflects year-by-year progress. Strong, analytical documents are particularly attractive to donors.
- Conduct a horizontal evaluation to feed into the consultant's analysis—to compare a project with others. The consultant may be able to act as a facilitator.
- Show commitment to capacity building by assigning someone from the organization to shadow the consultant.

Hiring a consultant demands due diligence. What kind of experience do they have in M&E or ET? Have they worked with a like-minded institution before? Do they understand exactly what is needed? Do they have a strong substantive knowledge of the work the organization does? And perhaps most importantly, does their personal style fit?[28] Never assume that a consultant knows what is wanted. Thorough briefing is essential, and a task-specific budget specifying a breakdown of time, travel, and other direct/indirect costs, can help to clarify expectations and roles.

Such work can be assigned internally but, as Patton says, "it takes clear conviction, subtle diplomacy, and an astute understanding of how to help superiors appreciate evaluation."[29]

Supportive Evaluative Thinking Environment

Connected to the results of self-assessment are changes that will foster better ET practice at the individual, project, and organizational level.

First, a commitment to capacity strengthening (training/fora) that will help institutionalize the ET concept. Second, ET can be extended from within an organization to its stakeholders. As Patton remarks, "training stakeholders in evaluation methods and processes attends to both short-term and long-term evaluation uses. Making decision-makers more sophisticated about evaluation can contribute to greater use of evaluation over time."[30] Third is a supportive technology environment that represents the degree to which an operation asks routine questions about how hardware and software contribute to effectiveness, conducts regular surveys to ensure the supportiveness of technology systems, and acts upon its collected data.[31]

BOX 3.1
Evaluative Thinking in Kenya and Malawi

In the Health Research Capacity Strengthening (HRCS) initiatives in Kenya and Malawi, ET is not just a tool—it is the very basis of the operations.

Their product is information for change. They are changing the way that information is gathered, stored and exchanged. Perforce, they must constantly monitor outcomes of the changes they make to inform their own evolution.

HRCS Learning will inform its two key audiences—HRCS itself, at the level of the funding partners (DFiD, Welcome Trust, IDRC) and the two country

(Box 3.1 contd.)

(Box 3.1 contd.)

initiatives, and the global community of those concerned with strategies for research capacity development. In the first instance, HRCS Learning will provide a rolling picture of HRCS's operations in order to inform and adjust HRCS's programming, both within and between Kenya and Malawi. The size and complexity of HRCS demands this kind of introspection to ensure that, over time, its activities evolve, learn and absorb lessons and experiences from other initiatives and contexts. In the second instance, HRCS Learning will capture these lessons and outcomes to inform other nascent research capacity strengthening efforts, many of which are already turning to the HRCS experience for guidance and expertise.

The "learning" process will involve a combination of internal and consultant-led analyses, workshops, exchanges, publications, open dialog, evaluation, "safe harbour" meetings, etc. It will elicit, document, synthesize and disseminate learning relevant to health research capacity development, both within Kenya and Malawi as well as to other similar initiatives.

Source: IDRC. 2006. "Health Research Capacity Strengthening." Available online at http://www.idrc.ca/en/ev-106713-201-1-Do_TOPIC.html (accessed November 8, 2010).

Budget

ET has a cost in time, finances, and human resources. Budgets for all three need to be dedicated and specific, not derived from or expressed as a percentage of other spends. Project proposals that include a well thought-out ET strategy is being encouraged by donors who are looking to support research that aims to be action-oriented and reflective in nature.

INSTITUTIONALIZING EVALUATIVE THINKING

ET is not and will not become a definitive process. It is by definition a learning—and therefore changing—concept. It is learning for change. It is learning to inform and shape action. It must therefore be a part of an organization's built-in culture rather than a bolt-on technique. It is a complement to—not a replacement for—M&E. To further understand particular M&E approaches, Frequently Asked Questions about M&E, discussing core concepts in both quantitative and qualitative M&E and tools can be found in chapter 15.

The *Guide to Monitoring and Evaluating Health Information Products and Services* "provides publishers, knowledge managers, programme managers, M&E specialists, and health information communicators with a standardized way to evaluate whether their print or electronic products and services meet the requirements needed to make them effective, used, and adapted by health care practitioners and policymakers in the field."[32]

NOTES AND REFERENCES

1. Davidson, E.J. 2005. "Evaluative Thinking and Learning-enabled Organisational Cultures," Presentation to the Canadian Evaluation Society & American Evaluation Association Conference, October 28, 2005.
2. Our definition draws upon the work of the Bruner Foundation. While the Bruner Foundation has issued a variety of bulletins and papers on Evaluative Thinking, their particular definition can be found in, Bruner Foundation. 2005. "Evaluative Thinking: Bulletin 2." *Evaluative Thinking in Organisations.* All 11 bulletins are available online at http://www.brunerfoundation.org/ei/sub_page.php?page=tools (accessed October 18, 2010).
3. Roper, L. and J. Pettit. 2002. "Development and the Learning Organisation: An Introduction," *Development in Practice*, 12 (3,4). Available online at http://www.developmentinpractice.org/oa/vol12/v12n03.htm (accessed October 18, 2010).
4. Patton, M.Q. 2006. "Evaluation for the Way We Work." *The Nonprofit Quarterly*, Spring 2006.
5. Patton, M.Q. 1999. "Utilization-Focused Evaluation in Africa." Evaluation Training Lectures delivered to the Inaugural Conference of the African Evaluation Association, 13–17 September 1999, Nairobi Kenya. Available online at www.preval.org/documentos/00552.pdf (accessed October 18, 2010). Also

see Patton, M.Q. 1997. *Utilization-Focused Evaluation.* Thousand Oaks, CA: SAGE Publications Inc.

6. Agarwal, A. 2005. "Learning Organisation," HR Folks International. Available online at www.hrfolks.com/ARTICLES/Learning%20Organisation/Learning%20Organisation.pdf (accessed October 18, 2010).
7. Senge, P. 1990. *The Fifth Discipline: The Art and Practice of the Learning Organisation.* New York, NY: Doubleday. This landmark work was extensively revised and reissued in 2006.
8. Agarwal, "Learning Organisation," and Senge, *"The Fifth Discipline."*
9. Agarwal, "Learning Organisation."
10. Dodge, C.P. and G. Bennett. 2010. *Changing Minds: A Guide to Facilitated Participatory Planning.* New Delhi: Academic Foundation; Ottawa: International Development Research Centre; Kampala: Fountain Publishing.
11. Davies, R. and J. Dart. 2005. *The Most Significant Change (MSC) Technique: A Guide to its Use.* Available online at www.mande.co.uk/docs/MSCGuide.htm (accessed October 18, 2010).
12. Hovland I. 2007. "Making a Difference: M&E of Policy Research," ODI Working Paper 281. Available online at www.odi.org.uk/rapid/Publications/Documents/WP281.pdf (accessed October 18, 2010).
13. Adapted from Davies and Dart (2005).
14. Adapted from Acosta, A. and B. Douthwaite. 2005. "Appreciative inquiry: An approach for learning and change based on our own best practices," ILAC Brief 6, July 2005. Available online at www.cgiar-ilac.org/downloads/Briefs/Brief6Proof2.pdf (accessed October 18, 2010).
15. Acosta, A. and B. Douthwaite. 2005. "Appreciative Inquiry: An Approach for Learning and Change Based on our Own Best Practices," ILAC Brief 6, July 2005. Available online at www.cgiar-ilac.org/downloads/Briefs/Brief6Proof2.pdf (accessed October 18, 2010).
16. Wikipedia. "After Action Review." Available online at http://en.wikipedia.org/wiki/After_Action_Review (accessed October 18, 2010).
17. Wallace, S. (USAID). 2006. "After Action Review: Technical Guidance." Available online at http://www.docstoc.com/docs/673425/The-After-Action-Review-Technical-Guidance (accessed September 29, 2010).
18. Mission-Centered Solutions, Inc. 2008. "Guidelines for the AAR." Available online at http://www.mcsolutions.com/resources/AAR_Wildland_Fire.pdf (accessed August 24, 2008).
19. Hovland, I. 2007. "Making a Difference: M&E of Policy Research," ODI Working Paper 281. Available online at www.odi.org.uk/rapid/Publications/Documents/WP281.pdf (accessed August 24, 2008).

20. Thiele, G., A. Devaux, C. Velasco and K. Manrique. 2006. "Horizontal Evaluation: Stimulating Social Learning among Peers," ILAC Brief 13, November 2006. Available at www.cgiar-ilac.org/downloads/Briefs/ILAC_Brief13.pdf (accessed October 18, 2010).
21. Hovland, "Making a Difference."
22. Westat, J.F. 2002. *The 2002 User Friendly Handbook for Project Evaluation.* National Science Foundation. Available at www.nsf.gov/pubs/2002/nsf02057/start.htm (accessed October 18, 2010).
23. Dodge and Bennett, *Changing Minds.*
24. Westat, J. F. 2002. *The 2002 User Friendly Handbook.* National Science Foundation. Available online at www.nsf.gov/pubs/2002/nsf02057/nsf02057.pdf (accessed August 23, 2008).
25. Westat, *The 2002 User Friendly Handbook.*
26. Molund S and G. Schill 2004. *Looking Back Moving Forward: Sida Evaluation Manual.* Stockholm: Sida.
27. Patton, "Utilization-Focused Evaluation in Africa."
28. Bruner Foundation. 2005. "Evaluative Thinking Bulletin 3: Board Members and Evaluation." Available online at http://www.brunerfoundation.org/ei/sub_page.php?page=tools (accessed October 18, 2010).
29. Patton, "Utilization-Focused Evaluation in Africa."
30. Patton, "Utilization-Focused Evaluation in Africa."
31. Bruner Foundation. 2005. "Evaluative Thinking Bulletin 7: Evaluation and Technology." Available online at http://www.brunerfoundation.org/ei/sub_page.php?page=tools (accessed October 18, 2010).
32. Sullivan, T.M., M. Strachan and B.K. Timmons. 2007. *Guide to Monitoring and Evaluating Health Information Products and Services.* Baltimore, Maryland: Center for Communication Programs, Johns Hopkins Bloomberg School of Public Health; Washington, DC: Constella Futures; Cambridge, Massachusetts: Management Sciences for Health. Available online at http://info.k4health.org/hipnet/MEGuide/MEGUIDE2007.pdf (accessed October 18, 2010).

SECTION

II

The Audience

The Context and the Contacts

Audiences—all audiences—have no interest in your aims except in the context of their own. Above any other factor, if you recognize and cater for this, your KT communication will probably work. If you do not, it definitely will not.

Philosophers have debated the subject of "altruism" for centuries, leading to a mountain of literature large enough to last a lifetime for those who wish to follow the trail all the way down to the selfish gene. Or there is a shorter way, by reading this one sentence:

For all practical purposes, the behaviour of nature in general and human nature in particular is motivated first and above all by a singular consideration: What's in it for me?

By all means keep searching for the exception, but meanwhile accept the rule. If you have a message to convey (e.g., a research finding), you can be certain that each and every person you wish to tell—the first, middle, and the last—is asking: What is in it for me?

As soon as the answer to that question is negative, the audience will stop listening. It will turn the page or look for the wastepaper basket. That applies equally to single individuals or complex institutions. For even if you think you are addressing a government, a ministry, a company, or a newspaper, you will not be talking to a building or a badge, you will be talking to a person.

If you understand the person—the audience—and their needs, you will be able to tailor the message appropriately to them. If you are able to do this, you have a better chance of getting them to listen. That is what is in it for you!

4

Context Mapping

Context must resound in all we do. It is the setting in which any action takes place, and it involves anything and everything from climate to politics, economics to culture, people, personalities and prejudices to history, technology, and fashion.

Without it, we might try selling fridges at the North Pole, frostbite remedies in the Sahara, and cabbages to carnivores. Context is a primary determinant of every *What, Where, Why, Who, When* and *How* of life.

Clearly, the more comprehensive our knowledge of the particular context of a specific plan, the more effective our action can be. Context is not just an accessory of KT. It is a fundamental of knowledge itself.

Context Mapping, Political Mapping, Power Mapping, Stakeholder Analysis, whatever the term, the idea connecting each is an appreciation of the setting that surrounds research. It is the tool KT uses to identify, express, and address relevant context issues. It starts by clearly defining "the objective" of a research project, then explores what forces may act upon that mission, positively or negatively, from the very outset (time, skills, resources) to the very end (stakeholders, target audience, policy-makers). This map is then used to design strategies that avoid problems, overcome obstacles, exploit opportunities, and deliver results with optimum impact.

"Context Mapping" is our preferred, politically neutral term for this process of understanding and adaptation, and in this chapter we will examine some of the theory and illustrate it through practical tools and examples.

THE DYNAMICS OF THE POLICY ENVIRONMENT

What are We Trying to Achieve?

The more specific an objective, the easier it becomes to understand a context and target audience. The target audience is by no means a side-bar—it is an essential part of research from the very outset. Followed by choosing the relevant messages, and appropriate tools and channels to reach them with precision and impact.

Who, Precisely, is the Target Audience?

In most cases, there will be a broad spectrum of individuals or groups who might have a vested interest in the project processes, findings, and proposed policy change.[1]

The importance and influence of each will vary, so the first task is to disaggregate (and prioritize) the audiences.

From a list of all stakeholders/targets, it is useful to create three categories:

1. Those with whom we MUST interact/communicate (usually those with overarching power to enable or prevent our objective);
2. Those we SHOULD interact/communicate with (usually those who can make the process easier or more difficult);
3. And those we would LIKE to interact/communicate with (those who might indirectly help or hinder, or represent some future or spin-off factor).[2]

Imagine these as three concentric circles and focus first on the inner ring.

FIGURE 4.1
Prioritizing Audiences

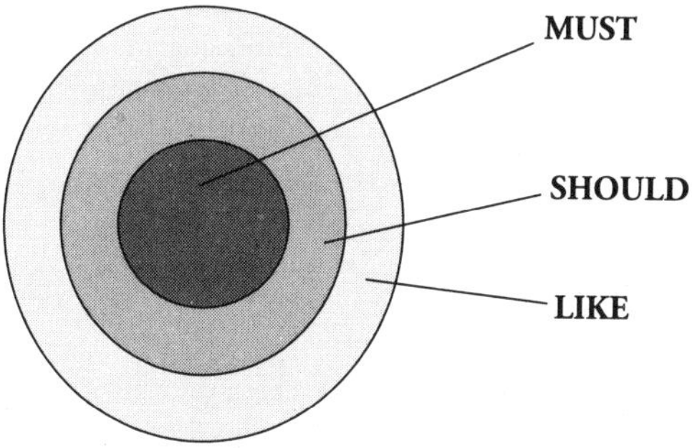

Who are the Most Important Actors?

If the objective is to influence a health policy, logically the organization that makes health policy will top the list. But even to such an obvious question, there is often not a clear answer. The Ministry of Health's decisions on a particular issue may be subject to preferences from multilateral donors or activities of single-issue national boards. These may, or may not, be harmonized and collaborative efforts.

BOX 4.1
Building Research Policy Links During an Economic Transition: The Vietnam Economic Research Network

The IDRC-funded Vietnam Economic Research Network (VERN), was formed to analyze the impacts of "economic renovation" (*Doi Moi*) on everything from managing inflation, food prices and fair trade to protecting the poor and building government capacity. Communication between researchers and policy-makers has been a key pillar of the process, and the network's Advisory Committee, which comprises officials from across the Vietnamese legislature and civil service, helps VERN

(Box 4.1 contd.)

(Box 4.1 contd.)

researchers to design projects that respond to current policy dilemmas and questions.

VERN, with support from ODI, has used a variety of techniques such as a website, policy and economic briefs and a policy workshop to connect their research to policy decisions. The research findings and their implications have also been cited in the Vietnam Development Report 2006. Two VERN researchers and three members of the VERN Advisory Committee have consequently been invited to join the official panel of economic advisors to the Economic Committee of the National Assembly, which has asked VERN to produce policy papers on pressing topics.

The process has led to a change in attitude about the role of economic research in Vietnam. Policy-makers are now demanding research to inform their policies. In turn, VERN researchers see their role in a new light and have found a new motivation to communicate their work.

This Network is coordinated by staff at the Centre for Analysis and Forecasting, under the Vietnam Academy of Social Sciences (VASS). More information on this IDRC-supported project is available at: http://www.idrc.ca/ggp/ev-107306-201-1-DO_TOPIC.html and at (http://www.vern.org.vn)

Sources: IDRC. 2006. "Vietnam Economic Research Network (VERN)." Available online at http://www.idrc.ca/ggp/ev-107306-201-1-DO_TOPIC.html (accessed October 14, 2010).

Vietnam Economic Research Network. Available online at http://www.vern.org.vn/ (accessed October 14, 2010).

And even if the Ministry does hold core power, exactly who within the Ministry wields it? The Minister, the Permanent Secretary, the Director of ... and who (at other levels or in other areas) has *their* ear? Broad target groups must be broken down as much as possible.

Policy-making is complex. As Stuart and Hovland suggest, "Where are the supporters, entry points, policy hooks, and opportunities to hang a proposal on in a timely and focused manner? Where are the detractors?"[3]

With careful analysis, the actors in any of the rings can be categorized as supporters, detractors or fence-sitters.[4]

What Level are We Trying to Influence?

There is a marked difference between proposing changes to national health policies and suggesting changes in the way services are implemented at a local level. It is essential to grasp this in order to achieve the stated objective.

How Politicized is the Issue?

No matter how sound or pressing a research initiative is, if it runs against the prevailing political wind, then either the project must be reframed to a less sensitive angle, or commitment made to the extra budget and time burdens of a contra-current concept.

What are the Information Needs of Target Audience?

The ways in which target audiences receive and absorb information is shaped by many factors, including their personal preferences and habits, literacy and education levels, degree of access to various media formats, and their level of understanding of the issue at hand. To communicate with any audience, we must consider *their* needs and *their* preferences—not only our abilities or desires. As discussed elsewhere in this book, a variety of tools can be employed to "package" information in a format well suited for any particular audience. These include policy briefs, systematic reviews, newspaper articles, newsletters, brochures, emails, radio spots, short video clips, and more.

BOX 4.2

Mercury in the Amazon—The Power of Opinion Leaders

Being one of the most poisonous natural substances on earth, mercury contamination and its connection to food, health and the environment was the focus of research by scientists from UQAM and the Universidade Federal do Pará in the village of Brasilia Legal. The mercury trail itself has done much to inform international discussion. Mercury in soil is usually harmless; because most plants cannot absorb it, but it becomes hazardous once it enters aquatic systems. Fish take up some of this methylmercury, through eating plankton. However, it is the fish which eat other fish that become most contaminated.

In time, the team not only sourced the deadly poison in the Tapajos River, but also traced where it went.

The villagers were involved from the outset in seeking solutions. A community workshop created the slogan "eat more fish that do not eat other fish." Posters were developed as a guide to safer and more hazardous species, and there was a cartoon strip entitled "O Mercúrio no Tapajós."

The results were spectacular. People were eating the same quantity of fish as before but their mercury levels had fallen by 40 per cent, leading to an improvement in nervous system function.These findings were followed by the recognition of the benefits of fruit consumption based on data from women who kept the year-long food diaries. The project also shed light on important contrasts between the families of people who were born and grew up in Tapajos and those of immigrants from the northwest, highlighting the influence of immigration on farmers' choices with respect to agriculture and extractive activity.

Workshops and other activities to achieve this brought together about 30 communities and numerous group affiliations—almost all led by those most central to the social networks and proactive in these communities: women. These networks blossomed in competence and confidence. They not only provided channels for further mercury research findings (such as the links between deforestation and Hg contamination) but also other local issues. The real focal points in the village—the "opinion leaders" whose views carried the most weight on important matters pertaining to health and environmental degradation—were once again, often women, rather than the official village chief or local priest one might have expected.

Source: CARUSO Project. Available online at http://www.unites.uqam.ca/gmf/caruso/caruso_home.htm (accessed October 14, 2010).

CONTEXT MAPPING TOOLS

Beyond common sense and other empirical approaches to assessing the overall research and policy environment, useful techniques have evolved to help map complex contexts. Such techniques can facilitate:

- an analysis of the different political actors in any given policy environment;
- an assessment of the power, position, and interests of those actors;
- an analysis of the degree of any actor's support;
- a graphic of the pressures for and against change; and
- an understanding of policy networks and policy influencers.

The following section gives an overview of some of the major mapping techniques. More information is contained in the links provided later.

Stakeholder Analysis

Qualitative data is needed to determine the interests, behaviour, intentions, agenda, inter-relations, and influence of different actors in a particular issue.

The "Stakeholder Analysis" tool is particularly useful in determining whose support should be sought throughout the project to ensure its eventual impact. It arose from "recognition among managers, policy-makers and researchers of the central role of stakeholders (individuals, groups and organizations) who have an interest (stake) and their potential to influence the actions and aims of an organization, project or policy direction."[5] Once results are available, as Stuart and Hovland explain, this tool can be used to determine "who needs to know about the research, what their positions and interests are and how the research should be presented and framed to appeal to them."[6]

What is actually being mapped?

1. The nature of stakeholders' interests.
2. The extent to which stakeholders' interests converge or overlap.
3. The stakeholders' importance with regard to the issue/policy/reform at hand.
4. The stakeholders' influence in this regard.

What are the steps in a Stakeholder Analysis?[7]

Creating a stakeholder table: This identifies all relevant stakeholders, often separating them into primary and secondary. Within these categories, there can be differentiation by occupation, income, gender, etc. Table 4.1 will help sketch out competing or hidden interests, and the impact of the project on those interests (typically as positive, negative, or unknown). The table can also indicate the priority of each stakeholder (one = high priority, four = low).

TABLE 4.1
Stakeholder Table[8]

Primary Stakeholders	*Interests*	*Potential Project Impact*	*Relative Priorities of Interest*
Ministry of Health	Implements project; provides funding; employs project staff	+	1
Communities	Receive intervention	+	2
Secondary Stakeholders	...		

Assessing each stakeholder's importance and influence: If "importance" is defined as a stakeholder's relevance to the project, and "influence" as their power over the project's success, they can be classified accordingly. A graph where x = importance and y = influence can help visualize the combination of both variables.

Identifying risks and assumptions: As any project depends on the strength and validity of core assumptions, sketching these out in advance can help depict relationships between stakeholders, potential conflicts of interest, and the appropriate level of stakeholder participation.

BOX 4.3
From Slum Dwellers to Urban Planners—The Power of Social Participation in Jakarta

Illegal and unruly slum settlements are a nightmare for large-but-poor cities everywhere. Jakarta, potential world champion of overpopulation in limited space and with scarce resources, has decided to turn the nightmare into a dream.

Space underneath an elevated toll-way in North Jakarta had been illegally occupied by more than 10,000 people, their homes and their businesses. They were forcibly evicted after a fire in 2007. However, they quickly returned.

With the support of IDRC and Mercy Corps in 2008, a group of settlers organized a participatory planning process to demonstrate to the local government that the community had a long-term vision for the space and should be allowed to administer it. More than 600 community members of all ages contributed knowledge and ideas, produced 65 scenarios of how the space could be used, including spaces for green, for community, for commerce, for transport, and for infrastructure. The community is currently developing partnerships with important stakeholders, including the local government and the private company that owns the toll road, and once a final plan is chosen, the community will work together with the relevant stakeholders to transform their space—building not only their environment, but also their capacity and confidence to engage the political system.

Source: IDRC. 2006. "Jakarta, Indonesia: Examining Economic Incentives for Improved Water, Sanitation, and Solid Waste Services." Available online at http://www.idrc.ca/en/ev-103126-201-1-DO_TOPIC.html (accessed October 14, 2010).

Resources

1. For an in-depth discussion of the method's origins and uses, *see* Brugha, R. and Z. Varvasovsky. 2000. 'Stakeholder Analysis: A Review.' *Health Policy and Planning*, 15(3): 239–246.

2. Andreas Wimmer explains the basics of the tool and provides an illustrative example: "Political Science Tools for Assessing Feasibility and Sustainability of Reforms." A Research Paper prepared for the Independent Evaluation Office of the International Monetary Fund. Bonn: Center for Development Research, 2002. Available online at https://www.internationalmonetaryfund.com/External/NP/ieo/2002/pu/052902.pdf (accessed October 14, 2010).
3. Hovland, H. 2005. *Successful Communication: A Toolkit for Researchers and Civil Society Organisations*. London: ODI. Also Available online at http://www.odi.org.uk/Rapid/Tools/Toolkits/Communication/Index.html (accessed October 14, 2010).
4. The World Bank's Poverty and Social Impact Analysis (PSIA) Source Book provides an overview of various Stakeholder Analysis Tools. Available online at http://go.worldbank.org/GZ9TK1W7R0 (accessed October 14, 2010).
5. Schmeer, K. 1999. *Guidelines for Conducting a Stakeholder Analysis*. Bethesda, MD: Partnerships for Health Reform, Abt Associates Inc. Also available online at http://www.phrplus.org/Pubs/hts3.pdf (accessed October 14, 2010).
6. "Health Systems Institutional Characteristics: A Survey of 29 OECD Countries." Available online at http://kuuc.chair.ulaval.ca/url.php?i=6346&f=News&l=En (accessed October 14, 2010). In 2008, the OECD launched a survey to collect information on the health systems characteristics of member countries. This paper presents the information provided by 29 of these countries in 2009.
7. "The Dissemination of Scholarly Information: Old Approaches and New Possibilities." Available online at http://kuuc.chair.ulaval.ca/url.php?i=6349&f=News&l=En (accessed October 14, 2010). Current methods of disseminating scholarly information focus on the use of journals that retain exclusive rights in the material they publish. Using a simple model, the authors of this paper explore the reasons for the development of the traditional journal model, why it is no longer efficient, and how it could be improved upon.

Force Field Analysis

This tool looks beyond actors to identify different forces of influence—pressures for and against a proposed change. The data comes from interviews, literature reviews, and stakeholder workshops. This tool is particularly useful to determine whether or not the initiative is feasible. If the analysis indicates the "forces for change" are many, the odds of success are high; if the balance favours those opposed to change; it is advisable to reconsider the objectives—or commit to long and in-depth advocacy work. Once the project is underway, this technique can help improve the chances of success by understanding who the supporters and opponents are likely to be.

Steps to undertaking a force field analysis:

1. In graphical format, place the plan, project or proposed change in the middle.
2. On either side, list the forces for and against the change.
3. Assign a numerical score for each force. Example: one = weak, five = strong.

FIGURE 4.2
Force Field Analysis

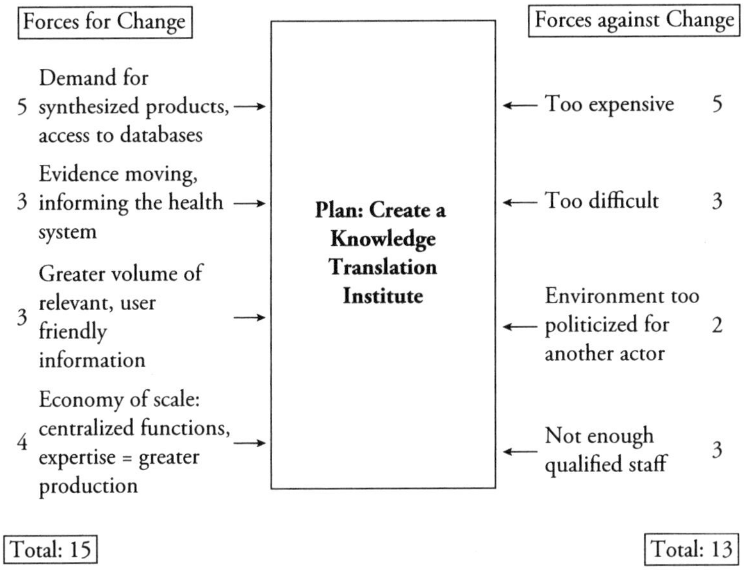

Source: Adapted from *Force Field Analysis: Understanding the Pressures for and Against Change*, Mind Tools, available online at http://www.mindtools.com/pages/article/newTED_06.htm

Resources

1. Hovland, H. 2005. *Successful Communication: A Toolkit for Researchers and Civil Society Organisations*. Available online at http://www.odi.org.uk/Rapid/Tools/Toolkits/Communication/Index.html (accessed October 14, 2010).

2. The Mind Tools website provides a good overview of the tool and provides a free worksheet to assist you in carrying out your own analysis. *See* "Force Field Analysis: Understanding the Pressures For and Against Change." Available online at http://www.mindtools.com/pages/article/newTED_06.htm (accessed October 14, 2010).
3. The Eureka Program of the Ohio Literacy Resource Center provides a concise 2-page brief on the topic. Available online at http://literacy.kent.edu/eureka/strategies/force_field_analysis.pdf (accessed October 14, 2010).
4. An in-depth description of the tool is provided in Section 2 of 2002. Dearden, P. et al. 2003. *Tools for Development: A Handbook for those Engaged in Development Activity.* 2002. Version 15. London: Department for International Development. Also Available online at www.dfid.gov.uk/pubs/files/toolsfor-development.pdf (accessed October 14, 2010).
5. For a discussion of Force Field Analysis by its creator *see* Lewin, K. 1951. *Field Theory in Social Science.* New York, NY: Harper and Row.

Policy Network Mapping

This helps to bypass less relevant actors and focus on those who are really concerned by, or can influence, projects, and proposals. Like Stakeholder Analysis, Policy Network Mapping can reveal personal and team relationships with individuals who wield political influence.

Elements to consider include:[9]

1. What are the different points through which a project or policy passes to become approved and implemented?
2. Who are the actors in charge of each step?
3. How is access to these actors achieved?
4. Are there other actors—not officially part of the process—who have substantial influence over those who decide?
5. In which ways can officials exercise influence over this process? Do they have particular skills or contacts that might help?

In situations where decision-making processes include complex, multi-actor issues, a policy network can sketch out relationships between players, show degrees of access, and lines of authority. This reveals how advocacy or evidence may need to move to achieve the desired influence.

FIGURE 4.3
Policy Network Map: HIV/AIDS in Country X

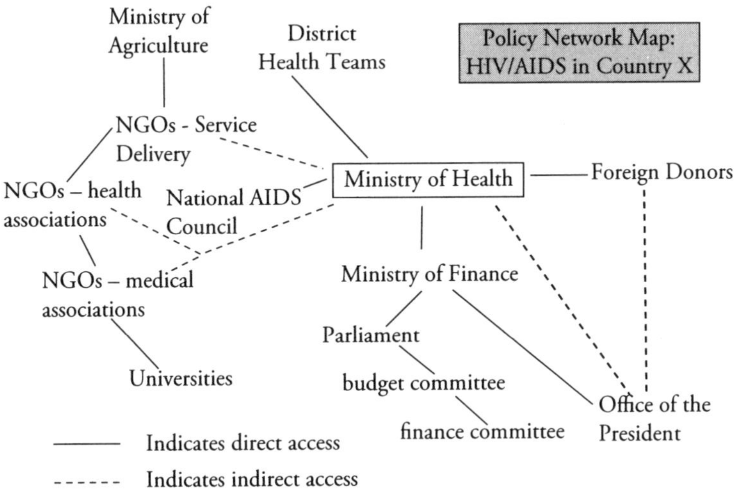

Source: Adapted from Crosby, B. 1992. "Management and the Environment for Implementation of Policy Change: Part Two, Policy Environment Mapping Techniques," *Implementing Policy Change: Technical Notes No. 5*, April 1992. Available online at http://www.usaid.gov/our_work/democracy_and_governance/publications/ipc/tn-5.pdf (accessed October 14, 2010).

Resources

1. Crosby, B. 1992. "Management and the Environment for Implementation of Policy Change: Part Two, Policy Environment Mapping Techniques," *Implementing Policy Change: Technical Notes*, 5 (April): 1–15. Also available online at http://www.usaid.gov/our_work/democracy_and_governance/publications/ipc/tn-5.pdf (accessed October 14, 2010).
2. Mikkelsen, M. 2006. "Policy Network Analysis as a Strategic Tool for the Voluntary Sector," *Policy Studies*, 27(1): 17–26.

Influence Mapping

This tool, also known as Stakeholder Influence Mapping, Power Mapping, or Arena of Influence, identifies "the individuals and groups with the power to effect a key decision." It also helps investigate "the position and motive of each player and the best channels to communicate with them."[10]

Influence Mapping is particularly useful in differentiating between decision-makers and those who can influence them (e.g., opinion leaders). The influencers are often more accessible, opening a channel to those who are not.

FIGURE 4.4
Influence Mapping

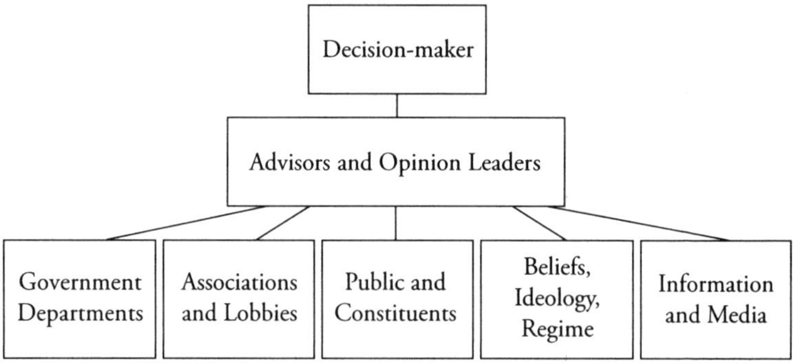

Source: Stuart, D. and I. Hovland. 2004. "Tools for Policy Impact: A Handbook for Researchers". Available online at www.odi.org.uk/rapid/Publications/Documents/Tools_handbook_final_web.pdf (accessed October 14, 2010).

Resources

1. Mayers, J. and S. Vermeulen. 2005. *Stakeholder Influence Mapping*. Power Tools Series. London: International Institute for Environment and Development. Also available online at http://www.policypowertools.org/Tools/Understanding/SIM.html (accessed October 14, 2010).
2. Stuart, D. and I. Hovland. 2004. *Tools for Policy Impact: A Handbook for Researchers.* Available online at www.odi.org.uk/rapid/Publications/Documents/Tools_handbook_final_web.pdf (accessed October 14, 2010).

THE POLICY CYCLE AND POLICY-MAKING THEORIES: AN OVERVIEW

Many scholars have studied the policy-making cycle, hoping to understand its workings and how to best influence the process. Policy making does not perfectly comply with the models developed to explain it, but such models are useful in separating the process into different stages, and generically understanding the influences that act upon each stage. For simplicity, five main stages are identified and discussed below. More discussion on this issue (including the role of evidence within the policy cycle) can be found in chapter 5.

FIGURE 4.5
The Policy-making Process

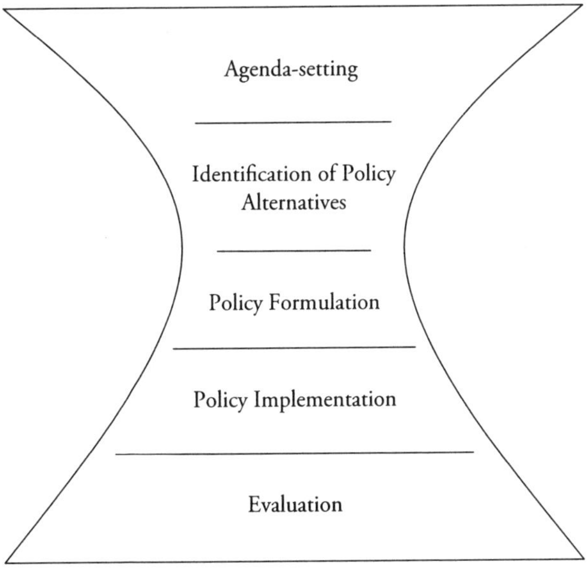

The hour-glass figure illustrates the potential degree of influence that we might have on each stage, from greatest at the agenda-setting and evaluation stages to least at the policy formulation stage. While many stakeholders can influence the agenda-setting stage, usually only a select group is involved in policy formulation. This is not to say that researchers do not have a potential role to play at each stage but that one should be aware of the challenges involved.

Agenda-setting

Not all problems will catch the attention of decision-makers. One challenge is to present information in a way that convinces them that particular ideas and proposals warrant immediate/priority consideration. As control of the agenda holds tremendous power over eventual policy outcomes, governments will try to command what is placed on the agenda. Others thus have little influence over the decision-making process unless they are highly organized into cause groups, lobby groups, networks, and the media—which exert pressure for agenda input.

Tools to raise the profile of an issue include public education and outreach, media campaigns, coalition building, and stakeholder meetings.

Identification of Alternatives and Policy Formulation

Decision-makers typically examine a variety of possible solutions before selecting one, leading to new or amended policy. Rationally, actors are expected to identify alternatives, gather information on each, analyze this against predefined criteria, and select the most efficient and effective option. However, decision-making is rarely so straightforward. Time-constraints, personal interests, lobby-group pressures, "colloquial evidence," and simple negligence can interfere.

Nevertheless, researchers can play a pivotal role in pushing a preferred solution forward, especially in helping decision-makers understand and use very specialized knowledge. This requires packaging the right information in the right format (for more on ways in which to best communicate research findings, please refer to Chapters 6, 7, 8 and 9).

BOX 4.4

Working to Improve Nutrition through Participatory Cropping Systems in Malawi

Science knows well enough the connections between soil fertility and nutrition; between nutrition and health. But how is this knowledge to be translated to communities in parts of Malawi where the soil is poor, 60 percent of the population cannot meet its basic daily needs, and 49 percent of under-five children suffer from stunting as a result? (2001)

One KT answer is to directly involve the subjects of a study in the research itself; so the process of getting the facts is—simultaneously—a public education exercise! Such a participatory ecosystem approach was used by the Nutritional Research Team (NRT)—getting farmers themselves to grow the crops the study wished to assess: in one step, experimentation and farmer-to-farmer learning.

NRT also brought together family members with influence on child nutrition and hospital and scientific researchers to look at agriculture, health, gender, and social relations. The dialogue not only identified the problems as findings, but solved them—through reflection, learning from doing, and discussion to foster long-term change. Key nutrition messages were discussed at recipe days, through dramas, role plays, informal chatting by the river, and house visits. In parallel, standard scientific data was collected from hospital visits, family surveys, crop yield figures, soil nutrients analysis.

Participants included more than 11,000 resource-poor smallholder farmers and their families, teachers, caregivers at nursery schools, and hospital staff, who also passed on seeds, food, information, and assistance to another 27,000 people in neighboring villages. The project could reach even wider as the Ministry of Agriculture agreed to bring farmers from other regions to see the work. The combination of agricultural intervention and a focus on food and health resulted in enhanced income and food security, increased social capital in the communities, and the extension of legume-based agricultural practices to communities outside the project area. Science brought knowledge to the project; and learned much from it. There have been numerous journal articles published on the project. See: http://soilandfood.org/ The project is also covered in a *National Geographic* article as an agro ecological alternative to the dominant agricultural model of fertilizers, hybrid seeds and pesticides being promoted for Africa.

Sources: Bourne Jr., J.K. 2009. "The Global Food Crisis." *National Geographic Magazine.* Available online at http://s.ngm.com/print/2009/06/cheap-food/bourne-text (accessed October 14, 2010).

"Soils, Foods, and Healthy Communities." Available online at http://soilandfood.org/ (accessed October 14, 2010).

Policy Implementation

Policy is only as effective as its implementation. As Anderson (1972) explains, administrative bodies charged with implementation typically "constitute a governmental habitat in which expertise finds a wealth of opportunity to exert itself and influence policy... Technical considerations and professional advice play an important part in most administrative decision making."[11] As experts, researchers can help set standards and criteria to increase the chances of policy implementation. In addition, regulatory and issue advocacy as well as litigation can be used to ensure that what is implemented complies with the policy decision.

Monitoring and Evaluation

Once a policy has been implemented, monitoring and evaluation strategies can measure effectiveness and capture lessons that will inform future policy decisions and their implementation. Research is useful in evaluating the extent to which policy has attained objectives and whether the desired outcomes were reached. Researchers further benefit from a degree of autonomy from decision-makers, allowing an objective assessment. For an in-depth discussion of different M&E techniques, please refer to the M&E Frequently Asked Questions, in Chapter 15.

BOX 4.5

Mapping the Policy Context in Zambia

As discussed throughout this chapter, often a number of different steps are required to get a full sense of the context. Sometimes, more ad hoc and informal methods can be quite useful. In Zambia, for example, a group of researchers and practitioners—under the coordination of the Zambia Forum for Health Research (ZAMFOHR)—conducted a number of context mapping exercises to better understand the overall context of health research, specifically focusing on who

(Box 4.5 contd.)

(Box 4.5 contd.)

was producing it, and how it had or had not been utilized. Several documents were commissioned to explore specific research, policy and political dynamics, including: Who is researching what? Who is funding what? How does research move to the policy arena? Who are the key actors within that arena? And, how could a Knowledge Translation Institute such as ZAMFOHR help to fill the gaps separating knowledge production, management, translation and utilization?

Today, these documents are available as a resource to any interested party, and are specifically targeted at Zambian researchers who are carrying out, or are planning to carry out, research in that country.

Source: ZAMFOHR website. Available online at www.zamfohr.org (accessed October 14, 2010).

NOTES AND REFERENCES

1. Hovland, H. 2005. "Successful Communication : A Toolkit for Researchers and Civil Society Organisations." Available online at www.odi.org.uk/publications/toolkits/rapid/tools2.pdf (accessed October 14, 2010).
2. Adapted from notes written by Metcalfe, J. 2002. "Communication Planning for Scientists and Engineers." *Workbook on Communication and Medial Skills for Scientists and Engineers*. Australia: Foundation for Education, Science and Technology. Available online at www.saasta.ac.za/scicom/pdfs/comm_planning.pdf (accessed October 14, 2010).
3. Stuart, D. and I. Hovland. 2004. *Tools for Policy Impact: A Handbook for Researchers*. Available online at www.odi.org.uk/rapid/Publications/ Documents/Tools_handbook_final_web.pdf (accessed October 14, 2010).
4. Meltsner, A. 1972. "Political Feasibility and Policy Analysis," *Public Administration Review*, 32 (6): 859–867.
5. Brugha, R. and Z. Varvasovsky. 2000. 'Stakeholder Analysis: A Review," Health *Policy and Planning*, 15(3): 239–246.
6. Stuart and Hovland, *Tools for Policy Impact*.
7. For more on Stakeholder Analysis, *see* Gavin, T. and C. Pinder. "Impact Assessment and Stakeholder Analysis." Available online at http://www.proveandimprove.org/new/documents/StakeholderAnalysis.pdf (accessed February 9, 2011).

8. Adapted from "Notes on How to Do a Stakeholder Analysis." (*See* note 7).
9. Crosby, B. 1992. "Management and the Environment for Implementation of Policy Change: Part Two, Policy Environment Mapping Techniques," *Implementing Policy Change: Technical Notes*, April (5).
10. Stuart and Hovland, *Tools for Policy Impact*.
11. Anderson, J. 1972. *Public Policy-Making*. New York, NY: Praeger Publishing.

5

Bringing in the Demand

Towards the Harmony of Push and Pull

The Mexico City Summit of Health Ministers in 2004 recognized the need for partnership between researchers and policy-makers, added the "know-do gap" to the popular lexicon, and saw how greater focus on "the demand side" would increase the influence of research on policy.

> *There is nothing a government hates more than to be well-informed; for it makes the process of arriving at decisions much more complicated and difficult.*
>
> **John Maynard Keynes**

But apart from realizing new partnerships, this watershed event explored such things as "knowledge brokering" and "involving the potential users of research in setting research priorities."[1] However, the Summit offered no formula for this new approach and no solution to the axiom above.

SUPPLY ⟷ **DEMAND**
Researchers — *Decision-makers*

This chapter synthesizes the ideas and theories that have emerged since then, looks at the theory behind both the policy process and the nature of evidence, and explores approaches—especially linkage and exchange, knowledge brokering, and KTPs—that have proven effective.

THE THEORY BEHIND THE HARMONY

The Enchantment with Rationality

> *Researchers search for truth by using a rational model... Policymakers search for compromise by using an intuitive model.*
>
> **Choi et al.**[2]

Caplan asserted that decision-makers and researchers are not natural partners.[3] Lomas coined the indicative "enchantment with rationality" to describe the researcher's typical mindset.[4] Whereas science solves problems to know, policy solves problems to satisfy.[5] Researchers demand logic, exactitude and replication; they are "rationalists."[6] Policy-makers are driven by intuition, constituents, and compromise; they are "realists."[7] Clearly, then, for the two to be partners, a "research-attuned culture" must grow in the policy world, and a "decision-relevant culture" must start to influence researchers.[8]

> *The two things one should never watch being made: sausages and public policy.*
>
> **Jonathan Lomas**

Researchers need to recognize that policy-making is not an event: it is a process.[9] It unfolds over time under the pressure of many different forces. Science is only one of these forces; only one kind of "evidence."[10] *Decision-makers* must appreciate that research is not a product; it, too, is a process. While there are useful "clearing houses" of research information, knowledge or evidence can take years to develop and in science there are usually no "quick fixes". *Both* sides need to understand the influence of "context" on what any piece of evidence might mean, and realize that they are trading not only in information, but also in values and beliefs.

Knowledge Translation is a meeting of complex processes within a social environment.[11] Its foundations are relationships. Personal contact between researchers and policy makers is crucial and is by far the best predictor of research processes influencing policy.[12]

BOX 5.1
Facilitators and Barriers to Research Utilization

In 24 studies, the most commonly mentioned *facilitators* of the use of research evidence in policy-making were:

- personal contact between researchers and policy-makers (13/24);
- timeliness and relevance of the research (13/24);
- research that included a summary with clear recommendations (11/24);
- good quality research (6/24);
- research that confirmed current policy or endorsed self-interest (6/24);
- community pressure or client demand for research (4/24);
- research that included effectiveness data (3/24).

The most commonly mentioned *barriers* were:

- absence of personal contact between researchers and policy-makers (11/24);
- lack of timeliness or relevance of research (9/24);
- mutual mistrust, including perceived political naïveté of researchers and scientific naïveté of policy-makers (8/24);
- power and budget struggles (7/24);
- poor quality of research (6/24);
- political instability or high turnover of policy-making staff (5/24).

Source: Innvaer, Simon, Gunn Vist, Mari Trommald and Andrew Oxman. 2002. "Health Policy-makers' Perceptions of their use of Evidence: A Systematic Review," *Journal of Health Services Research & Policy*, 7 (4): 239–44.

No matter what the setting—be it in a household or between countries—good relationships break down walls, they create understanding and trust, and they are the great facilitators for bringing radically different processes peacefully together.

The "Casual Empiricism" of the Policy Process

There are three broad types of policy-making:

1. Legislative policies provide organizational codes that govern an overall (health) system and its services.[13] Legislative decision-makers tend to be non-specialists, focused on impacts.
2. Administrative policies dictate how services are run and resourced. These decision-makers tend to have strong specialist knowledge and may use evidence to assist in programme planning.
3. Clinical policies centre on therapies and corresponding strategies. These clinical decision-makers are the greatest users of research evidence, and are receptive to "data on safety, clinical effectiveness, cost-effectiveness, and patient acceptance"—perhaps not simply because they are more attuned to research, but because research is more attuned to them.[14]

Policy-making (necessarily) is the messy unfolding of collective action, achieved mostly through dialogue, argument, influence, and conflict."[15] Stone concludes that "much of the policy process involves debates about values masquerading as debates about fact and data."[16]

In all three applications, different sources of information, different value systems, and different beliefs act upon the "evidence," the "decision," and the "outcome."

Science is not exempt. We trust the findings that most agree with our own values. The more aligned knowledge is with our value system, the more likely we are to accept it: some may accept abstinence as an evidence-informed AIDS prevention strategy, while others might brand this approach right-wing dogma. It all depends upon user perspective. The more challenging a piece of knowledge is to our value system, the more we will contest it—no matter its strength or relevance.[17] Research that challenges decision-maker values, ideas and ethics, will have a much harder time proving its validity.

A decision-maker's values (e.g., the spread of disease should be contained), can be further complicated by the values of culture (e.g., male circumcision should always be performed) and political ideologies (e.g., the state should provide free male circumcision to all who want it). Any argument that the researchers might present to the decision-makers must take these often intransigent "value layers" into account.

Respecting the immutable power of values and ideologies and focusing instead on changing decision-maker beliefs (e.g., believing that the African potato will cure AIDS) may well be a more promising approach.[18] Beliefs tend to be more flexible and fleeting—we all understand that knowledge is always evolving.

Scholars have tried to visualize this tangle of science, values, and beliefs with different metaphors and images. The policy process has "garbage cans," it's a "swampy world," it's a delta capturing the run-off of problem streams, policy streams, and political streams.[19]

Despite numerous studies of every facet of decision-making the road between where decision-makers get their information and the characteristics necessary for that information to infiltrate and influence their decision-making remains inscrutable. One clear bottom line is that research evidence must compete with all other types of "evidence" a decision-maker may find relevant, from common sense to "casual empiricism" to expert opinion and analysis.[20]

What We Talk about When We Talk about Evidence

"Evidence" means one thing to a researcher (what is proven to be true), quite another to a lawyer (what is said to be true),[21] and something completely different to decision-makers.[22] So what does the term "evidence-based" actually mean? Lomas et al. (2005) have distilled "evidence" into three different types.[23]

The first is *context-free evidence*, which is what works in general, or knowledge about the overall "potential" of something.[24] This is typically medical-effectiveness or biomedical research (e.g., male circumcision can be a strong preventative measure to HIV-acquisition in men).

The second is *context-sensitive evidence*, which puts evidence into a particular operational setting (e.g., male circumcision in LMICs may fail as an intervention owing to health system weakness and underlying poverty issues).[25] In ways, context-sensitive research can be thought of as where biomedicine meets social science, or where quantitative meets qualitative: Where the theory meets the reality. Both types of "evidence" are captured in systematic reviews (see discussion in chapter 7), in other syntheses (e.g., a policy brief—see chapters 7 and 11), in single studies, and in pilot or case studies.

The third and often most troublesome category is *colloquial evidence*. Roughly defined as any kind of evidence "that establishes a fact or gives reason for believing in something," it is typically a product of expert opinion (which can be biased) and first-hand experience (which may be anomalous or misinterpreted). What happens to the chances for research findings or policy if there is perceived "evidence" that "most experts agree that implementing a universal male circumcision policy is impossible because of the current cultural and political environment?"[26] Some commentators suggest colloquial evidence is useful for plugging the holes that the other types of evidence do not address; it may indeed be critical where other evidence is inconclusive or non-existent.[27]

If these three degrees of "evidence" typically inform the policy process, how and what weight should be given to each piece of evidence when making a decision? Are all pieces equal, or some more equal than others? The CHSRF has suggested that weighing up the evidence—assigning a value to each "piece"—is impossible. Where is the scale that will allow us to weigh experience (apples), expert opinion (oranges), and a systematic review (bananas)? Yet we clearly need to consider and assess all the pieces, and the only mechanism that seems to work is consensus through "deliberative dialogue."[28] Naturally, there are some important and contested issues here such as "what is consensus?" "who is a relevant stakeholder?" and "what is a participatory methodology?" Every deliberative process will have to answer these. We return to this important idea in the "Knowledge Translation Platform" section that concludes this chapter.

BOX 5.2
When it Comes to Research Evidence: What do Decision-makers Look For?

Credibility and reliability: evidence must come from trusted sources to eliminate need for the decision-maker to appraise and assess the evidence. This can be established through: authors' names, peer recommendations, source of research, familiarity of logos.

Quality: evidence must be current, jargon-free, and transparent; must include what worked and what did not; and must have recommendations ranked in order of effectiveness.

Cost: discussion must include a cost analysis.

Context: evidence must be presented within local/national/regional/global context.

Timing: evidence appears on issues they are already working on.

Connections: where can they get more information.

Customization: presented evidence must be flexible as it is often used for: cutting and pasting for presentations; passing on to colleagues; printing for their own use; saving and filing; composing a briefing note.

Modes of delivery: electronic format preferred but hard copy also desired.

Source: Adapted from Dobbins , M., T. DeCorby and T. Twiddy. 2004. "A Knowledge Transfer Strategy for Public Health Decision Makers," *Worldviews on Evidence-based Nursing*, 1 (2): 120–128.

BOX 5.3
Deliberative Dialogues

With an emphasis on creating and maintaining personal relationships, *deliberative dialogues* can take any number of forms and formats. They can involve any set of researchers, decision-makers, the media, civil society groups, and donors; can be officially "off-the-record" in that the "Chatham House Rule" prevails and no notes are taken, no quotations attributed; can focus on specific policies; can work to set a research agenda, and so on.

The Policy Pie

Different stakeholders have different notions of evidence, assign different weights to each piece, and scientific evidence (either context-free or -sensitive) is only one ingredient in the policy pie.

So this, then, frames everything we talk about when we talk about "evidence":

- The meaning of "evidence" is always defined by the *audience.*
- Evidence depends on *context* to become useful. It requires interpretation before it can become operational.
- No one "piece" of evidence can possibly address every point a decision-maker must consider in setting policy.[29]
- Evidence is *fluid* and evidence is *fallible.* What is true today is not always true tomorrow because context is ever-shifting and *science* is ever-evolving, there are flaws in the peer-review process, *context* can defeat replicability, and the underlying nature of knowledge is to question and improve upon itself.[30,31]

Nothing, we come to realize, is ever 100 percent true. Politics and decision-making may seem like irrational sports, but the fact is that they, like science, have evolved over centuries and have equally strong and compelling reasons for considering a wide range of "evidence" in their processes.

Perhaps pressing for "evidence-based policy" or even "evidence-based culture" might seem naive[32]—the subject is so slippery as to elude any sort of categorization, let alone represent a base for action. A growing chorus of authors is underlining this point, emphasizing that "there will never be a generalizable evidence base on which managers and policy makers will be able to draw unambiguously and to universal agreement" and that the idea of evidence-based policy "overlooks or plays down the role of power, uncertainty and chance."[33] One scholar adds that "the evidential base in support of the proposition that evidence-informed decision-making is, in broadest terms, a 'good thing' is itself distressingly thin."[34]

FIGURE 5.1
The Policy Pie

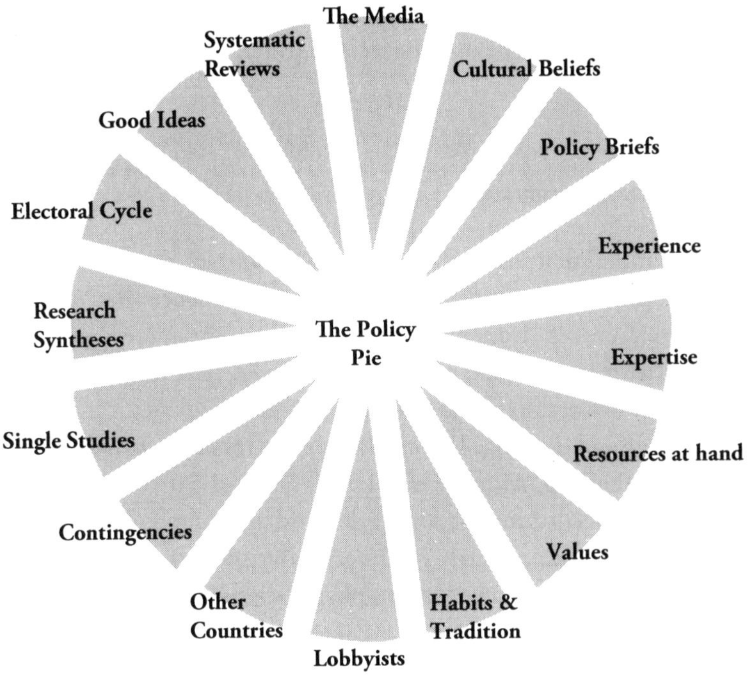

BOX 5.4
Viewing Evidence in Context

It is worth heeding the caution "evidence-based policy: proceed with care." For instance, while there may be extensive research on the effectiveness of health-care interventions, there is often less evidence on their cost-effectiveness, implementation, cultural appropriateness and effects on health inequalities, all of which are important considerations for policy-making.

Source: Haines, A., K. Shyama and M. Borchert. 2004. "Bridging the Implementation Gap between Knowledge and Action for Health," *Bulletin of the World Health Organisation*, 82: 724–732.

While there might be such a thing as "evidence-based practice" (e.g., incorporating context-free evidence into clinical practice and procedure), the compromised nature of decision-making all but disqualifies "evidence-based policy." "Evidence-influenced" or "evidence-informed" seem more realistic targets: they still aim to increase decision-makers' use of evidence, though in a more context-appreciative way.

$$\frac{\text{(Context-free + context-sensitive + colloquial) evidence}}{\text{(Debate + negotiation + compromise) experience}} = \text{Policy?}$$

The more that research can avoid fitting evidence into the decision-maker's context, and instead create evidence that respects the policy process from the very beginning—the more savvy and influential research work might be. As Davies puts it, we "need to encourage ownership of the evidence, not just the policy."[35]

Linkage and exchange becomes a primary model in achieving this type of ownership, with the creation of demand-based evidence reflecting the needed integration of demand and supply. Rather than trying to translate research results directly into practice, pursuing partnerships and creating robust linkages seems to offer the best set of choices in a KT agenda.

INTEGRATING RESEARCH AND POLICY

Towards Linkage and Exchange

Just as researchers may wish to co-produce policy, they must also encourage decision-makers to co-produce research—by identifying priorities, designing research, or utilizing findings—moving past researcher-driven processes into "co-production processes."[36] This section looks at linkage and exchange efforts through the researcher's lens.

How When Why

When it comes to "bringing in the demand," important variables include *how, when,* and *why* decision-makers are involved in the research process. Ross et al. outline the *how*:[37]

- As *decision-makers*, they are likely to not have direct involvement in the research, but do welcome and support it and can therefore confer an important air of legitimacy on the research process, and can open doors to further resources, information, and even other decision-makers.
- As a *responsive audience*, their participation rises, though it remains in response to actions initiated by researchers. They can help to craft the research design, be members of the research advisory team, give advice on tactics, and even help collect data, interpret results, and create KT strategies.
- As an *integral partner*, their level of participation increase dramatically. Decision-makers often initiate activities and shape key parts of the process. They are key team members with a role in executing core strategy.
- Another (and the "usual") category would be as *passive audience*—where decision-makers do not participate in the research process and instead passively receive findings and syntheses. They may even actively request these findings, but they play no role in the research itself. While this is clearly not as desirable as any of the other categories, finding the right decision-maker audiences and getting their ear is vital, and could be the precursor to more active and formal support.

When decision-makers become involved—at what stage in the research process—helps determine the nature of their involvement. Inviting a decision-maker to participate in the design of a research project is a smart, logical move, and several current Calls for Proposals have this type of requirement for any funding application.[38] While specific projects might make participation attractive to decision-makers, there are ideas researchers might use to encourage decision-makers to participate in or even create a research initiative.[39]

A decision-maker's potential role in the research process is often dictated by:

- the stage of the research process their participation is wanted;
- the time commitment required;

BOX 5.5

Public Sector Anti-retroviral Treatment in the Free State, South Africa

This multi-phased research program is a cutting-edge collaboration between the Free State Department of Health and several different research teams (one studying and training nurses, another the provincial health system, a third the impact of ART on communities). The FS Department of Health—initially the audience of research findings on the Practical Approach to Lung Health South Africa (PALSA) project—later sought PALSA's assistance in the development and implementation of training and an overall monitoring and evaluation programme for the Free State anti-retroviral therapy rollout. Through discussions with other researchers, the program was expanded to examine the effects on clients of health services, possible "system leakage," and the presenting policy context.

Close personal relationships, open lines of communication, and a decision-maker unafraid to receive "snapshots" of the health system are essential to this program. It aims to:

1. Support the government's effort to strengthen the primary health care system to deal with the HIV/AIDS burden in the Free State.
2. Build accountability and improve the effectiveness of the service offer to citizens through evaluating training of health workers and documenting the impact of the rollout at the institutional and community levels.
3. Inform and strengthen public health sector capacity to implement an effective, accountable and equitable ART rollout in the FS, potentially other provinces and other parts of Southern Africa.

Note: For more information, see http://network.idrc.ca/en/ev-59560-201-1-DO_TOPIC.html

- the alignment between decision-maker expertise and the research programme; and
- the presence of an already existing relationship.

Strong linkage and exchange strategies might include:

1. **Conceptualization stage:** Holding priority-setting exercises. These fora typically "translate priority issues into priority research questions."[40] They embrace a wide set of stakeholders and are guided by criteria of urgency and durability, the

existing stock of research, research capacity, and decision-maker capacity to participate and engage the findings. Just convening priority-setting exercises can cement partnerships.

2. **Production stage:** Designing collaborative research projects.[41] Denis and Lomas outline how collaborative research often works to amalgamate scientists and non-scientists in a true "cooperative endeavour" and produce knowledge that is ultimately usable.[42] It can bring the investigator into the policy and the policy into the investigation. Instead of a "client-contractor" relationship, collaborative partnership presents solutions, creates mechanisms to share issues and results, and designs broader KT strategies.[43] Ultimately, partnership must be characterized by a spirit of give-and-take, with fora and practices enabling collaborators to access and share their knowledge.[44]
3. **Dissemination stage:** Creating knowledge translation strategies. This goes beyond syntheses and into precise road-maps from findings to practice. Decision-makers know the context and how the policy system works. If researchers provide the science, decision-makers add how information flows, who needs to see it, and what consensus is needed to push action.
4. **Utilization stage:** Creating knowledge systems that can use, re-use and demand knowledge, backed by robust knowledge management systems to search, find, capture, extract, and even appraise knowledge and evidence. Deliberative fora unleash and share vital tacit knowledge.
5. **Stewardship:** Inviting decision-makers to participate in the governance of research processes by serving on a research organization's governing board or grant-selection panel.[45]
6. **Funding:** Inviting decision-makers to make a financial contribution to a research project. This investment reinforces a sense of real ownership, and CHSRF advises that funding arrangements should be one of the "first items to discuss" with decision-makers, establishing clear requirements and expectations up front.[46] Decision-makers, even if only silent partners,

then have a strong financial stake in any project's success. Joint-funding translates to mutual commitment.

BOX 5.6

Urban Ecosystems and Human Health in South Africa

Massive urban growth and health problems in slums prompted South Africa's Reconstruction and Development Programme to fund construction of enormous low-cost housing estates. Between 1994 and the start of 2001, more than 1.1 million cheap houses eligible for government subsidies had been built, accommodating five million of the estimated 12.5 million South Africans without proper housing.

But the people were neither happier nor (as research proved) healthier than the slum dwellers who struggled with poor sanitation, crowded conditions, unsafe water supplies, little electricity, and proximity to near industries with heavy emissions and busy roads.

The anomaly was addressed and understood when the team brought together key stakeholders—city planners, managers and community members—and tapped the local university's GIS capability, and mapped (and shared) the physical, environmental, and social aspects of the issue. The maps served as effective visual aids, and an interactive password-protected website served as a convenient medium for discussions between the research team and the municipality

The research team submitted articles in the local newspaper to share the vision and findings with local residents, (http://www.queensu.ca/sarc/ecohealth/publications.php) and encouraged them to react to the content of the papers.

The outcome was a significant investment shift from new estates (social dislocators) to improving existing slums (people's real homes, neighborhoods and workplaces), and the networks and concepts which achieved that now play a bigger part in all city planning and administration issues.

New collaborations and partnerships emerged as a result and consequently had a significant impact on the vision and policy of key stakeholders and institutions regulating the expansion of RDP housing. The University increased the relevance and reach of its work to the policy level. The Municipality gained as some of the gaps of information necessary to design more efficient policies were filled, while the Chamber of Business could position the agenda and priorities of the business sector on the municipal agenda and into the design of a new urbanization model. The partnerships established by the project are thus alive, well, and continue to influence political life.

BOX 5.7

Tobacco Control and Taxes: Win-win in Jamaica

After Jamaica ratified the Framework Convention on Tobacco Control (FCTC) in 2005, the Government contemplated a range of recommended policy measures to reduce tobacco consumption. Raising the price of cigarettes is well recognized as one of the most cost-effective interventions for reducing tobacco consumption but, despite the enthusiasm of the Ministry of Health, policy-makers within the Ministry of Finance feared that its success could reduce government revenues. These fears were stoked by the tobacco industry.

Research on the precise economic impacts showed that increasing tobacco taxes to about 72 percent of the retail price would deter consumption and increase government revenues and with schematics like the non-technical Laffer curve graphs they convinced policy-makers, including the minister of finance, of the "win-win" effect for both public health and the economy. Subsequent tax hikes reinforced the evidence, media campaigns reinforced support for the policy, and latest proposals commit 20 percent of tobacco revenue collections to the National Health Fund.

Note: For more information see, http://www.idrc.ca/tobacco/ev-86779-201-1-DO_TOPIC.html

Knowing the incentives for decision-makers to link and exchange with research processes, allows for informed "pitching" of the idea. One of the strongest pitches here rests on the question of impact—often the variable of primary interest to decision-makers. Why decision-makers may choose to become involved include:

- The ability to create evidence that aligns with policy needs. The more sensitive the issue, the more important evidence "ammunition" becomes.
- The wish for programmes that have been pre-validated by scientific (or "expert") scrutiny (e.g., synthesis work highlighting "best practice") or examples from other relevant contexts.
- The need to evaluate existing policies. This is one of the strongest arguments for linkage and exchange, as research can provide a "moving snapshot" of policies as they unfold, allowing

"mid-course" corrections. (For a pre-eminent example of this, see the Free State's Public Sector ART text box above.)

Context Mapping (*see* chapter 4) can greatly help efforts to link and exchange. Partnering with the wrong person or wrong department can squander time, resources, and reputations. Advance due diligence is essential.

Knowledge Brokering

In an ideal world, a web of vibrant linkages would connect researchers and decision-makers. In practice, there is often a disconnect that good intentions just cannot bridge. Enter the knowledge broker,[47] the "middle man"—either an individual or an institution—between the research and policy worlds.

The primary task of any broker is to network—using mediation and communication skills to put (and keep) people together. They must understand the variables of politics, power, and actors.[48] The terrain is research and politics and power dynamics. Knowledge-brokering characteristics that Jackson-Bowers et al. identify are trustworthiness, credibility, political neutrality, and subject expertise. Seniority, technical background (academics, policy officers, communication specialists), and location differ across contexts.[49] Beyond networking, the role of the broker can include:

- *synthesizing* research (through the creation of policy briefs, systematic reviews, briefing notes). The broker must have basic research skills and an ability to gather, appraise, analyze, synthesize, and package knowledge and evidence;
- *creating* partnerships around single studies, programmes of research, or systematic reviews to enable them to collectively ask and answer locally relevant questions;[50]
- *facilitating* access to data and evidence; and
- *convening* meetings (e.g., providing the space and neutrality for priority setting exercises or national policy dialogues).

BOX 5.8

What Distinguishes Brokering?

The researcher who takes the trouble to seek out a health system administrator with new findings is doing knowledge transfer but not brokering. That same individual running biannual meetings between researcher colleagues and the policy branch of a provincial health ministry is acting as a knowledge broker. A communications specialist who translates research into plain language and packages it in an accessible, quick-answer format is working on dissemination strategies but not brokering. The same communications specialist acting as a liaison for the ministry, building a network of academic contacts and helping policy planners to develop evidence-gathering projects, is brokering.

Source: CHSRF. 2003. "The Theory and Practice of Knowledge Brokering in Canada's Health System: a report based on a CHSRF national consultation and a literature review."

The "when" of decision-makers' interaction with research processes indicates specific entry-points for brokers. As one of their principal roles is encouraging a "continuous exchange on many levels—from sharing experiences and searching out existing knowledge to turning management problems into workable questions for researchers to study," brokers' work includes:[51]

1. **Priority-setting exercises:** Brokers offer neutrality (in both politics and in geography—i.e., occupying a neutral space) to convene this meeting, chair it, and mediate different needs and interests;
2. **Collaborative research:** Brokers can help define the terms for fusing research and policy, and neutrally negotiate partnerships;
3. **KT strategies:** As one of the core skills of any broker may well be evidence retrieval, appraisal and dissemination—as well as knowing the policy process—broker institutions could have searchable databases, clearing houses, and may also provide "rapid response" services that provide policy-ready responses (see KTPs below).

4. **Funding:** Through networking and personal contacts, brokers tend to know of funding opportunities and can help researchers and decision-makers negotiate the terms of funding or co-funding.

Knowledge Translation Platforms

"Knowledge Translation Platforms" (KTPs) are institutions committed to the arts of knowledge brokering. They aim to nurture and formalize the spirit of linkage and exchange. They exist to serve researchers, decision-makers, and other research-users—such as practitioners, the media, and civil society.

BOX 5.9
Attempts to Create KTPs

In Africa, there have been several noteworthy attempts at creating KTPs. One is the Regional East African Community Health Policy Initiative (REACH-Policy), currently based in Kampala, Uganda. Another is the Zambia Forum for Health Research (ZAMFOHR), based in Lusaka, Zambia. It is expected, however, that more and more KTPs will arise, particularly with continuing strong support from entities like EVIPNet, the Alliance for Health Policy and Systems Research, and IDRC.

Notes: More information on REACH-Policy available online at www.idrc.ca/uploads/user-S/11551301781REACH_Prospectus.pdf (accessed October 18, 2010)

More information on ZAMFOHR available online at http://www.zamfohr.org/ (accessed October 18, 2010).

More information on EVIPNet available online at http://www.who.int/rpc/evipnet/en/ (accessed October 18, 2010).

More information on the Alliance for Health Policy and Systems Research available online at http://www.who.int/alliance-hpsr/en/ (accessed October 18, 2010).

More information on IDRC available online at www.idrc.ca (accessed October 18, 2010).

KTPs are intermediaries between research and policy, smoothing movement between the two, connecting push and pull, infusing public dialogue with understanding of research processes, and with evidence. KTPs may find, present and synthesize information, convene meetings, and work to bring actors and processes together. If KT is a series of social processes, then KTPs are the meeting places.

Setting-up a KTP requires political manoeuvering and a broad stakeholder acceptance. This was done in both Zambia and the East African Community through deliberative dialogues. Such dialogues are crucial when discussing the terms of stakeholder buy-in, and for refining the technique of dialogue itself.

To be this convener of dialogues, optimally a KTP should be a physical place/space. The backdrop matters. KTPs need a room large enough for deliberative dialogues, and space for a resource centre. These ideas are explored in the three fundamental themes that wind through a KTP: the knowledge base, deliberative dialoguing, and capacity strengthening.

KNOWLEDGE DIALOGUE CAPACITY

The Knowledge Base

The knowledge base describes the role of a KTP in defining and identifying knowledge, and then harvesting, preparing, and synthesizing it. The term "knowledge" here includes any kind of data or information that a KTP deems relevant. If a KTP is to be a trusted source or clearing house of the knowledge that stakeholders want, it must have that knowledge on hand.

A dynamic knowledge base can see a KTP:

- determining the *type* of knowledge it wants to capture—e.g., single studies, systematic reviews, grey literature, project profiles, and reports. This could also take a more targeted

approach—e.g., capturing all research on malaria prevention and treatment;
- scanning the environment to *determine the knowledge other institutions already possess,* both electronically and in hard copy. This could include university libraries, UN agencies (e.g., UNAIDS), government parastatals (e.g., National AIDS Committees), and NGOs (both domestic and international);
- collecting all *relevant* knowledge (including research evidence, syntheses, reports, project profiles, etc.), through site visits to relevant organizations or individuals; and
- *creating systems* that allow users to search and access it (e.g., databases, websites, and dialogs for sharing tacit knowledge) in the understanding that the KTP need not duplicate other systems but rather find ways of tapping into or adding value to them.

Added value could include:

- **Synthesizing research:** Typically systematic reviews, meta-analyses and policy briefs, and user-demanded and other search services. The KTP may assess the quality and local applicability of evidence and contract out the production and regular updating of syntheses, especially where none exist or where quality is questionable.
- **Creating rapid response units:** Accessible by telephone, email or website, these units can rapidly provide up-to-date information for research-users searching for targeted evidence or expert opinion. Rapid response units may also conduct briefings with decision-makers based on the material they find in response to search questions.

KTPs are well placed to package and communicate key messages in user-friendly formats. Such strong knowledge bases can:

- develop *friendly front-ends* that provide "graded entry" for decision-makers. According to the CHSRF's formula, a "graded entry" reduces a complex issue, paper or body of evidence into one-page of "take-home messages," and a three-page executive summary adding benefits, risks, costs of policy alternatives, and factors influencing local applicability.[52] This is often called the 1:3:25 approach, with the "25" representing the full paper or synthesis. Clearly, each 1:3:25 is tailored for its particular target audience;

- producing a "Who's Who" Directory that documents all key health stakeholders domestically, including details of institutional affiliation, papers, grants, etc., and contact information; and
- developing annual reports or newsletters that discuss a range of issues, including gaps in research, "orphaned" research issues, features on successful instances of research and policy collaboration, and bringing in pertinent evidence-to-policy examples and personalities from other sectors or countries.

Deliberative Dialoguing

A deliberative dialogue is more than a meeting. It is almost always politicized and polarized.[53] Most deliberative dialogues tend to be issue-specific—"malaria treatment" rather than "health research." The CHSRF stresses that deliberative dialogs should include "criteria for the sources of evidence and their weight, and a mechanism for eliciting colloquial evidence," while acting as "guarantor" that scientific evidence will take priority.[54]

In order for KTPs to be trusted as neutral spaces for dialogue, incorporating sound deliberative processes is essential. These include:

- **Participation:** Who is invited? What institutions do they represent? What degree of inclusion is needed? Is civil society represented? Practitioners? How many expert disciplines are appropriate?
- **Evidence:** What evidence on the issue is out there? How can the dialogue weigh up and combine competing forms? How will the KTP (or the dialogue itself) resolve conflicts?

- **Facilitation:** Who will chair the meeting? Should an outside facilitator be brought in?
- **Logistics:** Is there material every attendee must read in advance? How will time for questions and space for dissenting or minority views be assured?

BOX 5.10
Addressing Maternal and Neonatal Mortality in Benin

In January 2007, a symposium on maternal and neonatal mortality in Benin, initiated by a research funder—IDRC—brought together, for the first time, health researchers, civil society organizations and decision-makers, who then committed to work together for the life and health of mothers and new-borns.

The Ministry of Health accepted the ensuing recommendation to integrate researchers and decision-makers into the process of developing a national strategy. This was then submitted to the Cabinet for official adoption; and the West African Health Organization is now looking to replicate and scale up the initiative across the 15 member states.

Note: For more information: www.idrc.ca/geh

Safe Harbours and Chatham Houses

Safe Harbours are informal meetings that allow "wild" ideas to be aired and potentially "stupid" questions to be asked—an ideal setting for people to admit they do not know or do not understand science, without fear of judgment. This is vital, because if decision-makers do not understand scientific evidence, they will not use it. They have plenty of "evidential" alternatives and other pieces of the policy pie.

These meetings often use the "Chatham House Rule," which dictates that the meeting may be discussed in the "outside world" but only on the condition that there is no attribution, no record of "who said what." As Wikipedia relates, "the Chatham House Rule evolved to facilitate frank and honest discussion on controversial or unpopular issues by speakers who may not have otherwise had the appropriate forum to speak freely."[55] While this would not be appropriate for all meetings, it has particular utility where decision-makers may feel intimidated or confused by the scientific evidence, or where they wish to discuss political pressures.

BOX 5.11
How REACH used "Safe Harbour" Meetings

The dialogue around the creation of the REACH-Policy initiative identified the need for "safe harbour" meetings. The EVIPNet teams have modified this into a "National Policy Dialogue" to emphasize the level (national) and the task (discussing a national policy).

Source: http://www.idrc.ca/uploads/user-S/11551301781REACH_Prospectus.pdf (accessed January 24, 2011).

Capacity Strengthening

The knowledge base creates a critical mass of information and resources, and deliberative dialoguing creates an open space to discuss and contextualize that knowledge. Capacity strengthening knits the two together.

Though a KTP contributes directly to capacity strengthening—through its knowledge base (good knowledge management systems and user-friendly content = accessible and understandable science), and through its deliberative dialog support (open spaces and multi-level networking = increased opportunities for learning)—regular and consistent training courses add significantly. These can be provided or brokered by the KTP which can also, on behalf of institutions like the Cochrane Collaboration or the CHSRF, identify individuals who would benefit from existing training opportunities elsewhere.

Deliberative dialogues may identify training needs for:

- **Decision-makers:** In acquiring, assessing, adapting, and applying research. Critical appraisal skills are commonly sought and demand for more know-how on organizational change theory and knowledge brokering is likely.[56]

TABLE 5.1
REACH-Policy: Knowledge, Dialogue, Capacity

Process	*Activities*	*Outputs*
Knowledge Base	Conduct searches for syntheses; connect with EAC partner state information bases; create clearing house for one-stop shopping; maintain website; create rapid-response unit to search, conduct, and commission syntheses. Develop friendly front-ends	Functioning clearing house. Databases. Website. Rapid-response unit. Packaged syntheses. KT strategies. Annual reports, newsletters
Deliberative Dialoguing	Hold priority-setting exercises; convene safe harbour and national policy dialogue meetings	Policy and research priorities aligned. Consensus on priorities. Policy-driven research syntheses. Evidence-informed policies created
Capacity Strengthening	Provide policymaker training in how to acquire, assess, adapt, apply research. Provide training for researchers in the policy context; how to create syntheses; how to lead or participate in KT activities	Training workshops. Briefings for high-level decision-makers

Source: REACH-Policy Initiative. 2006. "Prospectus." Available online at http://www.idrc.ca/uploads/user-S/11551301781REACH_Prospectus.pdf (accessed October 18, 2010).

- **Researchers:** In methodology, resource mobilization, knowledge translation, literature retrieval, and the policy process itself. Researchers tend to be very frank about what their training needs are, and how best a KTP might serve them.
- **The media:** In identifying subject experts, acquiring and assessing research, and in knowledge translation.
- **Civil society:** In the research cycle and in acquiring, assessing, adapting, and applying research.

BOX 5.12

The Zambia Forum for Health Research (ZAMFOHR): Resource Centre Plans

In February 2008, ZAMFOHR held a deliberative dialogue over its plans to launch a Resource Centre that would serve the many different research-users in Zambia, with a particular focus on capacity strengthening. With representatives from academia, civil society, the government, the media, and international donors, a facilitator from Tanzania guided the group through:

- a discussion of Resource Center examples in Africa and beyond; and
- a review of existing Resource Centers in Zambia itself.

Then the delegates discussed the core duties for the ZAMFOHR RC and decided that its priority service categories were to:

- harvest, filter, and synthesize research and evidence;
- disseminate and communicate research and evidence;
- build capacity at the interface connecting research with research users;
- provide reference information (collect, store, manage, make accessible).

Source: www.zamfohr.org

Some Concluding Thoughts

"Bringing in the demand" is still far from an exact art or science, and these chapters cannot be comprehensive. With that caveat, the "take-home" messages focused here are:

1. Context is all-pervasive and all-important. The more we know about any context, the greater our chances of influencing decisions.
2. Knowledge is fallible and fluid. Context is ever-shifting and science is ever-evolving.
3. Researchers rationalize and decision-makers compromise.
4. "Evidence" is slippery, elusive, and always user-defined. The challenge in KT is to make context-free and context-sensitive evidence as readily available as colloquial evidence so that all can be discussed and weighed in tandem.

5. All kinds of "evidence" compete for a place in the policy pie. If science cannot make itself understood, decision-makers will rely upon other kinds of "evidence."
6. The policy process has sharply different levels and actors of different capabilities.
7. Researchers need to focus more on changing beliefs and less on challenging values.
8. KT practitioners need to encourage ownership of the evidence, not just the policy; to move past old terms and start talking about demand-based evidence or even demand-based practice.
9. KT is a meeting of processes within a social environment. If research is not a product but a process, and policy is not an event but a process, KT works to bring those processes together, finding solutions by adding context and dialogue.
10. "Linkage and exchange" depends upon how, where, and why decision-makers are involved in the research process.
11. Knowledge brokers are neutral actors on a stage of politics and power. They are trusted resources for bringing together the worlds of research and policy.
12. Knowledge Translation Platforms are built on knowledge bases, deliberative dialogues, and capacity strengthening.
13. Deliberative dialoguing creates contextualized decision support for national research priorities and national policies. It can also determine the functions of a KTP, the nature of a KTP's knowledge base, and the capacity-strengthening courses offered through a KTP.
14. Capacity strengthening can expand the appreciation of research processes and scientific "evidence" among a range of research-users.

Resources

1. Guindon, G. Emmanuel, John N. Lavis, Francisco Becerra-Posada, Hossein Malek-Afzali, Guang Shi, C. Ashok K. Yesudian and Steven J. Hoffman for the Research to Policy and Practice Study Team. 'Bridging the Gaps between

Research, Policy and Practice in Low- and Middle-Income Countries: A Survey of Health Care Providers'. Available online at http://bit.ly/cbiyG7 (accessed October 18, 2010). Gaps continue to exist between research-based evidence and clinical practice. The authors of this article surveyed health care providers in 10 low- and middle-income countries about their use of research-based evidence and examined factors that may facilitate or impede such use.

2. Lavis, John N., G. Emmanuel Guindon, David Cameron, Boungnong Boupha, Masoumeh Dejman, Eric J.A. Osei and Ritu Sadana for the Research to Policy and Practice Study Team. 2010. "Bridging the Gaps between Research, Policy and Practice in Low- and Middle-Income Countries: A Survey of Researchers." *CMAJ*, June 15, 182 (9). Available online at http://bit.ly/aSyDcH (accessed October 18, 2010). Many international statements have urged researchers, policy-makers and health care providers to collaborate in efforts to bridge the gaps between research, policy and practice in low- and middle-income countries. The authors of this article surveyed researchers in 10 countries about their involvement in such efforts.
3. Lomas, Jonathan. 1997. "Improving research dissemination and uptake in the health sector: beyond the sound of one hand clapping," McMaster University Center for Health Economics and Policy Analysis. *Policy Commentary C97-1*, November. Available online at http://28784.vws.magma.ca/knowledge_transfer/pdf/handclapping_e.pdf (accessed October 18, 2010). As the former CEO of the CHSRF, Lomas investigated KT, the know-do gap and the demand side as much as anyone. Though he has written numerous excellent articles, this 1997 work remains the flagship.
4. The CHSRF website. Available online at http://www.chsrf.ca/ (accessed October 18, 2010). Reflecting the work of its former CEO, the CHSRF's website is loaded with papers, approaches, and projects that show the many different facets of linking supply with demand.
5. Davies, Philip. 2004. "Is Evidence-Based Government Possible?." Paper presented at the 4th Annual Campbell Collaboration Colloquium, Washington D.C. February 19. London: Government Chief Social Researcher's Office, Prime Minister's Strategy Unit, Cabinet Office. Available online at http://www.nationalschool.gov.uk/policyhub/downloads/JerryLeeLecture1202041.pdf (accessed October 18, 2010). Davies discusses and analyzes the different types of evidence jockeying to influence decision-makers.
6. Innvaer, Simon, Gunn Vist, Mari Trommald and Andrew Oxman. 2002. "Health Policy-makers' Perceptions of their use of Evidence: A Systematic Review," *Journal of Health Services Research and Policy*. 7:(4): 239–244. Innvaer et al. use a synthesis tool to look back on how syntheses—among other things—have influenced, or not, decision-makers.

7. Hammersley, Martyn. 2005. "Is the Evidence-based Practice Movement doing more Good than Harm? Reflections on Iain Chalmers' Case for Research-based Policy making and Practice," *Evidence and Policy*. 1(1): 85–100. While there are a number of texts challenging conventional wisdom of "evidence-based practice," Hammersley summarizes the argument for caution in assembling and relying upon an evidence base.
8. Lavis, John, Jonathan Lomas, Maimunah Hamid, Nelson Sewankambo. 2006. 'Assessing Country-level Efforts to Link Research to Action'. *Bulletin of the World Health Organisation*. 84 (8): 620–628. This paper provides a breakdown of the different "models" of knowledge translation—push, pull, linkage and exchange, and knowledge translation platforms.

NOTES AND REFERENCES

1. Keynes cited in Davies, P. 2004. "Is Evidence-Based Government Possible?." Paper presented at the 4th Annual Campbell Collaboration Colloquium. Washington DC. 19 February 2004. For details on the Ministerial Summit in Mexico City (2004), see the 'Mexico Statement on Health Research: Knowledge for better health: strengthening health systems'. At http://www.who.int/rpc/summit/agenda/Mexico_Statement-English.pdf
2. Choi, B., T. Pang, V. Lin, P. Puska, G. Sherman, M. Goddard, M. Auckland, P. Sainsbury, S. Stachenko, H. Morrison and C. Clottey. 2005. "Can Scientists and Policy-makers Work Together?" *Journal of Epidemiology and Community Health,* 59: 632–37.
3. CaplanN. 1979. "The Imo-communities Theory and Knowledge Utilization", American Behavioural Scientist, 22(3): 459–70.
4. Lomas, J. 1997. "Improving Research Dissemination and Uptake in the Health Sector: Beyond the Sound of One Hand Clapping." McMaster University Centre for Health Economics and Policy Analysis. *Policy Commentary C97-1*, November 1997. Available online at http://www.nationalschool.gov.uk/policy hub/downloads/JerryLeeLecture1202041.pdf (accessed October 18, 2010).
5. We have chosen to use the term "decision-maker" here because we believe it captures a greater range of daily activities and duties than does "policy-maker," as well as reflecting the many non-policy decisions made at the policy level. Text box quotation from Choi B., T. Pang, V. Lin, P. Puska, G. Sherman, M. Goddard, M. Ackland, P. Sainsbury, S. Stachenko, H. Morrison and C. Clottey. 2005. "Can Scientists and Policy Makers Work Together?," *Journal of Epidemiology and Community Health*. 632–37.

6. Lomas, J., T. Culyer, C. McCutheon, L. McAuley and S. Law. 2005. "Conceptualizing and Combining Evidence for Health System Guidance." *Final Report.*
7. Lawrence, R. 2006. "Research Dissemination: Actively Bringing the Research and Policy Worlds Together," *Evidence & Policy.* 2(3): 373–84.
8. Lavis, J., S. Ross, C. McLeod, A.Gildiner. 2003. 'Measuring the impact of health research'. *Journal of Health Services Research & Policy.* 8(3): 165–70. Also *see* Lawrence, *Evidence & Policy,* 2: 373, and Lomas, "Improving Research Dissemination."
9. Lomas, "Improving Research Dissemination."
10. For a fuller discussion see Black, N. 2001. "Evidence-based Policy: Proceed with Care." *BMJ.* 323. 4 August 2001.
11. Ginsburg, L., S. Lewis, L. Zackheim, and A. Casebeer. 2007. "Revisiting Interaction in Knowledge Translation". *Implementation Science.* 2(34). For a discussion of social processes and the "communicative perspective" see Golden-Biddle K, T. Reay, S. Petz, C. Witt, A. Casebeer, A. Pablo, C.R. Hinings. 2003. "Toward a Communicative Perspective of Collaborating in Research: The Case of the Researcher-decision-maker Partnership". *Journal of Health Services Research & Policy.* 8(2): 20–25.
12. *See* Lomas, "Improving Research Dissemination." Also *see* Innvaer S., G. Vist, M. Trommald and A. Oxman. 2002. "Health Policy-makers' Perceptions of their Use of Evidence: A Systematic Review," *Journal of Health Services Research & Policy.* 7(4). 239–44. Also *see* Jackson-Bowers, E., I. Kalucy, E.McIntyre. 2006. "Focus on Knowledge Brokering," *Primary Health Care Research & Information Service.* No. 4, December 2006. Available online at http://bit.ly/focusonkt (accessed December 14, 2010).
13. *See* Hanney S, M., Gonzalez-Block, M. Buxton and M. Kogan 2003. "The Utilization of Health Research in Policy-making: Concepts, Examples and Methods of Assessment," *Health Research Policy and Systems.* 1(2). doi:10.1186/1478-4505-1-2. Available online at http://www.health-policy-systems.com/content/1/1/2 (accessed October 18, 2010). Also *see* Dobbins, M., P. Rosenbaum, N. Plews, M. Law, and A. Fysh. 2007. "Information Transfer: What do Decision Makers want and Need from Researchers?". *Implementation Science.* 2(20). doi:10.1186/1748-5908-2-20. Available online at http://www.implementationscience.com/content/2/1/20 (accessed October 18, 2010). 2007. Also *see* Jacobson N, D. Butterill, and P. Goering 2003. "Development of a Framework for Knowledge Translation: Understanding User Context," *Journal of Health Services Research & Policy.* 8(2). 94–99. Finally on this point, *see* Lomas, "Improving Research Dissemination."
14. Lomas, "Improving Research Dissemination," for a breakdown and discussion of the respective decision-making "levels". Also *see* Dobbins et al., *Implementation Science* 2: 20.

15. Greenhalgh, T. and J. Russell. 2005. "Reframing Evidence Synthesis as Rhetorical Action in the Policy Making Drama," *Healthcare Policy*. 1(1): 34–42.
16. Stone cited in Greenhalgh and Russell, *Healthcare Policy*. 1: 1.
17. Ginsburg et al., *Implementation Science*. 2: 34; Jacobson et al., *Journal of Health Services Research & Policy*. 8: 94; and Davies, "Is Evidence-Based Government Possible?".
18. For more on this, *see* Black, "Evidence-based Policy."
19. For a recent discussion of Kingdon's various policy models, see Fafard P. 2008. "Evidence and healthy public policy: insights from health and political sciences". National Collaborating Centre for Healthy Public Policy. Also *see* Lawrence, *Evidence & Policy*, 2: 373 and Hanney et al., *Health Research Policy and Systems*. 1: 2.
20. Hanney et al., *Health Research Policy and Systems*. 1: 2 and citing Lindblom and Cohen in same.
21. For a fine quote from Eisenberg (2001): "Law relies on evidence of the instance; health care relies on evidence of the generalizable," *see* Cuyler T. [no date] "Deliberative processes and evidence-informed decision-making in health care".
22. For a full discussion of this, *see* Davies, P. 2007. "Evidence-Based Government: How do we make it happen?," presentation given to the Canadian Association of Paediatric Health Centres. Montreal, October15, 2007. Available online at http://www.caphc.org/documents_annual/2007/conference_ppts/15_10_2007/p_davies.pdf (accessed October 18, 2010). Also *see* Choi B, T. Pang, V. Lin, P. Puska, G. Sherman, M. Goddard, M. Ackland, P. Sainsbury, S. Stachenko, H. Morrison and C. Clotteyet. 2005. "Can Scientists and Policy Makers Work Together?," *Journal of Epidemiology and Community Health*. 59. 632–37.
23. Lomas et al. 2005. and Cuyler [no date]. Text box reference to Dobbins M., T. DeCorby, T. Twiddy. 2004. 'A Knowledge Transfer Strategy for Public Health Decision Makers'. *Worldviews on Evidence-Based Nursing*. 1(2). 120–28.
24. Lomas, J. 2005. 'Using Research to Inform Healthcare Managers' and Policy Makers' Questions: From Summative to Interpretive Synthesis'. *Healthcare Policy* 1(1): 55–71.
25. Lomas, *Healthcare Policy* 1: 55.
26. Davies, "Is Evidence-Based Government Possible?."
27. Lomas, *Healthcare Policy* 1: 55.
28. Hammersley M. 2005. "Is the Evidence-based Practice Movement doing more Good than Harm? Reflections on Iain Chalmers' Case for Research-based Policy making and Practice," *Evidence & Policy*. 1(1). 85–100.
29. For a discussion of issues around the peer-review process, see Grayson, L. 2002. "Evidence-based Policy and the Quality of Evidence: Rethinking Peer Review". ESRC UK Centre for Evidence Based Policy and Practice. For a discussion of

the failings of the evidence-based approach, *see* Hammersley, *Evidence & Policy*. 1: 85.

30. *See* Hammersley, *Evidence & Policy*. 1: 85.
31. *See* Hammersley, *Evidence & Policy*. 1: 85.
32. Greenhalgh (2005) and Hammersley, *Evidence & Policy*. 1: 85. Also *see* Davies, "Is Evidence-Based Government Possible?"
33. Cuyler, "Deliberative Processes and Evidence-informed Decision-making in Health Care".
34. Davies, "Evidence-Based Government: How do We Make it Happen?"
35. Lomas, *Healthcare Policy* 1: 55; and Haines A, K. Shyama, and M.Borchert. 2004. 'Bridging the Implementation Gap between Knowledge and Action for Health'. *Bulletin of the World Health Organisation*. 82. 724–32.
36. *See* Ross, S., J. Lavis, C. Rodriguez, J. Woodside and J-L. Denis. 2003. "Partnership Experiences: Involving Decision-makers in the Research Process". *Journal of Health Services Research & Policy*, 8(Suppl. 2): 26–34.
37. *See*, for instance, the periodic Calls for Proposals from the Alliance for Health Policy and Systems Research at http://www.who.int/alliance-hpsr/callsforproposals/en/ (accessed October 18, 2010).
38. Beyond any particular research project, we might do well to keep the big picture and the long-term in mind by trying to cultivate *system-level partnerships* that can reap benefits for years to come.
39. Lomas, J., N. Fulop, D. Gagnon, P. Allen. 2003. "On being a Good Listener: Setting Priorities for Applied Health Services Research". *Milbank Quarterly*. 81(3): 363–88.
40. CHSRF. [no date]. "How to be a Good Research Partner. A Guide for Health-system Managers and Policy Makers." Available online att http://www.chsrf.ca/other_documents/partner_e.php (accessed October 18, 2010).
41. Denis, J-L and J. Lomas. 2003. "Convergent Evolution: The Academic and Policy Roots of Collaborative Research". *Journal of Health Services Research & Policy*. 8(Suppl. 2): 1–6.
42. *See* CHSRF "How to be a Good Research Partner."
43. *See* Golden-Biddle, *Journal of Health Services Research & Policy*, 8: 20.
44. *See* Lawrence, *Evidence & Policy*, 2: 373; and Jackson-Bowers et al., "Focus on Knowledge Brokering."
45. CHSRF. "How to be a Good Research Partner." Also *see* Martens, P. and N. Roos. 2005. "When Health Services Researchers and Policy Makers Interact: Tales from the Tectonic Plates." *Healthcare Policy*. 1(1): 73–84.
46. CHSRF quotation cited in Jackson-Bowers et al, "Focus on Knowledge Brokering."

47. Cullen (2001) cited in CHSRF. 2003. "The Theory and Practice of Knowledge Brokering in Canada's Health System: A Report Based on a CHSRF National Consultation and a Literature Review."
48. Jackson-Bowers et al., "Focus on Knowledge Brokering."
49. Lavis, J., J. Lomas, M. Hamid, and N. Sewankambo. 2006. 'Assessing Country-level Efforts to Link Research to Action'. *Bulletin of the World Health Organisation*. 84. 620–28.
50. CHSRF, "The Theory and Practice of Knowledge Brokering in Canada's Health System."
51. For a discussion of friendly front-ends, *see* Lavis, J., H. Davies, R. Gruen, K. Walshe, and C. Farquhar. 2006. "Working Within and Beyond the Cochrane Collaboration to Make Systematic Reviews More Useful to Healthcare Managers and Policy Makers," *Healthcare Policy*. 2 (3): 373–384.
52. Lavis J. 2006. "Moving Forward on both Systematic Reviews and Deliberative Processes," *Healthcare Policy*. 1(2).
53. *See* Lomas, J., T. Culyer, C. McCutheon, L. McAuley and S. Law. 2005. "Conceptualizing and Combining Evidence for Health System Guidance." Final Report. Also *see* CHSRF. 2006. "Weighing up the Evidence: Making Evidence-informed Guidance Accurate, Achievable, and Acceptable." A summary of the workshop was held on September 29, 2005.
54. For more, *see* http://en.wikipedia.org/wiki/Chatham_house (accessed October 18, 2010).
55. Dobbins et al., *Implementation Science*, 2: 20.
56. Dobbins, M., T. DeCorby and T. Twiddy. 2004. "A Knowledge Transfer Strategy for Public Health Decision Makers," *Worldviews on Evidence-Based Nursing*, 1(2): 120–128.

SECTION

III

The Message

People interact with each other and the world around them by the exchange—at random or on purpose—of messages.

Because the volume of messages is so vast, we have extremely powerful internal filters that instantaneously judge the relevance of the message—is this for me, does it matter, does it present a danger or an opportunity, is it urgent?—and then either completely block it out, or allow a highly selective part of it, or absorb the complete picture.

Much of this exchange is random. Some of it is planned: a deliberate presentation of specific information, aimed at a specific audience, and aiming for a particular effect.

In the context of KT, the key point is this: the objective is the final, particular effect. So the message must reach the right audience, capture their attention amid a blizzard of other messages invading their space, and persuade them to take specific action. To get the message right, the target audience right, the channel right, and the timing right frequently, consistently, accurately and distinctively—needs a purpose, a plan, a strategy, and skills.

6

Communication Strategy

Every day, communication strategies unfold all around us. The billboards, radio jingles and storefronts, the countless logos and slogans, and advertisements all over the internet, our daily newspapers, the TV, are all clamouring for our attention. In this age of unparalleled choice, communication has to work especially hard to make one idea—in a great sea of ideas—stand out. Here is what separates our findings from all the others. Here is what makes our approach and our organization unique. And here is how our ideas can help you make a decision—whether you are choosing between two pairs of shoes or two policy options.

The making and implementation of a cohesive plan to deliver specific information, to a specific audience, for a specific reason, within a limited time frame, and with finite resources is "communication strategy." The information must not only reach the audience but must also catch their attention, capture their interest, penetrate their thinking, and inspire them to action.

An effective message leads to the action which brings the desired result. The keystone is the "message." The operative word is "effective." Organizations need to see effective communication as a vehicle that is not just helpful or required but essential to achieving core goals.

THE ESSENTIAL ELEMENTS

Addressing these 10 crucial steps gives a snapshot of who you are, what you have to say to the world, who you want to influence, and how you will do that—now, and in the months and years to come.

1. **Review:** How have you been communicating in the past? How effective has that been? How do audiences perceive the messages?
2. **Objective:** What do you want your communication to achieve? Are the objectives SMART?
3. **Audience:** Who is the key audience? Are there others? What information do they need to act upon the message?
4. **Message:** What is the message? Do you have one message for multiple audiences or multiple messages for multiple audiences?
5. **Basket:** What kinds of communication "products" best display and deliver your messages?
6. **Channels:** What channels will promote and disseminate your products?
7. **Resources:** What budget do you have for this? Will this change in the future? What communication skills and hardware do we have?
8. **Timing:** What is your timeline? Would a phased strategy be most appropriate? What special events or opportunities might arise? Does the work (or future work) of like-minded organizations or ministries, etc., present opportunities?
9. **Brand:** Are all of your communication products "on brand?" How can you ensure that you are broadcasting the right message?
10. **Feedback:** How will you know when your communication strategy is successful? What would have changed? How can you assess whether you used the right tools, were on budget and on time, and had any influence?

BOX 6.1
Communication—Not a "Soft" Element

"While policy research and formulation are given their due as tough, demanding areas of an organization's work plan, communication is seen as 'soft'. While programme development and practice are seen as requiring expertise and the thoughtful consideration of best practices, communication is an 'anyone can do it if you have to' task. It is time to retire this thinking. Doing communication strategically requires the same investment of intellect and study that these other areas of nonprofit practice have been accorded."

—**The Frameworks Institute**

Source: Cited in Hershey, C. 2005. *Communications Toolkit: A guide to navigating communications for the nonprofit world.* Available online at www.cause-communications.org/clients-cause.php (accessed October 14, 2010).

The essential elements illustrate some core truths of communication:

- Communication is a two-way process. The better you listen to and know the audience, the better you will relate to their needs and thus the more your messages will be listened to, believed, and acted upon.
- Effective communicators know what an audience wants to know, what "language" they understand, and where and when they look and listen.
- Communication is the single most visible activity we engage in, requiring extra delicacy—say the wrong thing or present badly and the damage could be severe and lasting.
- Tools and channels must fit the message and the audience.
- Messages must recognize the cultural context of audiences.
- Good communication is time- and skill-intensive work.
- There is no certain, catch-all formula. Every communication must be tailored to a particular situation, and constantly learn from feedback.

Review—Performance and Perception

How have you been communicating in the past? How effective has that been? How do your audiences perceive you?

An *audit*—a rigorous and structured review or assessment—can help assess past performance[1] and perceptions[2] (credibility) of an organization through both internal brainstorm and external research.

The evaluation can be absolute or, per Hershey's competitive analysis, judged in comparison with others. She notes: "A big part of the 'who are you' question is determining what makes you unique. What do you do that no one else can do? And one of the best ways to answer that crucial question is to look at how you compare with institutions that serve the same core constituency."[3] She cites the work of Tom Peters and his suggestion that every organization initiates such a competitive analysis by asking itself: who are we? (In one page, then in 25 words), how do we uniquely serve our constituents (again in one page, then in 25 words), and what are three distinct differences between our organization and our competition?

BOX 6.2

Survey Questions to Assess External Perceptions

1. How have you come to learn about organization X in the past?
2. In your opinion, what do you think is most unique about organization X?
3. What is organization X best known for?
4. What is the most compelling reason for supporting this organization?
5. What are the strong reasons for not supporting this organization?
6. Do you find that this organization's papers, ideas or products stand out from those of other research organizations?
7. What could this organization improve about its communication?
8. Are there any other issues regarding this organization and its plans that you would like to comment upon?

Source: Adapted from Hershey, C. 2005, and [no author]. 2001. "Report on Communication Strategies and Information Technology," Mexico City, Mexico. Available online at www.wingsweb.org/download/communication_strategies.pdf (accessed October 14, 2010).

Objectives—Making Them SMART

What do you want communication to achieve? Are the objectives SMART?

All strategies must start with an understanding of objectives.[4] Communication can be expensive in resources and time, so the more precisely you can state your objectives or reasons for communicating, the better you will be able to spend those precious resources.

Many research organizations might state their communication goal as: "In communicating our results and processes, we are seeking to influence or change X," or more generally, "We want people to understand the significance of our research." **Influence is typically the central objective of most research institutions.**

A one-line summary is an important guide, but it must be more specific: "We want communication to make our research understandable and to ultimately influence policy." These can be further defined by ensuring that they are SMART:

Specific;

Measurable;

Attainable;

Results-orientated; and

Time-bound.

In the end you want to evaluate what you have done, so the SMARTer you can be, the easier it will be to ultimately assess and adjust your activities. As the World Wildlife Fund (WWF) offers, examples of strong, specific, clear, and measurable communication objectives could include: building awareness of a project or programme among a tightly defined audience; securing the commitment of a defined group of stakeholders to the project's aims; influencing specific policies or policymakers among key and defined aspects; and encouraging increased stakeholder participation on specific issues.[5]

Take a mission statement example:

To influence the health system, national malaria policies, and to raise anti-malaria awareness in communities.

To test for SMARTness, challenge each word/phrase.

Influence: Does that mean change? In what way(s)?

Health system: Which parts of which health system?

Malaria policies: Would that be malaria "control" policies?

Raise awareness: How indicated, how measured?

Communities: What sort, where?

And all this by *when*?
A SMART mission would therefore be:

To develop a communication strategy that will ensure government adoption of evidence-informed policies in its malaria control strategy by 2011.

BOX 6.3
Communication Objectives in Action: The International Monetary Fund

The IMF's communication strategy seeks, above all, to "strengthen the Fund's effectiveness"—principally by "raising understanding and support among key constituencies of the Fund's mission and reform agenda, and using communication as a tool in the delivery of the Fund's operational activities." Its communication objectives aim "to build understanding and support for the IMF's reform agenda...further integrate communication with operations, raise the impact of communication tools, and rebalance outreach efforts." Each of those areas is large but well defined, and the remainder of its Communication Strategy elaborates on each of these objectives. These are IMF's communication objectives as means to an end, not an end in itself. This distinction is crucial.

Source: The International Monetary Fund. 2007. "The IMF's Communication Strategy". Available online at https://www.imf.org/external/np/pp/2007/eng/052907.pdf (accessed October 14, 2010).

Audience—Primary and Secondary Targets

Who is the key audience? Are there others? What information do they need to act upon your message?

Each audience has its own likes, needs, and abilities. These particularities need to be understood and appreciated in order to reach the various audiences effectively.[6]

The (communication) objectives determine which audiences we need to reach. From there on, the chosen audience determines what and how you communicate—the content of the message, the language, the style, the medium that is best for them, that is most likely to achieve the results you want.

And that applies to each and every audience. For example, where the primary audience is the Ministry of Health, it is likely that secondary audiences might include the general public and the international community. (*See* chapter 4 on Context Mapping for more on mapping audiences)

Neither the best message nor the best medium is the same for any of those. Then there are specific individuals within each broad audience: within the Ministry, the Minister personally, the Permanent Secretary, the Director of Medical Services? Each has a separate personality, level of understanding, and different priorities.

Messages must be designed and delivered accordingly, whether tailoring for a single target or for a mass audience. The following example shows how policy-makers as well as the general public were targeted with the same information but in different ways.

BOX 6.4

TEHIP: Affecting Policy and Practice Simultaneously

One of the key requirements for any successful health systems strengthening project such as the Tanzania Essential Health Interventions Project (TEHIP), is how best to expand the successful strategies and findings to cover the entire country as quickly as possible. "The National Expansion of TEHIP Tools and Strategies through Zonal Rollout (NETTS/ZORO)" project was developed and implemented between July 2006 and June 2009 in Tanzania.

(Box 6.4 contd.)

(Box 6.4 contd.)

In order to ensure uptake of the roll-out results and the role of Zonal Health Resource Centers (ZHRC) several KT tools were employed. Following release of the final evaluation report, a PowerPoint presentation was crafted to identify the main findings and recommendations. The presentation was first presented to the full Ministry of Health and Social Welfare Directors' meeting chaired by the Permanent Secretary (PS) in September 2009. As a result of this high level meeting, the presentation of the evaluation was again made, at the request of the PS and the Chief Medical Officer (CMO) to the Joint Annual Health Sector Review.

Consequently, and with strong senior level support, full activation of the Zonal system has been called for by the PS and the CMO including its clear articulation on the medium-term expenditure framework. These presentations have re-established the importance of the zonal structures and the Ministry of Health and Social Welfare has now re-named the eight centres as ZHRCs in anticipation of further strengthening and devolvement of responsibilities from the central ministry into this zonal system. The evaluation and its initial products were thus timely and appear to have reactivated a strong commitment for their consolidation.

Further communication products include newspaper articles which have appeared in the Tanzanian Citizen and Guardian newspapers with another coming out in the regional, weekly East African newspaper.

- Lobulu, W. *Tanzania:* "Health Sector Rolls Out 'Survival Tools'." *The Arusha Times*. Tanzania. http://allafrica.com/stories/200912220394.html
- Lobulu, W. *Future Looks Bright for Health Sector*. The Citizen Newspaper. Tanzania. http://allafrica.com/stories/201001070377.html

The articles describe the pivotal role of ZHRCs in relieving Tanzania of its staggering burden of disease and realizing the country's Millennium Development Goal for health by 2015. They have been published by the *The Guardian* (January 9, 2010), *The Citizen* (January 7, 2010) and The *Arusha Times* (a Weekly, on December 19, 2009). AllAfrica.com disseminated the article internationally and it was published by many agencies and some newspapers including India Times.

As a result of the numerous media articles, a number of agencies have picked up the story including NGO News Africa and the India Times. These KT products therefore have already raised the issue to a high level with corresponding support and a call for renewed action.

Source: www.idrc.ca/tehip (accessed October 16, 2010)

Guidelines and rules for communication with the press (media) are detailed in chapter 7. In terms of overall communication strategy, it is vital to recognize:

- "The media" is not one big entity, nor is it just the press. It is a huge number of different publications and broadcasting stations, and can also refer to different types of communication technology and sources of information.
- The internet is no longer an emerging medium. It is becoming the most dominant.
- You will never meet or talk to "the press." You will meet and talk to individual people who work for the Press.
- The media/press has potentially enormous power—to help, to harm, or to ignore.

Note that the media may not always be a particularly helpful target. As Media Trust observes, "Everyone would like a higher media and political profile, yet activities aiming towards this may ultimately be self-serving and only communication driven, with no wider impact."[7]

Message—Problems, Possibilities, Policies

What is your message? Do you have one message for multiple audiences or multiple messages for multiple audiences?

Even the most "singular" objective is likely to involve communication with several audiences, each requiring a tailored message, each of those requiring different tools. In every instance, the principle of IGM (Inform, Guide, and Motivate) applies. This is amplified by the AIDA rule[8] of:

A Attract the **attention** of the target

I Raise **interest** in the message or evidence

D Encourage a **desire** to act or to know more

A Prompt **action** and present a solution

The power of a message might be computed as:

Visibility × Clarity × Relevance × Practicality = Impact.

Whatever numerical factor is assigned to each of those, if one of them is zero, the impact will be zero. As the objective is to trigger an action, the message must provide a solution to a problem (practicality) that the audience cares about and can relate to (relevance).

All this can be catered for by creating a "core message" that can then be adapted to each specific audience. The Core Message could include:[9]

1. Analysis of the problem.
2. The problem's cause.
3. Who could or should solve it.
4. Why change is important.
5. Proposed solution.
6. Actions we ask others (message recipients) to take to bring this change about.

For example:

Every year, malaria claims more than one million lives worldwide, and three-quarters of these deaths occur among African children under the age of five. Even among survivors, malaria can lead to low birth weight, weakness, blindness, anaemia, recurrent fever, and other problems, in addition to representing a high economic burden for individuals, families, communities, and health systems. Yet there exist proven, cost-effective interventions that can help curtail the ravages of malaria if only they are made available to those who need them. By subsidizing the distribution of insecticide-treated bed nets at the local level, all-cause child mortality can be reduced by as much as 20 percent.[10]

BOX 6.5
Top Tips for Developing Messages

- Develop some simple messages and model how these might work in different contexts: a press release, a report, a newspaper article, a web page. Be succinct without "dumbing down." Make sure the project is branded in line with communication objectives.
- Consider using the *grandmother test*: would she understand the message? If it is too complex for her, perhaps it is too tricky for the audience as well.
- What if the message were on the back of a cereal box? "Cornflake Papers" are short, simple and sweet, and can be read by a rushed individual over breakfast.

As discussed in chapter 7 and chapter 11's consideration of the Two-Pager messages, which briefly explain the *problems*, the *possibilities* for solving those problems, and the potential *policies* follow the "problem—solution—action" maxim.[11] These component "parts" should each be no longer than 35 words, and must cater to the comprehension of each target audience. An exercise in logic and brevity.

Basket—Tools and Products

What kinds of communication "products" will best capture and deliver the messages?

The choice of communication "basket" depends on the type and content of message, available resources, and how the audience likes to receive information (What newspaper do they read? What radio station they listen to? Where do they gather? How can you marry scientific content with the right dissemination channel?)

Single messages rarely achieve an overall objective. A phased "build" of awareness, understanding, argument, persuasion, and indirect pressures is usually needed. The 1:3:25 graded entry format, with each product matching an anticipated rise in audience interest, can be especially useful.

BOX 6.6
The Graded-entry (Staged) Format

1 = a one-pager of clear and concise *take-home messages* for skimming or time-pressed decision-makers; Exciting facts. A tone of "hear this—and there is evidence to prove it" Tempts the decision-maker to learn more.

3 = a three-page executive summary or *main message discussion* (such as a policy brief) with more details and resources aimed at those now "open" to the possibilities. Shows the concept is more than an idea. It is real, it stands up to scrutiny, and it is backed by authoritative experts. Persuades the decision-maker that action is required and will be beneficial—indeed, that failure to take action could backfire.

25 = a twenty-five-page scientific paper or synthesis—the *evidence* for administrators or implementers. Shows the proof. Shows the context. Shows how policies can solve problems. Indicates other resources, and what still needs to be done. Assures the decision-maker that the time is right, the issue is pressing, and credible solutions are at hand.

Source: Canadian Health Services Research Foundation. 2001. "Reader-Friendly Writing—1:3:25." Ottawa. Canadian Health Services Research Foundation. Available online at http://bit.ly/fEgiyV (accessed January 24, 2011).

A communication "basket" includes face-to-face meetings. There is no substitute for them. These can be phone calls, seminars, workshops, focus groups, conferences, and multi-stakeholder fora, which can in turn be used to *create* products like a policy brief.

Within this idea rests another truth: no matter how well research processes and findings are packaged and communicated, they alone will not change policy but will likely contribute to it.

Local communities in LMICs often do not possess a computer or television and may never see a newspaper. Indeed, many cannot read. Tools to reach them include marketplace buskers, village-level meetings with community leaders, and women's associations etc., to explain the issues at hand; "town-hall" meetings and lively posters to support or illustrate claims, radio spots on vernacular stations, and videos for mobile cinemas.

BOX 6.7
EVIPNet—Triggering National Policy Dialogues

In February 2008 in Addis Ababa, Ethiopia, an EVIPNet workshop brought together seven African teams, each composed of a senior decision-maker and researcher. In plenary and group work, each team developed a policy brief focused on how to support the use of artemisinin-based combination therapies (ACT) to treat uncomplicated falciparum malaria. Through the work of EVIPNet's Global Resource Group, country teams drew on a wealth of systematic reviews (on ACT; on delivery, financial and governance arrangements; on behaviour change) and single studies conducted in their own country or region. Following the one-week workshop, teams returned home to stage a national policy dialogue (NPD) at which the policy brief featured prominently in a discussion among key officials and stakeholders.

Source: EVIPNet. 2008. "Report of the 1st EVIPNet-Africa Policy Brief Workshop." Addis Ababa, Ethiopia. February 18–22. Available online at http://bit.ly/cDVDRs (accessed November 8, 2010).

The press can be direct targets of these outputs and also reporters of these events and/or their outcomes. International audiences are best reached through conferences, newsletters and websites (more information on creating a website is provided in chapter 13).

Channels—Promotion and Dissemination

What channels will you use to promote and disseminate your products?

Having the right message, the right audience, and the right products is one thing. Delivering them is another. All too often, researchers spend too much time on the products and not enough on the channel. The channel is essential. The medium—be it TV, newspaper, or a meeting—dictates who receives the message. If one must pay for a service, (e.g., satellite TV), one who does not pay is not likely to receive it. If one must attend a meeting to receive the message, one who does not attend will not receive it.

Each message must be tuned not only to your subject and the audience, but also to the channel that will be used to deliver it. A

Communication Strategy considers this in parallel with all the other elements, from the outset.

BOX 6.8
Connecting the Dots: Public Health and Privatization of Public Services in South Africa

The post-Apartheid government of South Africa made equitable access to water and other basic services a high priority, but at the same time they moved to allow local authorities to pursue cost-recovery, privatization and corporatization. As a result, many poor people were soon cut off from these services due to non-payment.

Research findings can be hard enough to sell even in a neutral context. When the recommendations are contrary to a huge national policy trend the task can be enormous. When researchers from Rhodes University in South Africa and Queen's University in Canada showed the resulting negative health impacts of a nationwide initiative to privatize essential municipal services, they had to use almost every KT tool in the book to get a policy shift.

They used a diverse and impactful communication and KT strategy in their participatory research, including engaging diverse technical and community groups, publishing booklets, papers, newsletters, journal articles, radio series (in six languages), newspaper features, television documentaries, art, music, and poetry.

And it worked. The project was influential in the decision to guarantee each household a minimum 50 litres/day of potable water and the team has been solicited by the Ministry of Health to identify solutions to on-going challenges raised by privatization. The project team is now focusing efforts on an enhanced website as the central feature of their Knowledge Translation strategy. An enhanced, multilingual and interactive website allows researchers and practitioners around the world to post relevant material and engage in discussion, as well as access material produced by the Municipal Services Project itself.

Source: http://www.queensu.ca/msp/ (accessed October 16, 2010).

Resources—Materials, Finances, People

What budget do you have for this? Will this change in the future? What communication skills and hardware do you have?

The potential cost of effective communication is open-ended. Commercial organizations spend trillions of dollars, not only to design and deliver a message, but especially to ensure it is heard by everyone who needs to know, and even more especially to ensure it "stands out" amid the competition of everybody else's attempt to reach their audiences. (For a mock budget for radio spots *see* Chapter 8).

Remember that everybody is constantly bombarded with messages and has to have a "spam" filter to survive the onslaught. So a key principle of a Communication Strategy (often on a very limited resource budget) is to focus on what you can do well—well enough to get noticed. This is even more demanding on audience identification and tool selection. The strategy must get them absolutely right—and prioritize them perfectly.

To illustrate, imagine you decorated the walls of a large hall with hundreds of the most exquisitely designed posters and cuttings from superbly crafted magazine articles, examples of newsletters, framed policy briefs, a bank of video screens etc. Then, in the middle of the hall, you seated an artist's model wearing nothing but a top hat.

Now, bring your audience to the front door of the hall. Open it, let them look in for 30 seconds, and then close the door and take them to have a cup of tea somewhere else and discuss football, or climate change, or the latest ipod.

After the tea and talk, ask them what they saw in the hall. And what did all the papers on the walls say? That puts the challenge of getting an audience's attention into perspective.

Timing—Events, Opportunities, Planning

What is your timeline? Would a staged strategy be the most appropriate? What special events or opportunities might arise? Does the work (or future work) of like-minded organizations or ministries, etc., present possible dissemination opportunities?

Communication Strategies must consider both internal and external deadlines, allowing for planning, preparation of materials, delivery logistics, budget constraints, graded-entry sequences, possibly prolonged advocacy campaigns, and feedback—set against possibly fixed dates for impending legislation, or subject-centred conferences, or media seasons, or funded project expiry etc.

Baeyaert frames his vision of a phased (stage-by-stage) approach with "do not play all your cards at once," urging organizations to "map out who you will approach first (influencer cascade), plan for a regular flow of information rather than one-shot announcements, [and] build in 'highlight activities' with high impact."[12] Phased strategies often let audiences determine their own exposure to research: in the graded-entry 1:3:25 formulation, reading the one may convince the audience to progress to the three, and in turn to the 25. Whatever the case, once you announce yourselves and make your message heard, you need to keep yourselves known, and your knowledge available within the resource budget.

A second timing point relates to any events you might capitalize on—conferences bringing together key stakeholders, a change of government, the scheduled writing of a government plan, an anticipated policy shift. One team member should be assigned to monitoring the external event context. S/he would need to subscribe to listserves, like PAHO's Equity List, which sends out three–five emails per day, highlighting recent papers, toolkits, and upcoming conferences and events (on global issues). It can be joined at http://listserv.paho.org/Archives/equidad.html, and accepts submissions. (For more information on listserves see chapter 13).

The more a team is aware of all such contexts, the more creative and opportunistic it can be.

BOX 6.9

Fighting Second-hand Smoke in Guatemala

When Guatemala ratified the WHO Framework Convention on Tobacco Control (FCTC) in 2005, it agreed to reduce exposure to tobacco smoke in "workplaces, public transport, and indoor public places." At the time, Guatemalan law

(Box 6.9 contd.)

(Box 6.9 contd.)

prohibited smoking in schools and hospitals, but had only partial bans in private workplaces and restaurants. There were no restrictions in bars.

In 2006, a research team from Fundación Aldo Casteñada found that nicotine concentrations in restaurants and bars were as much as 710 times higher than equivalent spaces in Guatemalan public schools. Designated non-smoking areas and expensive ventilation systems were found to be largely ineffectual.

Armed with this information, the team worked closely with the Guatemalan Congress Health Commission in 2007 to draft evidence-informed legislation for an outright ban on smoking in restaurants and bars. However, against a strong tobacco industry lobby, the law languished for lack of debate in Congress.

Publication in a respected medical journal, *Cancer Epidemiology Biomarkers and Prevention*, lent credibility to their research, but in order to excite action, the team needed to "translate the knowledge" with a public awareness programme. They cultivated media contacts, and numerous newspaper articles included a full-colour spread in January 2008 in the largest newspaper in Guatemala. The team leader provided frequent written and oral policy briefings to various members of Congress. By December 2008 a new law was passed—imposing a comprehensive ban on smoking in all public places, including bars and restaurants.

Source: http://www.idrc.ca/tobacco/ev-140615-201-1-DO_TOPIC.html (accessed October 16, 2010).

Brand—Creating One and Being On it

Are all your communication products "on brand"? How can you ensure that you are broadcasting the right message?

Consider the logos and products of Toyota, Nike, Heinz, and Barclays. These brands translate not only as car, shoes, food, and bank (what they are) but also give us an association of status, quality, and size (what they're like—the feelings their products create in us). A brand tells the world, at a glance, who, and what you are. It is what you want to be seen, known, and remembered as. "Being on brand" means that whatever you do, say, or produce is consistent with the image and quality your brand represents. *Your brand represents everything you do, so everything you do must reflect the brand.* This includes consistency in style and message.

BOX 6.10
Message Checklist

Before any of your products are disseminated, you must go through a checklist to ensure that your messages are of high quality and are "on brand:"

Does your message, in two sentences or less, capture the importance of your work?

Does your product show your honesty and trustworthiness?

Does it show, in concrete terms, what you have achieved?

Does it frame your issue and your research within the issue's broader perspective?

Does your message inspire? Does it convince an audience of its worth?

Does it lead an audience to further resources?

Source: Adapted from WWF. [no year]. *International Communications Department. Programme/Project Communications Strategy Template.* Available online at http://smap.ew.eea.europa.eu/test1/fol597352/International_Communications_Strategy_Template.pdf/download.

Three simple "being on brand" strategies include:

1. **Creating a "communication committee" to review messages and products before they are disseminated**—not necessarily composed entirely of our own staff; individuals from like-minded organizations (or a donor organization) may be happy to quality-check the consistency, "honesty," and perspective in your messages, and at the same time offer other useful feedback.
2. **Media/promotional (PR) training**—of everybody in the organization, so they understand the brand is built (or broken) by everything they do, and how the "corporate image" of the organization influences external relationships and how people listen to its messages.
3. **Hiring a professional to create a logo and a style guide.** These design issues are central to a perceived "professionalism:" just

as your personal appearance speaks to your professionalism (imagine wearing a T-shirt and shorts to a board meeting), so do the small details of design contribute to the "look and feel" of your organization.

Tips for developing a style guide include:[13]

- Uniform use of the logo must be incontestable—when to use it, when not to use it, how to use it, whether it is in black-and-white or colour, and so on.
- Create a preferred "house style" for all print communication, setting out rules for font type, font size, capitalization, punctuation, and abbreviations.
- Choose a reference work (e.g., the Chicago Manual of Style) and a preferred dictionary to resolve any spelling or grammatical issues.
- Describe acceptable variations to the house style.
- Create a nomenclature for projects, programmes, and documents (especially collaborative documents) and consistent codes to identify different versions.
- Create a good glossary of terms.
- Create a list of frequently misspelled or misused words/phrases.

Consistency and simplicity need not be dull. For example, "one color" does not necessarily mean black-and-white. Messages get to the reader's brain via the reader's eye. Templates (starting with an electronic letterhead on which any correspondence can be imposed) assure consistency most time efficiently. Even more complex documents, like an entire newsletter lay-out, can be templated.

Feedback—Evaluative Thinking

How will you know when your Communication Strategy is successful? What will have changed? How can you assess whether you used the right tools, were on budget and on time, and had any influence?

Chapter 3's investigation of ET explores these questions in much detail, particularly "feedback loop" mechanisms. This is essential to knowing which products and tools are hitting their targets, and which are missing, how audiences receive them, and how "perceptions" might be changing.

FIGURE 6.1
The Communication Feedback Loop

Source: Adapted from Principia Cybernetica Web, "Feedback" http://pespmcl.vub.ac.be/feedback.html

Communication is not a subordinate part of overall M&E, and can be assessed by impact logs, formal surveys, key informant interviews, as well as other ET tools described in chapters 3 and 15.

Some form of action-orientated learning document can (should) be an intrinsic part of a Communication Strategy, informing not only communication performance but all aspects of the organization.

For examples of Communication Strategies used by other organizations, see Section V on The Toolbox. Chapter 10 has templates, guides, and resources on Communications Strategies.

TABLE 6.1

Example of a Communication Strategy

OBJECTIVE: "Develop a Communication Strategy that will Ensure Government Adoption of Evidence-Informed Policies in its Malaria Control Strategy by 2011"

AUDIENCE	***Primary:* Ministry of Health** since it has the most power to make the changes required.	***Primary:* Local communities** as they are the most affected by the disease, the interventions, *and* any national malaria control policy. They can become excellent advocates for policy recommendations, and if amplified well, have a voice that will resonate in any decision-making forum.	***Secondary:* Media** because they are absolutely essential in conveying messages around social change and in stirring up policy debates.	***Secondary:* International community** as they can become vehicles of dissemination as well as powerful global voices.
INSIGHT	Issue knowledge: 7/10	Issue knowledge : 4/10	Issue knowledge: 2/10	Issue knowledge: 8/10
STRATEGY	Need "targets" that have a decent understanding of both malaria and health systems. *(Director of Research, the Director of Public Health, and also on several of the Ministry's mid-level "desk officers" responsible for working with foreign donors around malaria initiatives)* Need to understand the ministry's policy formulation process (individuals and structures) and policy windows.	Bias of design and delivery towards individuals or cadres deemed most "influential"—those most likely to transmit effect to others. *(influential subgroups, focus on women's group)* Recognize that, some may be illiterate, some may not have access to TV.	Print and radio.	Those interested in Malaria issues *(NGOS, bilateral, donors, GFATM, WHO etc.).*

(Table 6.1 contd.)

(Table 6.1 contd.)

OBJECTIVE: "Develop a Communication Strategy that will Ensure Government Adoption of Evidence-Informed Policies in its Malaria Control Strategy by 2011"				
MESSAGE	Needs to a) emphasize the importance of the health systems aspects of malaria control; b) suggests solutions.	Reducing malaria control into digestible "bites" of education (i.e., promoting prevention-savvy techniques, training of district health staff), systems (i.e., delivery mechanisms, gender analysis, equity of access) and economics (i.e., who should pay for these interventions).		
BASKET	Staged approach: 1:3:25 pager, policy briefs, face-to-face meetings; bi-annual newsletter.	Posters; radio spots; meetings with community leaders, bi-annual newsletter.	Newspaper articles, radio interviews, radio spots bi-annual newsletter.	bi-annual newsletter, website, conference presentation.
CHANNELS	Personally hand-out the 1:3:25 page documents; Mail hard and soft copies; Mount them on website; Send to all of email contacts (perhaps via a listserve).	Marketplace buskers; town hall meetings; waiting rooms at health clinics; churches; health and fitness clubs.	CD-ROM or DVD of radio spots for dissemination (at the Ministry; conferences) upload onto website.	Global List-serves; Showcase radio spots at a Conference on Information and Communication Technologies; website uploads.

RESOURCES		
TIMING	Change in Minister of Health in March.	Weekly women's meetings, bimonthly vaccination days.
BRAND	Catchy, punchy, simple, include logo, two colours only (dark and light blue).	
FEEBACK	Were the right tools used to reach the right audience? Was the ultimate goal of policy influence achieved? How did policy shift as a result of the campaign? Was the budget adequate? Did the audiences understand the message? And, ultimately, did the communication work to change national malaria policy by the year 2011?	

Resources

1. Young, J. and Enrique Mendizabal. 2009. *Helping Researchers Become Policy Entrepreneurs.* Overseas Development Institute. Available online at http://www.odi.org.uk/resources/details.asp?id=1127&title=become-policy-entrepreneur-roma (accessed October 14, 2010). Donors spend billions of dollars on development research each year, but what is the impact on policy? This Briefing Paper summarises ODI's work on understanding how policy processes operate in the real world, as part of its mandate to inspire and inform policy and practice that lead to the reduction of poverty. The paper presents six key lessons that are essential to any researcher or organization wishing to generate evidence-based policy change, and an eight-step approach for policy entrepreneurs wishing to maximize the impact of research on policy. This is known as the RAPID Outcome Mapping Approach (ROMA).
2. Hershey, R. Christine. 2005. "Communications Toolkit: A Guide to Navigating Communications for the Non-profit World." Available online at http://www.causecommunications.org/clients-cause.php (accessed October 14, 2010). This toolkit has many strong suggestions and examples on designing a strategy.
3. Behague, D. Charlotte Tawiah, Mikey Rosato, some Télésphore and Joanna Morrison. 2009. "Evidence-based Policy-making: The Implications of Globally-applicable Research for Context-specific Problem-solving in Developing Countries," *Social Science & Medicine.* 69(10): 1539–46. Using the maternal and neonatal subfield as an ethnographic case-study, this paper explores the effects of these divergences on EBPM in five developing countries (Bangladesh, Burkina Faso, Ghana, Malawi and Nepal). In doing so, the analysis aims to explain why EBPM has thus far had a limited impact in the area of context-specific programmatic policy-development and implementation at the national and sub-national levels.
4. Baeyaert, P. 2005. "Developing an External Communications Strategy." Presentation at Communicating European Research, November 14, 2005. Also available as a PowerPoint presentation with several excellent slides on http://ec.europa.eu/research/conferences/2005/cer2005/presentations14_en.html.
5. World Wildlife Foundation. International Communications Department. Programme/Project Communications Strategy Template. Available online at http://smap.ew.eea.europa.eu/test1/fol597352/International_Communications_Strategy_Template.pdf/download (accessed October 14, 2010). Though brief, this document breaks down the many tasks within a communication strategy.
6. Bessette, G. 2004. "Involving the Community: A Guide to Participatory Development Communication," Canada's International Development Research Centre. Available online at http://www.idrc.ca/en/ev-52226-201-1-DO_

TOPIC.html (accessed October 14, 2010). This guide introduces participatory development communication concepts, discusses effective two-way approaches, and presents a methodology to plan, develop and evaluate Communication Strategies at a community level.

7. "Report on Communication Strategies and Information Technology." Conference Proceedings. Mexico City, Mexico. 2-4 April, 2001. Available online at http://www.wingsweb.org/download/communication_strategies.pdf (accessed October 14, 2010). These bullet points on "best practices in internal communication" draw useful distinctions between internal and external strategies.
8. Gauthier, J. 2006. "Field Sheets on Effective Development Communication," International Development Research Centre. Available online at http://www.idrc.ca/en/ev-104545-201-1-DO_TOPIC.html (accessed October 14, 2010). These 14 quick-reference "field sheets" present guidelines for developing a communication strategy for rural- or village-based projects. This includes the use of "small media" such as photographs, illustrations, leaflets, and working with media specialists in theatre, radio, video, etc.
9. Media Trust. "Developing a Communications Strategy." Available online at http://bit.ly/comstrategy (accessed February 8, 2011). This website divides core tasks within a communication strategy. Though not as intricate as the Big Eleven Questions, it is useful in thinking through needs and abilities.
10. The SPIN Project. 2005. "Strategic Communications Planning." Available online at http://www.spinproject.org/downloads/StrategicCommunications.pdf (accessed October 14, 2010). This brochure gives an overview of the components of strategic communication, with good diagrams and suggestions.

NOTES AND REFERENCES

1. Some large organizations may wish to pay particular attention to internal communication perceptions, noting the sharp differences between internal and external communication.
2. Again, the issue of internal vs external communication is an important one. For reasons of space, this chapter will mostly focus on external Communication Strategies.
3. Hershey, C. 2005. "Communications Toolkit: A Guide to Navigating Communications for the Nonprofit World." Available online at http://www.cause-communications.org/clients-cause.php (accessed October 14, 2010).
4. Baeyaert, P. 2005. "Developing an External Communications Strategy," Presentation at Communicating European Research, November 14, 2005. Available online at http://ec.europa.eu/research/conferences/2005/cer2005/presentations 14_en.html (accessed October 14, 2010).

5. World Wildlife Foundation. *International Communications Department. Programme/Project Communications Strategy Template*. Available online at http://smap.ew.eea.europa.eu/test1/fol597352/International_Communications_Strategy_Template.pdf/download (accessed October 14, 2010).
6. This toolkit does not explore issues of culture and communication, though this is an extremely important aspect of any communication initiative. For a strong treatment of this issue vis-à-vis health research, *see* Matthew Kreuter and Stephanie McClure. "The Role of Culture in Health Communication." *Annual Review of Public Health*, 25: 439-55. Available online at http://arjournals.annualreviews.org/doi/abs/10.1146/annurev.publhealth.25.101802.123000 (accessed October 14, 2010).
7. More from the Media Trust can be found at http://www.mediatrust.org/training-events/training-resources/online-guides-1/guide_developing-a-communications-strategy
8. Stuart, D. and I. Hovland. 2004. *Tools for Policy Impact: A Handbook for Researchers*. Overseas Development Institute. Available online at www.odi.org.uk/rapid/Publications/Documents/Tools_handbook_final_web.pdf (accessed October 14, 2010).
9. de Toma, C. and L. Gosling. 2005. "A Collection of Tools to Help Plan, Implement, Monitor and Evaluate Advocacy." Save the Children. Available online at http://www.mande.co.uk/docs/AdvocacyInitiativesToolkit2005.pdf (accessed October 14, 2010).
10. Lengeler, C. 2002. "Insecticide-treated Bednets and Curtains for Preventing Malaria (Cochrane Review)." In The Cochrane Library, 2002. Available online at http://www.cochrane.org/reviews/en/ab000363.html (accessed October 14, 2010).
11. The SPIN Project. 2005. "Strategic Communications Planning". Available online at http://www.spinproject.org/downloads/StrategicCommunications.pdf (accessed October 14, 2010).
12. Baeyaert, "Developing an External Communications Strategy."
13. Adapted from Hershey, "Communications Toolkit."

SECTION

IV

The Medium

Print, Multimedia, and Social Media

A completed research project is like a seed. Getting the findings published in a scientific journal is like putting that seed in a packet, with a label on it. Well done! But is it "job done"?

KT suggests it is only job begun, because while it remains a seed, it is only data; when it is packaged and labeled it is only information. To become knowledge, it must be taken out of the packet and planted in a place where it can grow (the right soil, the right climate, the right care) and become something useful. Even the most brilliant scientific paper becomes something useful only when it is planted in the mind of someone with the power to do something about it. The message of research findings must not only be written. It must be read, understood, and acted on.

KT offers numerous ways to take what you know, what you have researched and written, and put it where it will serve a practical purpose. The transport is provided by some form of media.

7

Print Media

Despite a plethora of options in modern communications technology, print remains a very powerful and important medium. While "push" strategies such as journal publications certainly have their uses, they generally have a limited influence on the decision-making process. The value of print media, therefore, rises tremendously when used in conjunction with "pull" or "linkage and exchange" strategies described in Chapter 1.

As in all things KT, the more you know about your message and your audience, the better the chances that you will select the right tool (or set of tools). In this section, we discuss seven different tools and indicate which audience they are best suited for, tips on how to make best use of them, as well as links to further resources.

Print media tools can be put to effective use *before*, *during*, and *after* a project, in order to optimize its reach and impact. This chapter discusses seven different print media tools: *peer-reviewed articles, newspaper articles, press releases, policy briefs, newsletters, brochures*, and *cartoons*—all of which can be used at various times in the research cycle, hence serving as primers or teasers for eventual findings and recommendations. Each has its pros and cons for capturing messages and reaching audiences.

The choice of medium—from moment to moment in a project cycle—thus depends on *what* your message is and *who* you want to deliver it to. In turn, the choice of audience (the medium and its readership profile) dictates *content*, *style* and method of *delivery*. For media you personally own and control (policy briefs, newsletters, brochures, etc.), *delivery* means getting through the right office door, or building the right mailing list, or selecting the right display points. For media owned by someone else (journals, newspapers, magazines, etc.), it means obeying their rules, knowing specifically "who" to approach, and how to persuade them to publish.

ARTICLES IN SCIENTIFIC JOURNALS

This tool can capture, in its fullness, the science of any study. Peer-reviewed articles are often the litmus test of a researcher's success, determining tenure or "fundability." If the only goal of research is to influence the state-of-the-art or target only other researchers, then this is all you need. However, many scholars in low and middle income countries (LMICs) are unlikely to have full access to peer-reviewed publications. One way of getting around this problem is to publish in open-access formats (*see* Chapter 13 for more on this). It is also worth noting that the sheer quantity of articles—about three million and more each year—makes it extremely difficult for even the most devoted scholar to keep up. A scholar would need to read approximately 17–20 new articles every day just to keep abreast of the latest developments.[1]

If, however, the aim is to change or influence policy, this tool is woefully inadequate. Beyond scientists and academics, the audience for scientific journals is approximately zero. To non-scholars (the majority) the language of journals is somewhere between deadly dull and incomprehensible. Often the articles are frustrating in that they lack concrete recommendations.

Some useful tips for maximum impact when writing for scholarly journals include:

- **Clear and simple:** Even if the audience is broadly jargon-savvy, your subject area may be unfamiliar.

- **Short and precise:** Use sentences that are crisp and direct.
- **Easily translatable:** Do not use idioms, colloquial speech, contractions or convoluted syntax.
- **Active:** Avoid the passive voice, i.e., use "new research shows" not "it was shown by new research that…"
- **Thoughtful and thorough:** As carefully written as the study itself, and considerate of the readership's needs and interests.

Most scientific journals publish a set of "instructions for authors," generally:[2]

- **Title:** Clearly and briefly describe the content. Think about keywords that will be picked up by search engines and lead readers to the paper.
- **Abstract:** A short section summarizing the purpose of the study, the research methods, the main results, and principal conclusions; enough for readers to decide on their agenda—whether to read on or move on.
- **Introduction:** Again briefly presents the question being asked (statement of purpose), the context (background information about what is already known), and the hypothesis.
- **Methods:** Explain why and how each method or procedure was used, providing sufficient information to allow others to reproduce the study.
- **Results:** Presented without comment, bias or interpretation, using verbal summary, and, if appropriate, figures and tables.
- **Discussion and conclusion:** Analyze the data, evaluate their meaning, highlight significance in terms of the original question, and explain how they relate to other studies. Conclude by summarizing key points and note areas for further study.
- **Acknowledgements** (if any)
- **References:** A list of the references that were cited in the body of the paper The *Vancouver Style* is used in most biomedical publications.

BOX 7.1
Sections of a Scientific Paper

What did I do, in a nutshell?	**Abstract**
What is the problem?	**Introduction**
How did I solve the problem?	**Materials and Methods**
What did I find out?	**Results**
What does it mean?	**Discussion**
Who helped me out?	**Acknowledgements** (optional)
Whose work did I refer to?	**References**
Extra Information	**Appendices** (optional)

Source: Home Department of Biology. 2003. "The Structure, Format, Content, and Style of a Journal-Style Scientific Paper," in *How to Write a Paper in Scientific Style and Format*. Lemistan, Maine: Bates College. Available online at http://abacus.bates.edu/~ganderso/biology/resources/writing/HTWsections.html (accessed October 14, 2010).

Resources

1. The website of the United States National Library of Medicine provides 41 citation examples using the *Vancouver Style*. Available online at http://www.nlm.nih.gov/bsd/uniform_requirements.html (accessed October 14, 2010).
2. The International Committee of Medical Journal Editors publishes the *Uniform Requirements for Manuscripts Submitted to Biomedical Journals*. Available at: http://www.icmje.org/ (accessed October 14, 2010).
3. The websites of various scientific journals provide guidelines for authors. See for example:
   (*a*) *The Lancet*. http://www.thelancet.com/authors (accessed October 14, 2010).
   (*b*) The *British Medical Journal*. http://resources.bmj.com/bmj/authors?resource_name=Authors (accessed October 14, 2010).
   (*c*) The *Oxford Journal of Public Health* http://www.oxfordjournals.org/pubmed/for_authors/index.html (accessed October 14, 2010).

NEWSPAPER ARTICLES AND EDITORIALS

Articles in newspapers—news items, features, or editorials—are an obvious choice if a research message needs to get to the general public. The audience is wide, generates public debate, transmits "public education," and represents the electorate (so policy-makers are pressured by their opinion). Newspapers can be powerful allies ... or opponents.

BOX 7.2

Truth and Reconciliation Commissions: A Global Reality Check

The success of South Africa's Truth and Reconciliation Commission is a model many other countries might use to address deep historic conflicts, promote peace and prevent a resurgence of violence. But South Africa's pioneering version, and others that followed, were not necessarily without fault and had no formal analysis to make them easily replicable. In response, an IDRC-supported research project, led by the Nairobi Peace Initiative-Africa (NPI-Africa), is documenting diverse experiences, lessons-learned, and valuable insights on such commissions.

To encourage dialogue, NPI shared this knowledge through local and regional newspaper articles, academic papers, and an international conference. These KT processes have developed awareness, promoted understanding, and provoked discussions not only in Kenya but around Africa, hence contributing significantly to global peace building field.

Source: http://www.npi-africa.org/ (accessed October 14, 2010).

The only way to be certain that a newspaper will publish an article, fully and accurately, is to buy advertising or advertorial space. Otherwise the fate of an independent article will depend on your relationship with the editorial staff and *their* perception of newsworthiness, public interest, technical authority, content, style, length, and timing.

The ink is theirs, the paper is theirs, and the decisions are theirs. The last word is theirs! You need to know the personality, practices, and preferences of the people and the paper to maximize the chances of the article being published at all. You need to know which editor of which paper to take a particular subject to. Alternatively, if budget permits, it may be possible to commission a reporter to write the article; that gives it an inside track. There are ethical issues to be observed here.

BOX 7.3
Who's Who in a Newspaper Office

Editor in chief – determines overall editorial policy;

Chief sub-editor – selects stories, decides prominence, assigns processing to sub-editors;

News editor – trawls news sources, assigns reporters;

Department editors – control specific sections of the paper (e.g., Sport, Business, Features, Fashion, Health etc.);

Reporters – some are generalists, others focus on specific subject areas.

FIGURE 7.1
Inverted Pyramid Writing

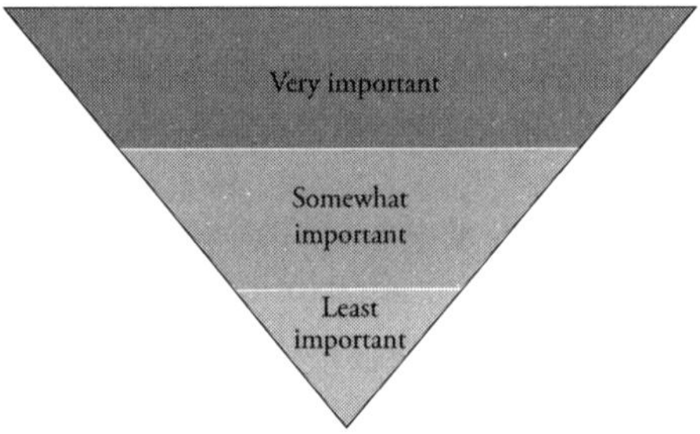

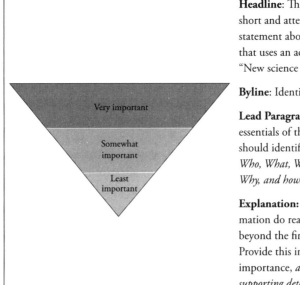

Headline: This should be a short and attention-grabbing statement about our story that uses an active verb (e.g., "New science reveals…")

Byline: Identifies the author.

Lead Paragraph: This is the essentials of the story and should identify the six Ws: *Who, What, When, Where, Why, and how.*

Explanation: What information do readers need beyond the first paragraph? Provide this in order of importance, *and finish with supporting details and any additional information that is not crucial.*

Writing a Newspaper Article[3]

Articles for newspapers and magazines fall into three broad categories: news items (reporting recent events), features (analyzing subject areas), and commentaries (opinion pieces, columns, editorials, letters).

News items in newspapers have a fixed formula: the headline is the shortest, clearest possible description of something important that has just happened. The "intro" gives the key facts (usually the six W's of Who, What, Where, When, Why and hoW.) Just one paragraph—the first—gives the reader all the key information. It gets straight to the point. All succeeding paragraphs are amplifications of the core facts, presented in descending order of importance. The origins of this are that a news story can be cut, instantly and without even reading it, simply by removing paragraphs (starting at the bottom and working up) until what is left is the required length.

Feature articles in newspapers or magazines can sometimes follow a similar pattern, but more often start with a cryptic headline to arouse curiosity and lure the reader into the message with indirect or tantalizing information. For example, a headline like *The killer in our midst* tells you nothing, but certainly makes you stop and look. The first paragraph may reveal all (*Malaria is killing 72 children every day in…*) or may use a more teasing start (*It is silent. It is everywhere. And it is looking for your child…*) before coming to the central point is what is called a "dropped intro."

Commentaries are similar to features, but with more emphasis on interpretation of facts than just presenting them. They too, often have cryptic headlines and usually start with a single statement that takes a challenging position and commands attention. They then take whatever roundabout route they wish to build a case and prove a point, ending with a final punch line that is the most important part of the story. For example, a headline such as *They do not have to die* and an opening statement like: *A treated net costing less than $1 is too high a price to pay for a child's life. Or so we are led to believe.* Then argument of the issue, both citing evidence and giving opinion on its accuracy, significance, awareness, and bottom-line meaning, perhaps ending with a punch line like: *Can you think of a better way to spend $1*?

These are the different tools available to researchers with knowledge to share, to be used singly, or in sequenced combination to reach the right audience, in the right way, at the right time.

Irrespective of the type of article, there are common rules:

Presentation: Any article submitted to the media should:

- Use double-spaced typing.
- Number every page at top right with a "catchline."
- Type "more…" at the bottom of each page if there is continuation.
- Type "ends" at the conclusion of the article.
- Followed by the name, position, and contact details (telephone, e-mail) of the author.
- Whether and what byline is given is at the editor's discretion.

General style tips:

- Keep sentences plain and simple.
- Keep paragraphs short.
- Do not waste words, do not ramble.
- Use straightforward vocabulary and avoid jargon and acronyms.
- Use active verbs (e.g., "research shows", not, "it was shown by research").
- If possible, use some quotations to add life and attribution.
- All news quotes can be qualified by the word "said." So-and-so said, He said, She said, as many times as need be.
- Literary variety with words such as "indicated," "quipped," "related," "observed," "mentioned," "commented," are neither necessary nor appropriate, unless they add substantively to the sense.

Delivery: Newspaper articles must be delivered in the right form, to the right person, in the right way, at the right time.

- **The right form:** As described under "Presentations" (chapter 8).
- **The right person:** Newspaper and magazine content does not go directly from source to print. The press release must go the editor of the right department (news, features, etc.) according to its subject matter. It will then be "copy tasted" for relevance and priority level before being passed to a Chief Sub-editor for page selection, positioning on that page, and determination of length and headline size. (If the content is contentious, the News Editor may assign a reporter to research issues and gather alternative—and possibly opposing—views).
- **The right way:** Call the appropriate editor and forewarn that you are sending the piece, using the opportunity to sell-in its relevance and importance. Send it (or better still personally deliver it) in an envelope marked for the attention of a particular individual, but addressed to a position, not the person. That way, if the particular person is out when the envelope arrives, it will still be opened and processed by someone else. Make a follow-up call to confirm receipt, assess interest (likelihood of publication), and answer any initial questions.
- **The right time:** Means the right day and the right hour. Even daily papers have weekly and indeed seasonal rhythms; special business or subject-specific feature sections are usually weekly; some days are generally "thinner" on news, other days on overload. Major events (scheduled or not) consume extra space and detract from reader attention to other subjects (yours).

Press Releases

Like policy-makers, practitioners, and the general public, the media are also inundated by the daily flow of information and will need to be convinced that a story merits coverage. It is absolutely fundamental to examine the news content of different newspapers, the audiences they reach, as well as the frequency at which they are published.

The level of news activity varies considerably, and often with cyclical regularity, from very quiet to hyper active—at different hours of the day, on different days of the week, and in different seasons of the year. Getting the timing right improves the chances of your story being given attention and space.

There are obvious benefits to a researcher who is respected and trusted by journalists as a reliable expert in a particular subject area, but being contacted and quoted as a source can have pitfalls, too.

BOX 7.4

Format of an Embargoed Press Release

Date or embargo: An embargo enables a journalist to receive a release in advance on the condition that it may not be used before a specific date and time. The word EMBARGO, the time, and date the limit ends should be clearly written at the top of the first page. Beware—embargoes are not always honored. A judgment call on the integrity of both the paper and the journalist are needed.

Heading: This should be short (three to seven words) use an active verb and capture the most interesting aspect of the story.

Introductory paragraph: The intro should answer the "who," "what," "why," "when," "where," and "how" questions.

Text: As with a newspaper article, the paragraphs should be written in descending order of importance, closing with the word "ends."

Details: Contact information for your spokesperson; relevant website address.

Sub-editors work throughout the day to progressively fill pages—after 10 am, available space shrinks by the hour. Some weekly feature sections are completed a day or more in advance, and you need to know their "pre-print" deadlines.

BOX 7.5

Roles the Media can Play in the Research Process

- To inform the general public that research is underway;
- To disseminate important findings;
- To act as a conduit between groups with similar interests;
- To provide a forum for debate and dialogue; often shaping debate by providing the parameters of discussion and highlighting particular issues;
- To provide the non-scientific context and colloquial evidence around the issue at hand;
- To market the research, the research institute, the programme or the researchers, building their profile and reputation; and
- To build accountability by communicating findings with those who participated in or supported the research; to allow the public to hold decision-makers to account.

Source: Adapted from Panos Institute. 2005. "Getting into the Kitchen: Media Strategies for Research," Background paper produced for the Chronic Poverty Research Center by the Panos Institute, London; and Laney, M.L. 2005. "Tips for Using the Media," Commsconsult.

POLICY BRIEFS

Policy briefs communicate with officials, bureaucrats, politicians, development practitioners, donors, and more. As always, the characteristics of audience determine format, content, and style. The audience will have a variety of constraints on time and comprehension, so the brief must be absolutely concise in conveying the importance, relevance, and urgency of the issue—all in the space of two-pages or less. The brief should pass the "corn-flakes test"—whether a politician [can] identify its main points in the time it takes to eat a hasty breakfast.[4]

A policy brief should identify a problem, cite new evidence which informs policy on the matter, propose optional solutions, and present a compelling recommendation—move from *problems* to *possibilities* to *policies.* Facts and science alone are not enough. The implications for people and communities are an essential ingredient. As Hovland explains, "the presentation of the outcomes of [our] data analysis will probably not be enough to make an impact in the policy debate on a particular issue, but through the use of this data as evidence in a comprehensive and coherent argument of [our] position, [we] will give [our] work the best possible chance of having this impact."[5]

Tips for an effective policy brief:[6]

- write for a specific audience;
- use a professional as opposed to an academic tone;
- ground the argument in strong and reliable evidence;
- limit the focus to a particular problem or issue;
- be succinct, using short and simple sentences and paragraphs;
- provide enough information to allow the reader to follow the argument effortlessly;
- make it accessible by subdividing the text;
- make it interesting but not overdone through the use of colors, images, quotes, boxes, etc.;
- avoid jargon or acronyms;
- provide an overview of cost implications (optional);
- make sure the recommendations are practical and feasible (recommendations are optional in a policy brief and should be considered based on the needs of the decision-maker); and
- consider the supporting documents behind a policy brief.

BOX 7.6

Supporting a Policy Brief

"Our interviews with health care managers and policy-makers suggest that they would benefit from having information that is relevant for decisions highlighted for them (e.g., contextual factors that affect a review's local applicability and information about the benefits, harms/risks and costs of interventions) and having reviews presented in a way that allows for rapid scanning for relevance and then graded entry (such as one page of take-home messages, a three-page executive summary and a 25-page report)."

Source: Lavis, J., H. Davies, A. Oxman, J.L Denis, K. Golden-Biddle and E. Ferlie 2005. "Towards Systematic Reviews that Inform Health Care Management and Policy-making". Journal of Health Services Research & Policy. Vol 10 Suppl 1. (Emphases added).

Components of a Policy Brief

The length of a brief depends on the intended audience and the stage of the issue.

1. **Title**: Brief and attention-grabbing.
2. **Executive summary**: An overview of the problem, its relevance, the reasons why action is necessary (and specific recommendations). On the first page.
3. **Statement of the problem**: A question that requires a decision. Avoid "Why" and focus instead on "What," "How," "When," etc.
4. **Background and/or context to the problem and its importance**: The essential facts to convince an audience that the problem requires urgent attention and action.
5. **Pre-existing policies:** What has been done in the past or what is in place now, if anything, to deal with the problem.
6. **Policy options**: Some alternative ways to address the problem.
7. **Critique of policy options**: The pros and cons of each alternative from the perspective of the target audience.
8. **Policy recommendation (optional)**: A preferred alternative, providing a convincing argument and imperatives for action.
9. **Sources consulted or recommended**: An annotated bibliography (in the graded format, this would appear in the 25-page version).
10. **And remember "delivery"**: Who should the brief be given to, and how is it to get onto that desk?

BOX 7.7

Policy Brief on Support for Scaling up Artemisinin Combination Therapies (ACTs) in Treatment of Simple P. Falciparum Malaria in Burkina Faso

Policy issues

The resistance of *P. falciparum* to conventional antimalarial drugs is well attested by a number of studies throughout the world and in Burkina Faso. The efficacy of artimisinin-combination therapies (ACTs) has also been proven in various studies

(Box 7.7 contd.)

(Box 7.7 contd.)

and the large-scale use of ACT is recommended by WHO. Like other countries, Burkina Faso opted to change its drugs strategy for treatment of simple malaria by substituting ACT for chloroquine treatment in February 2005. At the time of writing, this scaling up of ACTs has not been applied to all age groups.

Scale of the problem

Malaria is a major public health problem in Burkina Faso, with more than two million recorded cases and over 4,000 deaths every year, especially among children under five. The majority of medical consultations, hospital admissions and deaths are malaria-related. Proper management of malaria requires the use of effective treatment. However, the socioeconomic status of the population, limited public resources and poor health service infrastructure prohibit large parts of the population from accessing this life-saving treatment.

Policy options

Given this situation, there is urgent need for policies to improve universal and equitable access to ACTs for treatment of non-complicated malaria. These include:

- Urge private-sector stakeholders to comply with national directives on subsidized pricing of ACTs (pharmacies, clinics, and surgeries).
- Motivate community health workers responsible for home-based management of simple malaria.
- Withdraw the antimalarial drugs used in monotherapy to treat simple malaria.

Implementation considerations

To implement any of these three policy options, it is essential:

- To provide information to and raise the awareness of the principal malaria control stakeholders.
- To ensure that ACTs adapted to each age group are available countrywide.
- To train the staff tasked with dispensing ACT.
- To review certain regulatory arrangements relating to policy implementation.

Source: Adapted from EVIPnet Burkina Faso policy brief (www.evipnet.org)

Note: Pursuant to producing this policy brief, a team of researchers and decision-makers convened a National Policy Dialogue on malaria treatment policy. The very composition of the multi-sector team gave the "linkage and exchange" strategy a window into the tone and language needs of its audience. This brief was not the result of researchers advocating change but rather the product of an already successful union.

To learn more about how to write a policy brief, work through an example and adopt existing templates, see chapter 11.

NEWSLETTERS

Newsletters can be tailored for either an external or an internal audience (but not both at the same time). Internal newsletters are to inform and motivate staff; they help build and maintain an organization's culture. External newsletters are used principally to increase the visibility of an organization and its activities, and establish a regular communication channel with selected audiences. Chapter Fourteen provides more discussion of the newsletter, and how to integrate this with information technologies.

As ever, the audience will determine content and presentation. Newsletters should generally be two-to-four pages long and be produced often enough to build regular anticipation, but not so often that they cause irritation. Newsletters are like shop windows of an organization, and should represent its image in name, design, content, and material quality. It might be prudent to look at a variety of professional publications and mimic a preferred style.

Writing rules are the same as for newspapers and magazines.[7] Without going into a full design lecture, the aim is to ensure the newsletter is clearly identified, attractive/interesting to look at, and easy to read. Design pitfalls include being too monotonously plain or too ambitiously decorated. Establish "house rules" on each element—a balanced and consistent set of fonts and sizes for headlines, body text, and captions; a limit on number and size of panels/illustrations per page, and stick to them. Be innovative while keeping it short and sweet. Do not be afraid of using white space: it gives the reader's eyes a rest and emphasizes the separation between different items.[8]

A newsletter can be professionally commissioned or, if the internal skills exist and/or the level of sophistication required is not too demanding, produced in-house using a programme like InDesign or, as a last and lowest resort, even a word processing programme like MS Word.

What might be included in a newsletter?[9]

- **Digest:** Edited versions (a "snippet-list") of press releases.
- **Progress:** Update of activities, projects, plans.
- **Reports:** On conferences or meetings.
- **Goals:** Achievements, milestones.
- **Plans:** Info about forthcoming events.
- **Tips:** Technical advice.
- **Links:** To project results, articles, and further information.
- **People:** Profiles of researchers.
- **Graphics:** Images, cartoons, and pictures.
- **Features:** Meatier analysis of an issue.

Distribution: Will be influenced, once again, by audience. Rural communities will need a hard copy; researchers, decision-makers, and global colleagues might prefer something via email or posted on a website. A List-serve is a useful aide to mailing lists.

Newsletter examples:

- *Research Matters* (*see* www.research-matters.net)
- *NIH News in Health* (*see* http://newsinhealth.nih.gov/)
- *Links*, the Newsletter of the Canadian Health Services Research Foundation (*see* http://www.chsrf.ca/other_documents/newsletter/index_e.php)

BROCHURES AND LEAFLETS

These are similar to newsletters but best at presenting a single product, service or issue in one cover-to-cover summary. They can also be used to profile an organization. They have a longer shelf-life and can also be used to capture "unknown" audiences—by placing brochures in public display areas rather than mailing them to individuals.

- Content aligns more closely to that of a policy brief (but for wider consumption), with added graphics throughout and extra information that will not be outdated.

- Links to further sources of information, and the producer's contact details.

An added design challenge for brochures and leaflets is that they are usually on a single sheet of paper, with multiple folds and therefore the reading sequence needs to be considered:

FIGURE 7.2
Sample Brochure/Leaflet Layout

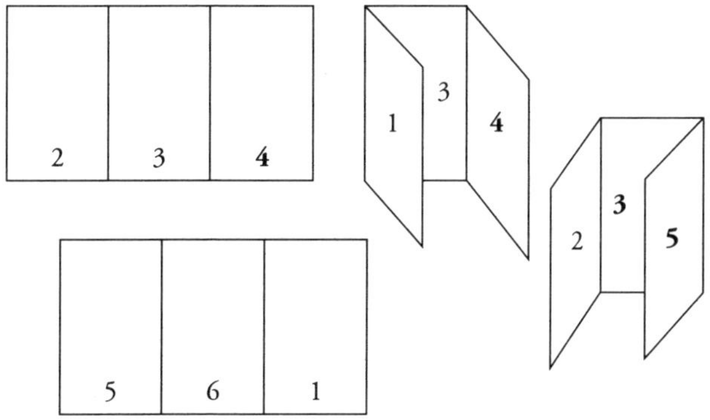

The front cover (**1**) should be eye-catching and provide enough content to encourage the reader to look inside. Consider using an image that illustrates the subject, a logo, and possibly a slogan. Avoid using the back cover (**6**) for much more than contact information, as this is the panel the audience is least likely to pay attention to. Include most information the **2–4 spread**, with overspill or reference information on page **5**.

BOX 7.8
Promoting Women's Rights within Decentralized Systems

It is commonly assumed that the global trend towards decentralization of public decision-making and allocation of resources is necessarily good for women. Projects carried out by IDRC partners in South Asia, Sub-Saharan Africa, and Latin America—using in-depth interviews, focus group discussions, and story telling—both tested the assumption and developed tools to ensure it.

(Box 7.8 contd.)

(Box 7.8 contd.)

In 2008 IDRC co-hosted the first international forum (500 participants from 50 countries) on comparative analysis of women's rights, citizenship, and governance under decentralization systems and processes. IDRC also organized an event for researchers to present their findings at the UN Commission on the Status of Women in March 2009.

The conference produced an array of resources for action, and a working group developed a booklet of policy recommendations. This booklet is now informing governments and institutions all over the world.

Note: The video—Decentralization, Local Power and Women's Rights can be viewed at http://www.idrc.ca/decentralization/ev-139631-201-1-DO_TOPIC.html.

BOX 7.9

The Power of a Pamphlet: Health Warnings about the Narghile (Waterpipe)

Across large parts of the Middle east and southern Asia, the "narghile," "sheesha," "hubbly-bubbly" or waterpipe is a popular means of using tobacco. Narghile use is all the more insidious as it is typically a social activity, shared among friends in cafés and homes and enjoys the prevailing belief that it is less hazardous than other forms of smoking. But research at the American University of Beirut found that in a typical one hour session, the user inhales as much tar as that produced by a whole packet of cigarettes, and is exposed to large quantities of the carcinogens and toxins that make cigarette smoking dangerous.

These research results influenced the WHO, in 2006, to issue a Scientific Advisory Note on Waterpipe Tobacco Smoking: Health Effects, Research Needs, and Recommended Actions by Regulators. Furthermore, primary translation of this crucial new knowledge came through a WHO conference in 2008, where the research team distributed a pamphlet that captured the interest of delegates from Malaysia, Germany, Oman, Bahrain, Saudi Arabia, Turkey, and Djibouti, all inquiring about copyright and implementation issues related to the use of the warning labels. Their research also received coverage in radio and newspaper media in South Africa.

This single document—a pamphlet, at just the right place and time—helped the research team reach and interact with public health practitioners and decision-makers around the world, and lifted an issue from "unknown" to "clearly and widely received and understood" policy information at a single stroke.

Note: For more information contact Dr Rima Nakkash, American University of Beirut, email: rn06@aub.edu.lb

CARTOONS AND IMAGES

The saying "a picture is worth a thousand words" exists for good reason. While images are not always the best tool to explain the complex science behind a specific research project, they are brilliant at bringing to life—with nuance and texture—the kernel of an idea or the spirit of a project. A recent review of research has shown that "pictures closely linked to written or spoken text can, when compared to text alone, markedly increase attention to and recall of health education information."[10]

As highlighted in Box 7.10, cartoons and images get a message across in a way that captures and keeps an audience's attention.

Cartoons may not have been necessary had the researchers been working with medical groups and the government from the outset, using research as an on-going policy and planning tool, as constant feedback on progress. This may not always be possible, and is unlikely for any study that investigates an issue like corruption. The cartoons thus highlight another aspect central to KT—overarching context.

Corruption is not an issue that can be dealt with over a friendly lunch with a government official. The researchers understood the authorities would be hostile to their results. Printing their findings in newspapers and papering cartoons on the walls of clinics forced many different audiences to respond. They could not afford not to.

Professional cartoonists not only give the graphic more impact, but also have the mind-set to make the situation more appropriate and amusing. Additionally, local artists tend to strike a much more accurate chord for a community audience. Alternatively, you can easily use pictures and other images that have already been produced, as long as you obtain permission from their creator or from whoever holds the copyright.

BOX 7.10

Reducing Petty Corruption in Senegal's Health System

Petty corruption was well known and widespread in Senegal's health system for many years—in full knowledge of the government.

With high-level political support and in the general political climate of the time, Le Forum Civil (in English, Transparency International) was able to launch a multi-disciplinary team of sociologists, jurists, and economists to examine petty corruption in the health system. The study took place in six villages, and examined a range of hospitals and other health facilities. Using interviews, focus groups, and direct observation, the study revealed a "pathogenic governance of health structures," featuring "profound distortions" in the hierarchy and the system of control. The result was that the health system operated through informal networks based on personal connections, rather than clearly delimited roles and responsibilities.

Results were made public through a final report and a national forum, then repackaged in a DVD and as cartoons into a form easily understood by doctors and health workers, ministry officials and citizens.

Under the glare of attention, a number of hospitals changed recruitment procedures and created sanctions for inappropriate behaviour.

"Everything is here! I'll even give you a half-price special!"

How am I supposed to cut the umbilical cord? The scissors need grease. Please take what you need from my purse. And hurry!

This success hinged on identifying high-level political support (without which the study would not have been possible), using the media to bring research results to the general public, and cartoons which struck such a clear and strong public chord, that policy-makers could not ignore.

Source: IDRC. 2006. "Corruption and Good Governance in the Health Sector (Senegal). Available online at http://www.idrc.ca/en/ev-83062-201_101914-1-IDRC_ADM_INFO. html (accessed on November 8, 2010).

NOTES AND REFERENCES

1. Shea, B.J., G. Grimshaw, M. Wells, N. Boers, C. Andersson, A. Hamel, A. Porter, P. Tugwell, D. Moher and L. Bouter. 2007. "Development of AM-STAR: A Measurement Tool to Assess the Methodological Quality of Systematic Reviews," *BMC Medical Research Methodology*, 7:10.
2. Adapted from "Appendix E: Guidelines for Writing Scientific Papers." Available online at http://www.bms.bc.ca/library/Guidelines%20for%20writing%20Scientific%20papers.pdf (accessed October 14, 2010).
3. Panos Instit.te. 2005. "A Researcher's Guide to Working with the Media." Produced for the Chronic Poverty Research Center by the Panos Institute, London. Available online at http://www.odi.org.uk/cspp/activities/PPA0211/docs/4.1_6-Researchers_Guide_Working_Media.pdf (accessed October 14, 2010).
4. Nath, C. "How do I Brief Policymakers on Science-related issues?", Sci-DevNet, Available online at http://www.scidev.net/ms/sci_comm/index.cfm?pageid=227 (accessed October 14, 2010).
5. Hovland, I. 2005. "Successful Communication: A Toolkit for Researchers and Civil Society Organisations." Available online at http://www.odi.org.uk/RAPID/Tools/Toolkits/Communication/tools.html (accessed October 14, 2010).
6. Adapted from Young, E. and L. Quinn. *The Policy Brief*, LGI training materials, available online at http://www.policy.hu/ipf/fel-pubs/samples/PolicyBrief-described.pdf (accessed October 14, 2010).
7. London Community Recycling Network, "Guide to Writing a Newsletter". Available online at www.lcrn.org.uk/images/531.pdf (accessed October 14, 2010).
8. London Community Recycling Network, "Guide to Writing a Newsletter."
9. Adapted from, European Commission. 2004. *European Research: A Guide to Successful Communications*. Luxembourg: Office for Official Publications of the European Communities. Available online at http://ec.europa.eu/research/science-society/science-communication/index_en.htm (accessed October 14, 2010).
10. Houts, P.S., Cecilia D. Doak, Leonard G. Doak and Mathew J. Loscalzol. 2006. "The Role of Pictures in Improving Health Communication: A Review of Research on Attention, Comprehension, Recall, and Adherence," *Patient Education and Counseling* 61 (2006): 173–190.

8

Multimedia

VIDEO

Video as a method for communication should be chosen according to goals, not because of its inherent attractiveness. Short films or video clips allow absorption of a general idea faster, easier, and more clearly and therefore secure better retention of the nuggets of "action." Video "animates" an issue and makes it more tangible by showing real people and real examples, even if they are not fully representative. In sum, videos contain less meat, but are more appetizing.

This is best suited for audiences who are not highly literate, or too busy or bewildered to read lengthy texts. Video makers must therefore select just the right key messages and illustrate them in just the right way for a particular audience—and the context in which the film will be watched.

Audience

Once again there is no substitute for knowing the intended audience. All good communication hinges on this understanding. Final audience must be the guide before the screenplay is written, before

BOX 8.1

From Tobacco to Bamboo

The Government of Kenya ratified the Framework Convention on Tobacco Control (FCTC) on 25 June 2004 which calls on Parties to the treaty to promote economically viable alternatives for tobacco growers. Tobacco control may be improving health, but it is leaving former tobacco farmers jobless.

The School of Environment and Earth Sciences at Maseno University in Kenya is researching bamboo cultivation as an alternative. The research has piqued the interest of the Ministry of Information and Communications (MIC), which has begun filming interviews with small-scale farmers involved in the study. The video will document problems associated with tobacco production and farmers' optimism about the potential benefits of switching to bamboo.

Farmers are also being taught to craft bamboo, in order to gain new skills and income before their first crop harvest. The video documentary may be broadcast on national television to transfer the knowledge to the general public.

The researchers reached the scientific community through publication in international journals while simultaneously contributing to WHO Working Groups on Alternative Livelihoods. While considering scale-up to 10 tobacco-growing regions, the Kenyan project's success has impacted WHO and FCTC (Framework Convention on Tobacco Control).

Source: IDRC. 2009. "IDRC on Tobacco Control." Available online at http://www.idrc.ca/en/ev-140493-201-1-DO_TOPIC.html (accessed October 14, 2010).

Note: For more information see www.tobaccotobamboo.com

the field tapes are shot, before the footage is edited, before the script is overlaid, and before the final format is set.

Does one version have to be a catch-all, or will different lengths and composition be needed? What languages are involved—for interviewees as well as listeners? Will sub-titles be necessary—and can all the audiences read? What type of video players, if any, do they have? Will it be watched in a private or public setting?

It is possible—but not yet common—to produce various versions of the same video tailored to the variety of factors affecting the various target audiences. The staged approach for papers described in chapter 7 (e.g., 1:3:25) can be emulated for videos, where the number of pages is replaced with minutes of length (e.g., 1:5:10 minutes). People interested in the technical details, tables, and a thorough background will therefore be encouraged to access the version that suits their needs.

Cautions and Precautions

Shooting, editing, and dubbing a video (all digitally) is now technically simple, flexible, and quick. Doing it well is highly specialized, complex, and time consuming. And even in the professional market, video makers familiar with the research world are rare. It is therefore recommended to have a balance of content expertise as well as technical expertise on the team.

The most effective "message" videos are no more than nine minutes long, preferably less. Even with a tight screenplay, this can involve several hours of field footage taken at several dozen different sites, later edited (over days) into several hundred separate but interlocking clips. Serious computer power is needed to process many gigabytes of source and final material.

Complex subject matter often demands lots of "talking heads"—yet care must be taken not to turn the film into a series of mini lectures. While comfortably and clearly showing the speakers for a few introductory seconds, their voice continuity can be overlaid on shots of what they are talking about, balancing direct speech with background commentary, etc.

Further, all people in all videos equate the process with "being on television" and therefore inherently prestigious; that makes many key subjects nervous, some are very clumsy on camera, and virtually all become much more sensitive to their status/political position when on tape. So do institutional stakeholders.

Despite these and other difficulties, videos are still a popular and highly recommended medium—because they can be so potent.

Distribution: How to Get a Video to the Intended Audience

Streaming online video is one of the fastest-growing sectors on the internet.[1] The leading platforms are social sites like YouTube but there are also specific platforms for scientific content—probably the most developed at time of writing was www.scivee.tv, a web-portal that allows researchers and institutions to upload videos about their activities and findings and to classify them according to topic and target audience.

Online networking and video publishing platforms are evolving rapidly, and both method and material must stay up-to-date.

Many peer-reviewed journals now enable a video-annex with published articles, high impact journals like JAMA, The Lancet, New England Journal, and PloSmed are among them[2]. Links to uploaded videos can be added to electronic newsletters and emails, or on website home pages, or by producing video-podcasts that research-users can subscribe to. For some audiences, videos produced as DVDs can be attached to written documents, or mailed like brochures.

Other media or venues suitable for video-dissemination include:

- for rural populations, existing or portable TV sets or mobile cinemas, even a projector, a white bed-sheet, and car battery;
- for academic peers, short videos can be shown during presentations at conferences or as complement to a poster;
- for young, urban audiences (including policy-makers), the screen of mobile phones is increasingly used;
- for all, public screenings at exhibitions, etc.

Broadcast television is an obvious route, but this demands very high technology and—unless the slot is sponsored by related commercial interests (which can compromise perceptions)—high cost in air time.

Budget

Costing a video is like costing a car. In both cases—from very little to a fortune—even with due diligence you generally get what you pay for. There are no short cuts to good quality.

Every video budget will have to include some costs for:

- **Pre-production:** Development of a draft script, a derived screenplay and shooting schedule, and possibly search for and advance visits to locations.
- **Filming:** Equipment, personnel time (crews of three are common), and possible travel and accommodation costs. There may be filming license fees in some places.
- **Production:** Editing equipment, final script, voice-over (the choice of narrator voice is a key ingredient of success) titling, and other animation.
- **Post-production:** Packaging and distribution.

Additional Considerations

While it is true that the time it takes to produce a good video should not be underestimated, the costs of making videos have rapidly decreased with new digital technology for filming and editing. You may be fortunate to have special in-house skills and semi-professional equipment that has become less expensive; there is even free amateur software. If there is no in-house skill base, then a few days of training in video making in a well-planned and purposeful manner (as opposed to a "shoot-and-run" methodology, i.e., just filming "whatever happens"), followed by camera operation, editing, and "storytelling", may be a viable option. Making simple videos at low cost is now possible, and useful for in-house illustration. But beware, external broadcast of a sub-standard or bad video can do more harm than good (professional television has given most audiences high standards of expectation).

The objectives of videos should be very clearly defined—general goals such as "making X visible" or "raising the awareness of Y" lack measurability and real focus; objectives must be as specific, realistic, and concrete as possible.

It is better to be liberal with credits and logos in the video, rather than allowing too many stakeholders to shape the content. It is advisable always to include a two-second disclaimer that the contents do not necessarily represent the official view of the institutions involved.

BOX 8.2
Cochabamba, Bolivia—Urban Solid Waste: Using TV to Engage the Public

Bolivia offers one of the most striking examples of government power devolution to the municipal level. Large-scale decentralization has been on-going since the early 1990s. The city of Cochabamba,—situated in the middle of an inter-Andean valley—is a fragile and vulnerable urban area with a population of more than 600,000. The city produces 400 tons of solid waste each day. The material is transported to the K'ara K'ara dumpsite, 10 km outside the city, where informal low-income settlements have developed.

Upon reaching the city of Cochabamba, and after feeling rural poverty, hundreds of women find themselves on a dumpsite—literally—scraping a living from filth. The Society for Environmental Management Bolivia have started to make this most marginalized population an economic retrieval service, as part of better solid waste management and improved conditions. The research project ensured parliament involvement right from the outset and in 2009 received public Recognition from the Bolivian Parliament for their work on solid waste management. (http://www.idrc.ca/upe/). This was followed by a national symposium on solid waste management. (*Source:* http://www.idrc.ca/en/ev-142034-201-1-DO_TOPIC.html)

As a result, El Porvenir, a Women's Card Makers Association, composed of former waste pickers, have not only mastered recycling techniques but now successfully commercialized recycled cars and bags (*Source:* http://www.sgab-bolivia.org/pdf/catalogo%20de%20tarjetas.pdf). Furthermore, the project has engaged the private sector in so far that the recycled bags are being used by a Bolivian Airline souvenir for passengers. For an interview with the airline, see http://www.youtube.com/watch?v=9IiQmvdrIkY

The Cochabamba project has placed particular importance on outreach and result dissemination with the general public, policy makers and members of parliament, through national media. At least seven TV interviews (http://www.sgab-bolivia.org/eventos.html), newspaper articles (http://bit.ly/cochabambaproject (accessed on December 14, 2010)

These KT efforts completely transformed the response when the management program asked Cochabamba residents to pre-sort their rubbish. They understood; they co-operated. The project gained in a very practical way by telling people what it was doing.

This pilot project is now part of the national policy agenda.

Source: http://www.sgab-bolivia.org/cfcochabamba/ (accessed October 16, 2010).

Resources

1. www.scivee.tv has a list of video professionals specialized in scientific productions.
2. *Insight into Participatory Video: A Handbook for the Field* by Nick Lunch and Chris Lunch. Available online at http://www.comminit.com/en/node/187674/38 (accessed October 14, 2010). Written by the directors of InsightShare, a United Kingdom/France-based organization using Participatory Video (PV) as a tool for empowering individuals and communities. It offers an outline for facilitators to use video to encourage a lively, democratic process. Descriptions of games and exercises to introduce PV are given, and a selection of video films made by local people and a training film are included in an accompanying CD-ROM.
3. Participatory Video Research Network. Available online at http://community.eldis.org/.5993f371/ (accessed October 14, 2010). This group aims to share, discuss and reflect on using participatory video as a tool for research and not just for KT.
4. Soul Beat Africa. For more information on film and video and their role in development in Africa, go to the ALL SECTIONS area on the Soul Beat Africa website at http://www.comminit.com/en/nodes/38 (accessed October 14, 2010).
5. Videmus: a video production company specialized in communicating research-related issues on video for targeted audiences. They offer international services for the dissemination of research findings, support for on-going research projects and video and digital content for instructional purposes (www.videmus.tv) (accessed October 14, 2010).
6. Tutorials on how to make video: available online at http://www.sf.tv/var/VideoGuide/lang_fr/loader.php (accessed October 14, 2010). (Note that this is by Swiss TV and is available only in French or German.)

RADIO SPOTS, PODCASTS

A radio spot is a short commercial slot between major programs. These spot times are generally purchased from the radio stations.

A podcast is a digital audio (or video) file that can be downloaded from the internet. Since 2004, it has become a popular means of sharing multimedia files—widely and quickly—through the web. Audio files recorded for radio purposes have found, in the internet, an alternate means of mass dissemination.

In communities where the culture of knowledge-sharing is primarily oral—and/or where written material (even the daily newspaper) does not reach or is too expensive—radio can be a powerful mechanism for all communication, including distilling research results into lay terms. The messages need to grab the attention of the listener immediately and ensure that the key points are all covered in a very short time.

Community radios have played a large role in raising awareness, educating the public, and allowing citizen expression. They have also explained to the listeners and populations, the concept of democracy, of citizenship, and of good governance.[3] Often, radio promotes the participation of communities in decision making and has at times also led to establishing a social dialogue between leaders and followers.

BOX 8.3

The EQUINet Story—Radio as Part of a Multi-pronged Approach

A network of professionals, researchers, members of civil society organizations and policymakers have come together as EQUINET, to promote equity in health in southern Africa. They launched a four-day seminar to raise the profile of health equity in the Southern African Development Community (SADC).

Using book and article publication, the web, and conferences, they have changed their image from a "left consciousness" organization to a key advisor to SADC on health equity.

EQUINET provided scientific input supporting SADC's position at World Trade Organization talks in 2003. It has assisted SADC chart a position on international intellectual property law that was in the interests of southern Africa. It helped inform SADC policy on HIV/AIDS

EQUINET had less immediate success at the national or local level—direct one-to-one linkage between research and health policy change may be hard to detect and may hang on too narrow a definition of "impact." EQUINET has since expanded policy capacities and broadened policy horizons within the region, altering the climate of health policy even when its direct participation is absent.

More recently, in September 2010 it used the power of radio to strengthen the media profile and outreach of messages and actors in EQUINET on fair financing. It has also strengthened the capacities and learnings throughout the network on use of mass media for message dissemination. Since the show was broadcast,

(Box 8.3 contd.)

(Box 8.3 contd.)

the National Health Insurance issue in South Africa has been getting increasing attention (due to the political climate, as well as coverage by the show), and several radio stations have research leaders in this work, to be studio guests on the topic. It is clear that the EQUINET production was both timely and well received and has been able to make a positive contribution to the current debates.

The **EQUINET** radio spots and debates on fair financing for health were featured on the African Labor Radio Project and on South Africa FM in September/October 2009:

- "*Public Healthcare Financing*" http://www.equinetafrica.org/bibl/docs/alrpfinoct2009.mp3 The show reached an estimated audience of 796,000 across South Africa. In addition, the show was downloaded 111 times since it was put on the EQUINET website in September 2010, with 27 downloads in September, 50 downloads in October and 34 in November, 41 distinct hosts were served.
- *Healthcare Financing: The State of Healthcare and the Working Class* http://www.equinetafrica.org/bibl/docs/audiodump.mp3 The pre-recorded 15 minute slot had content from South Africa, Malawi, Zimbabwe, Nigeria and Ghana. The show reached an estimated 12,000 listeners across Africa.

Sources: www.equinetafrica.org (accessed October 14, 2010).

http://www.idrc.ca/uploads/user-S/12808453701EQUINET_Radio_project_1_pager_FINAL.pdf (accessed October 14, 2010).

Radio is particularly well-suited if the audience has any or all of these characteristics:

- relies on verbal information;
- has limited access to print or visual media;
- communicates in the vernacular;
- does not have time or disposition for lengthy reading;
- is only superficially interested in a topic;
- has limited literacy or low affinity to reading; and
- finds the topic too complex to read about it.

Similar to video distribution, audio messages can be used in presentations or as complement to a poster, sent to mobile phones, played at exhibitions and road-shows through portable radio sets, or formally broadcast.

Budget

Despite all the high-tech visual options, radio remains an extremely wide-reaching medium—in urban areas and among affluent audiences because they can listen (gather information) while doing something else (driving, ironing, washing up) and in rural areas and among poor audiences because it is the most available, most accessible, and lowest cost source of news or entertainment.

As a KT tool, it is generally much less expensive than video-TV, but that does not mean it is cheap. Below (Table 8.1) is a rough guide for planning a budget for 18 radio spots.

TABLE 8.1
Budget for 18 Radio Spots

Item	*Number*	*Cost*	*Total Cost (USD)*	*Notes*
1. Pre-production				
(*a*) Radio spot concept (incorporating research) and creation of 6 episode scripts	10 hours	$50 per hour	$500	Writing fees to hire professional writers
(*b*) Editing of script	2 hour	$50 per hour	$100	To hire outside editor
Translation of six scripts into local languages X and Y	6 scripts × 2 languages = 12 translations	$100 per script	$1,200	Languages will be: English, X and Y. The script will be the same for all languages
Sub-total Pre-production Costs			**$1,800**	

(Table 8.1 contd.)

(Table 8.1 contd.)

Item	*Number*	*Cost*	*Total Cost (USD)*	*Notes*
2. Production Costs				
(*a*) Interviews	20	$20	$400	To cover transportation fees for interviewees
(*b*) Voice talent	2	$100	$200	Small honorarium for two voice-actors
(*c*) Various production costs	18	$200	$3,600	Covering all technical inputs, rental of recording studio, etc.
(*d*) Content supervision and editing			$500	Honorarium for our own staff
(*e*) Technical editing			$500	Honorarium for radio staff
Sub-total Production Costs			**$5,200**	
3. Post-production Costs				
(*a*) Air Time	18 spots	$100 per 10 minutes	$1,800	Each spot is 10 minutes long
(*b*) CD creation: duplication of CDs (incl. master); labeling CDs, etc.	180	$2	$360	180 CDs in total: 60 per language. To be produced in-house.
Sub-total Post-production Costs			**$2,160**	
GRAND TOTAL			$9,160	

Resources

1. The Communication Initiative—Community Radio Theme Site: http://www.comminit.com/en/africa/community-radio/ (accessed October 14, 2010).

2. Center for International Media Assistance, National Endowment for Democracy. 2007. *Community Radio Social Impact Assessment—Removing Barriers, Increasing Effectiveness.* Washington: CIMA. This evaluation report details a long-range participatory action research process launched in 2006 by AMARC, to identify the barriers to the positive impact of community radio, and to explore ways to increase its effectiveness in poverty reduction, development, inclusiveness, and democracy-building in local communities around the world. http://www.ned.org/cima/CIMA-Community_Radio-Working_Group_Report.pdf (accessed October 14, 2010).
3. AMARC. 2008 (December). *Citizens Empowerment and Good Governance through Community Radio in Western Africa.* Legislative and Policy Frameworks. Compilation of Documents for an Action Research to Remove Barriers and Increase Social Impact of Community Radio. AMARC, Africa. AMARC (World Association of Radio Broadcasters) is an international non-governmental organization serving the community radio movement, with almost 3,000 members and associates in 110 countries. Its goal is to support and contribute to the development of community and participatory radio on the principals of solidarity and international co-operation. http://www.amarc.org/ (accessed October 14, 2010).
4. Farm Radio International: This is a Canadian-based, not-for-profit organization in direct partnership with some 300 radio broadcasters in 39 African countries, fighting poverty and food insecurity. Their materials are also available electronically to broadcasters and to rural development organizations in Africa, Asia, and Latin America. http://www.farmradio.org/ (accessed October 14, 2010).
5. The Panos Institute. 2006. *Heeding The Voiceless: A Guide to the Use of Oral Testimonies for Radio Documentaries.* Dakar, Sénégal: Institut Panos Afrique de l'Ouest. Available online at *http://www.radiopeaceafrica.org/assets/texts/pdf/pdf Heeding the voiceless.pdf* (accessed on December 14, 2010). The Oral Testimony is a new format in community radio, adapted from a social research tool set up by Panos London. It is an inverted interview because it is guided by the interviewee and not the interviewer. It stems from the principle that to know what is really going on in a community, you have to listen patiently to the people at grassroots level, instead of asking only the leaders of that community as is usually the case. These leaders tend to hide problems in their efforts to present a nice face of their community to outside eyes and ears. The consequence is the vast majority of community members, who effectively shape social trends, never get a chance to say their views, perceptions, experiences, priorities, values.

INTERNET: SOCIAL NETWORKING, WEBSITES, AND BLOGS

Social Networking

The internet enables and extends social networking in ways previously unimaginable and we have not even come close to seeing its full potential yet. Colloquial evidence suggests that—in the developed world—people of all ages now spend more time surfing the net than watching television. Social sites are the overwhelming leaders.

So as Satterfield remarks, "Although popularly known as places where people make friends and find romance, social networking sites can also play a key role in helping any organization (reach people to) achieve its goals."[4]

BOX 8.4
Internet Behaviour is Fundamentally "Social"

When you look at the history of any new medium, it takes a decade or more for people to figure out what the native behaviour of that medium is. For the first 15 years of television, they were actually filming radio shows. And it really took 10–20 years to start seeing native TV programming like the Today show, which nobody thought was going to be successful because people did not watch television the first thing in the morning. What is becoming very, very clear…[is that] when you look at what the fundamental or native behaviour of what the Internet is, it is social. It is two-way communication.

Source: Gina Bianchini, quoted in Mayo, K. and P. Newcomb. 2008 (July). "How the Web was Won: An Oral History of the Internet," *Vanity Fair*.

A host of Friend-Of-A-Friend (FOAF) platforms are now used to share ideas, content, photos, alert each other to excellent websites, and videos and—most critically for KT purposes—often group people together to promote causes and even to fundraise.

Facebook is possibly the most successful social networking phenomenon with more than 100 million members, each member having a free, personalized website allowing interaction with millions of others.

Facebook's "Causes" application currently has more than four million users, allowing people to browse NGOs and charitable organizations, and then directly contribute funds. While this is currently only available to US 501(c) (3) organizations, it will surely extend to other countries. As one example, UNICEF's "Causes" page shows almost 700,000 members, who have donated more than $33,000 to date.

Creating a Web Presence

In chapter 6, we outlined the essential elements that any organization should consider in designing a Communications Strategy. Developing a web presence is no different—strategically—from developing print tools, videos or radio spots: considering audience, designing message, producing materials, and delivering them.

A website can at once be a "brochure" profiling an organization, its topical "newsletter," a repository of its reports, a "policy brief" and advocacy forum, a photo library, a showcase of multimedia video and radio spots, and an active interface with anybody. It can archive all previous material of these types and be the front-line display of all new material the organization generates.

The cost in equipment and skills is relatively modest, but essential to not only create an effective site, but also to monitor, maintain, troubleshoot, and update it. The most accessed sites are updated every minute. Some element of addition, deletion, modification at least once a week is a recommended minimum. Expertise in design and structure of a site can be outsourced until in-house capability is established.

Creating a Blog

Beyond social networking and more formal (e.g., www.xxxx.org) websites, another simple online presence is a weblog or a "blog."[5] Like an electronic journal or diary, blogs allow posting of entries on a website, from quick messages and photographs to more in-depth articles. These posts are typically sorted by date, meaning the most recent entry is displayed first. Many blogs are interactive, encouraging visitors to leave a comment.

BOX 8.5
Why Create a Blog?

- A blog (or a website more generally) can extend an institution's influence by attracting audiences in a way that is far more interactive than email. But we must be careful: blogs and websites must be routinely updated to be effective;
- Blogs can create a forum for expert commentary and analysis on hot policy issues;
- A blog's easy-to-read, informal writing style can demystify key concepts;
- Blogs can help set the media agenda—authoritative comment and analysis on under- or unreported issues can lead journalists or others to follow up and write about it;
- For those interested in a specific topic, relevant blogs could eventually become a leading supplement to traditional print and online news;
- The "feedback loops" created by the blog could lead to new audiences and collaboration opportunities.

Source: Hovland, I. 2005. "Successful Communication: A Toolkit for Researchers and Civil Society Organisations." Overseas Development Institute.

There are a range of options at the disposal of the aspiring blogger. Blogs can be freely created at: www.civiblog.org; www.blog.co.uk; www.livejournal.com; www.mindsay.com; www.blogger.com

BOX 8.6
Five Common Web Mistakes

1. No clear identification of what we want from our site;
2. Not understanding the importance of good design;
3. Not editing or updating content;
4. Failing to use the web as an interactive platform;
5. Not assembling an in-house web team.

Source: Adapted from Hershey, C. 2005. "Communications Toolkit: A Guide to Navigating Communications for the Nonprofit World." Available online at http://www.causecommunications.org/clients-cause.php (accessed October 14, 2010).

PRESENTATIONS

"The conference" is an unparalleled moment to network, present, source funding, solve problems, and soak up new knowledge. Such events are also time- and travel-expensive and can degenerate into a mound of giveaways, buffet lines, dreary lectures, followed a month later by an unabridged organizers' report heavy enough to bend a wheelbarrow.

Too often, conferences do not measure their overall contribution to the field—because no one is even trying to. While organizers organize, and presenters present, veteran delegates know what really matters: who you meet and what you hear and say over a coffee or a drink between sessions.

The "next wave"—the Conference 2.0—aims to turn every conference into a dynamic learning environment, where solid oral and poster presentations easily flow into proceedings that capture strong messages and action points.

To that end, this chapter focuses on:

- **Oral presentations** — how to make speeches and talks more memorable, and how to use supporting technology responsibly (without letting the technology become the speech).
- **Poster presentations** — how to choose the right content, the right look, and the right size.
- **Conference presentations** — how to streamline and improve the conference's final record of proceedings, how to nurture better rapporteurs, and how to amplify the participation of session chairs in capturing main messages.

Oral Presentations

Fact one: The average adult attention span is around 20 minutes. Chances are high that 16 percent will fall asleep.[6]

Fact two: Nobody in the room is interested in knowing everything you did.

Fact three: Nobody will leave a presentation saying, "I wish that presentation had been longer!"

Fact four: At any conference, people may see 20–30 presentations. Any excuse to stop listening and they are gone!

The speech

Like a two-pager, a video or a newsletter, a speech should be an appetizer; it should leave the audience hungry for more information. A good speaker impresses the importance of an issue, "sells" a core idea, and then points the way to follow-up details, the paper, hand-outs, brochures, DVDs, etc., that are "up here by the lectern" or available on the internet or will be mailed directly to all interested parties.

A speech is not an academic paper. It is not an opportunity to discuss the finer points of methodology and, most of all, a speech is not a PowerPoint. If, one minute after a speech—never mind a week or a year later—the audience can recall three major points, the job was done well.

This section discusses the "three-message speech," provides some tips for presenting, and concludes with the responsible use of Microsoft's PowerPoint application.

The "Three-message speech"

The audience must be the starting point—a speech must satisfy their experience, not your own.[7] Effective speeches grab attention, communicate audience-relevant arguments and evidence, persuade an audience they are true, and are memorable and entertaining. The easiest way to structure a speech is to create three "pegs" that capture the essential points and then hang the talk on them. This clearly does not resemble the abstract-introduction-hypothesis-methods-discussion-conclusion format of a paper, and nor should it. A speech is not a paper. In a speech, the content must be organized in a way that is easy to follow and recall at one "reading."

In the "typical" speech as shown below, an audience's attention is high at the beginning (hopeful) and at the end (grappling for key

FIGURE 8.1
The Three-message Speech

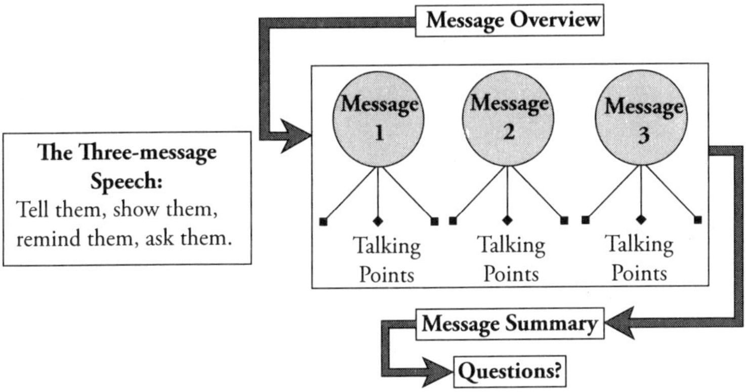

messages). Structuring around three take-home messages works to maintain an audience's attention throughout, as it promises and delivers regular "peaks."

- **Tell them** what the three messages are.
- **Show them** those three messages in action and with detail.
- **Remind them** what the three messages were.
- **Ask them** for their questions or concerns.

While some have re-spun the "tell them, show them, remind them, ask them" directive as "tell them what you're going to tell them, tell them, tell them what you told them,"[8] these pointers are a useful way to structure the "three messages" approach.

Using "brevity, levity, and repetition" really does work.[9] There may be three "sub-messages" explaining each of our three major messages, but so long as a speech delivers the three major "pegs"—briefly, and memorably—the audience will get the message. For a step by step guide on how to give an effective speech, see chapter 12 on Conference 2.0.

BOX 8.7
The "Nodding-off" Indicator

While attending lectures on dementia, doctors Kenneth Rockwood, David B. Hogan and Christopher J. Patterson kept track of the number of attendees who nodded off during the talks. They found that in an hour-long lecture attended by about 100 doctors, an average of 16 audience members nodded off. "We chose this method because counting is scientific," the authors wrote in their seminal 2004 article in The Canadian Medical Association Journal. The investigators analyzed the presentations themselves and found that a monotonous tone was most strongly associated with "nod-off episodes per lecture" (NOELs), followed by the sight of a tweed jacket on the lecturer.

Source: Carey, B. 2008. "You're Checked out, but Your Brain is Tuned in." *The New York Times*, August 5.

BOX 8.8
Emotional versus Intellectual Content

Ultimately, people are not at all rational; they 'hear' the emotional content of the lecture more clearly than they 'hear' its intellectual content. Therefore, the emotional content establishes the context in which they receive the intellectual content. If the emotional context is solid, then they are receptive to the intellectual content, they understand it better, and they take away more. If the emotional context is weak, then they just do not pay enough attention to really absorb the intellectual content.

Source: Hecker, C. "How to Give a Good Presentation." Available online at http://chrishecker.com/how_to_give_a_good_presentation (accessed October 14, 2010).

PowerPoint "do nots"

PowerPoint slides can help animate a speech, and can be legitimately used to "illustrate" with graphs or pictures. Text can be used, but only in very brief bullet points (few words each, and few per page, in large and legible type) to deliver hear-AND-see emphasis. It is vital to be familiar with the programme and equipment, and to ensure its reliability in advance, so intermittent use of slides is seamless with the content of what you are saying.

And…

- *Never* distribute a print-out of the PowerPoint in advance (delegates will read it, totally and rapidly, instead of listening).
- *Never* read out the text on screen—delegates can read faster than you can speak (up to 10 times faster). Use on-screen text as your own triggers, but always amplify using different words.
- *Never* depend on the technology—be ready to continue even if the system fails.

Concluding thoughts on oral presentations

An oral presentation—like a two-pager or a press release or a brochure—is designed to convince an audience to seek more information. So "more information" must be on hand, preferably on a table in the presentation room. Tell the audience what material will be available and where, but give them nothing in advance, or they will be reading it while you are talking. Supporting information includes print-outs of the presentation (having too many is better than running out), any printed material relevant to the talk (papers, briefs), and perhaps some general information on your organization (brochure, newsletter, DVD). You are on stage and this is the time to highlight your work.

BOX 8.9

From Waste Sorters to Policy Stokers… The Case of the Mbeubeuss Landfill

All Africa's big cities have massive waste landfills. These bring important benefits (thousands of livelihoods through scavenging, urban agriculture, and recycling) and problems (health risks to dumpsite workers and pollution of groundwater). The Mbeubeuss landfill, receiving about 500,000 tons of waste each year, is the only facility of its kind in Dakar.

The city of Dakar is addressing the pros and cons through multi-stakeholder platforms to gather facts and perspectives—and other KT tools to make the key messages availably both locally and universally.

(Box 8.9 contd.)

(Box 8.9 contd.)

In addition to contributing to the creation of a Municipality "Local Consultation Framework," the leaflets, posters, a special issue of "Vie, Vert–Information Environmentale" and video materials, a special issue of the Environmental Information Journal was distributed at the IV World Urban Forum. A 10-minute video documentary was used to convey key messages from the local communities and researchers to policy makers at the conference, to development agencies, and to scientific communities within Senegal and beyond.

And, as so often happens, community involvement on one issue has led to general community empowerment on many others.

Source: http://www.idrc.ca/en/ev-103125-201-1-DO_TOPIC.html (accessed October 14, 2010).

Links to videos of excellent presentations are listed below. How do expert presenters stand? Use gestures? Structure a speech? Create simple but stylish presentations?

Resources

1. *Presentation Skills: World Champion of Public Speaking.* This award-winning speaker is very, very good. His secret? "Get them to want to know the point before they know the point." Available online at http://www.youtube.com/v/HOSADvJnrG8&hl=en&fs=1 (accessed October 14, 2010).
2. *Steve Jobs Introduces the iPhone.* Watch this speech from one of the pre-eminent business speakers introducing a new product. Available online at http://www.youtube.com/watch?v=vZYlhShD2oQ (accessed October 14, 2010).
3. *Death by PowerPoint (and how to fight it).* This online PowerPoint presentation (irony?) walks us through the necessary (and unnecessary) Powerpoint ingredients. Available online at http://www.slideshare.net/thecroaker/death-by-powerpoint (accessed October 14, 2010).

Poster Presentations

A successful poster presentation summarizes selected work in easy, captivating nuggets. It is an advertisement, an eye-catching visual presentation. Like other KT tools, a good poster inspires desire for more information: further resources should be immediately at hand.

Further, a poster must stop a "strolling audience" from walking by.[10] There are about 11 seconds to grab and retain their attention, then less than 10 minutes to use that attention to deliver a message.[11]

According to Connor, a good poster is a combination of compelling science, an uncluttered and colorful design, with text that is legible, brief, and organized in a straightforward fashion.[12] Some argue that it is better than giving a talk: it works even if we are not there, it can go to multiple conferences unchanged, it can compensate for the presentation-shy; and it can provide valuable opportunities for students or other up-and-comers to make an impact.[13]

A poster demands careful choices of what to include and what to leave out, bearing in mind that a full reading should take between five and 10 minutes.

FIGURE 8.2

Capture Attention; Deliver Instant Impact

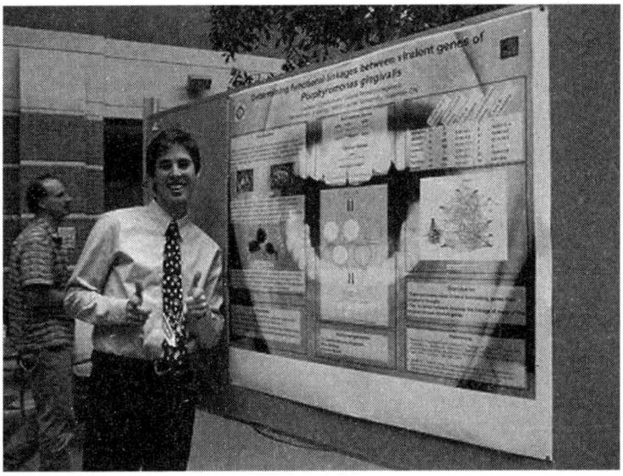

Source: Baker, N. 2006. "Snazzy Cam." Photograph. Available online at http://www.flickr.com/photos/imdreaminggreen/133619408/ (accessed October 14, 2010).

Note: Please note the synchronization of poster and presenter. The poster also has innovative graphics and a good balance of information and visuals.

For a step by step guide on how to structure a poster, *see* chapter 12, "The Conference 2.0: Making Most of Conferences".

Resources

1. Colin Purrington's "Advice on designing scientific posters" is an excellent place to start. It has great pictures and sound advice. www.swarthmore.edu/NatSci/cpurrin1/posteradvice.htm (accessed October 14, 2010).
2. Carol Waite Connor, "The Poster Session: A Guide for Preparation" has excellent tips as well, especially in capturing the attention of the "strolling audience." www.aapg.org/meetings/instructions/prepguide.pdf (accessed October 14, 2010).
3. The University at Buffalo Libraries also has a strong collection of links in "Poster Presentations: Designing Effective Posters." http://library.buffalo.edu/libraries/asl/guides/bio/posters.html (accessed October 14, 2010).

Conference Presentations

In this section we will examine the role conference organizers could play in capturing messages primarily by producing better, more dynamic conference records. Two different strategies for producing better conference reports are:

- **Synthesis:** Making the final report a dynamic synthesis incorporating presentations, interviews, discussions, workshops, and so on.
- **Rapporteuring:** Selecting rapporteurs, helping them capture the key messages, and convincing session chairs to contribute to the rapporteurs' work.

BOX 8.10

***Conference Report:* Implementing the Comprehensive Care and Treatment Programme for HIV and AIDS Patients in the Free State: Sharing Experiences**

Bloemfontein, South Africa March 30–April 1, 2005

This report is intended to share the experience of the Free State in expanding ART in the province, and aims to develop lessons and recommendations for the Free State and elsewhere. The document is directed at four specific user-groups: policy-makers and planners; health workers; researchers; and civil society.

(Box 8.10 contd.)

(Box 8.10 contd.)

This report was compiled by four researchers commissioned by the Health Systems Trust. They attended the conference and took notes throughout. Information gathered was supplemented by notes from rapporteurs and discussions with conference delegates.

A draft report was presented by the researchers at a subsequent one-day workshop held in Johannesburg on May 5, 2005. Participants included policy-makers, planners, researchers, health workers, and representatives of civil society from different provinces in South Africa and regionally. The participants provided feedback on the report content and made further contributions to the recommendations of the report.

Source: www.hst.org.za/publications/677 (accessed October 14, 2010).

Synthesis

South African Health Systems Trust[14] began with the expected audience: *policy-makers* and *planners*; *health workers*; *researchers*; and *civil society*. Participants from within as well as outside of South Africa were expected.

With the audience established, the planning group then identified (from submitted papers and speaker lists) three major themes:

- The Process of Implementing the ART Program in the Free State.
- Resource Requirements for the ART Program in the Free State.
- The Impact of Implementing the ART Program in the Free State.

And following production of the synthesis, they held a one-day "feedback workshop" to ensure they had got it right.

Beyond a strong blend of presentations, workshops, seminars, and other discussions—and its audience segregation—what really makes a synthesis stand out is its action-oriented focus. Each chapter concludes with "Lessons and Recommendations," stating specifically what should be done and who, among the four types of participants, should do it.

Disseminating the synthesis is the final ingredient for success. All-important distribution was through mailing to all who attended the conference, those impacted by the key lessons and recommendations (e.g., prominent HIV/AIDS policy-makers, health NGOs, journalists), and posting a copy on a website alongside all presentations, creating links to the finished, polished products and every presenters' PowerPoint, paper or poster.

Rapporteuring

Capturing "key points" is a subjective judgement, so the quality and briefing of rapporteurs and the guidance they receive from session chairs is important.

- **Careful rapporteur selection:** Typically, rapporteurs are students with an academic background aligned to the conference's theme. But what about journalists (given their skills at writing and interviewing) or primary health care workers or members of a research team (given their knowledge of the subject area)? The HST team of rapporteurs drew on all of these.
- **Rapporteur training:** Several training sessions alert rapporteurs to core messages that need to be captured. The training helps them navigate the tremendous volume of content and range of people that the conference will throw at them, arms them with relevant lists and documents, and enables individuals to be matched to sessions according to their preferences or the organizers' assessment.
- **Session chairs as rapporteurs:** Session chairs have unique insights and usually provide a highly qualified perspective. While rapportage is not their task, they often use their opening and closing remarks to provoke the speakers, summarize main points, and provide their insights. These in turn steer those compiling the synthesis.

Concluding Thoughts

At this very moment, speakers are reading their slides, shooting all kinds of bullets, drowning an audience in color and detail, and putting 16 percent to sleep.[15] The world is teeming with dreadful presentations. It is important to try to understand what makes presentations good or bad, in the hopes of correcting flaws. Conferences are becoming ever-more prevalent and ever-more important. From organizers to presenters to spectators to chairs to donors, we all have a role to play in creating the Conference 2.0—that sees and delivers the big picture, distills messages, links to more information, and captures the meaning and purpose and outcome of an event in a short, high-impact report.

NOTES AND REFERENCES

1. See for example, http://www.comscore.com/Press_Events/Press_Releases/2009/9/Google_Sites_Surpasses_10_Billion_Video_Views_in_August (accessed October 14, 2010); and http://www.investmentpitch.com/advertise/ (accessed October 14, 2010).
2. JAMA: http://jama.ama-assn.org/misc/multimedia.dtl (accessed October 14, 2010).; *New England Jounal*: http://content.nejm.org/misc/videos.dtl (accessed October 14, 2010).
   The Lancet: http://www.thelancet.com/ (accessed October 14, 2010).
   PloSmed: Videos are published on www.scivee.tv
3. AMARC. 2008. *Citizens Empowerment and Good Governance through Community Radio in Western Africa.* Legislative and Policy Frameworks. Compilation of Documents for an Action Research to Remove Barriers and Increase Social Impact of Community Radio. AMARC, Africa.
4. Satterfield, B. 2006. "What Can Social Networking do for Your Organisation?" Techsoup. Available online at http://www.techsoup.org/learningcenter/internet/archives/page9215.cfm (accessed October 14, 2010).
5. "Blog" is a derivative of "weblog".
6. Figure cited in Carey, B. 2008. "You're Checked Out, but Your Brain is Tuned in." *The New York Times*, August 5, New York.
7. Ferriss T. "From Al Gore's Chief Speechwriter: Simple Tips for a Damn Good Presentation (plus: breakdancing)." Available online at http://bit.ly/i7N051 (accessed on December 14, 2010).
8. Cash, R., "Elements of a Talk." Also *see* Atwood J. 2006. "How not to give a good presentation." Available at: www.codinghorror.com/blog/archives/000504.html
9. Ferriss, "From Al Gore's Chief Speechwriter…"

10. Connor, C.W. "The Poster Session: A Guide for Preparation." US Geological Survey. USGS Open-File Report 88-667. Available online at http://www.aapg.org/meetings/instructions/prepguide.pdf
11. Mandoli D. "How to Make a Great Poster." University of Washington. www.aspb.org/education/poster.cfm
12. Connor, "The Poster Session: A Guide for Preparation." (accessed October 14, 2010).
13. Purrington, C. "Advice on Designing Scientific Posters." Swarthmore College. Available online at www.swarthmore.edu/natsci/cpurrin1/posteradvice.htm (accessed October 14, 2010).
14. This report was partially funded by Research Matters.
15. Statistics from *Death by Powerpoint (and how to fight it)*. Online presentation. Available online at http://www.slideshare.net/thecroaker/death-by-powerpoint (accessed October 14, 2010).

9

Social/Popular Media

Often, the target audience are best able to repackage information for themselves and their peers. In communities, particularly, the public uses popular means of sharing stories such as storytelling, theatre, dance, and song.

STORYTELLING

Storytelling is an ancient art, but it has a significant application in modern KT. KM Expert Steven Denning uses stories as a tool, especially to capture tacit knowledge, and to effect change within organizations through innovation, individual growth, community-building, and appropriate technology. He uses springboard stories to enable "a leap in understanding" by the audience.[1]

A Good Story

According to Prusak, a good story should possess the following attributes:[2]

- **Endurance:** While stories are likely to change over time, the lessons they convey should stay the same.

- **Salience:** Good stories should appeal to their audience, be witty, pithy, and touch an emotional chord. The story must be short enough for people to remember it.
- **Coherence:** Stories should explain something and make sense. They must also be believable—avoid exaggeration.
- **Character:** Stories tend to hinge around the values and actions of characters the audience can easily identify with.

In addition, stories should be simple and concise but with sufficient background information; be plausible, lively, and exciting; be told with conviction and, always, end on a positive note.[3]

BOX 9.1

Managing Storytelling

How to go about it (as a storyteller)?

1. Be clear about the key message you want to convey with a story.
2. Build your story on a personal experience. Note key-words, from the beginning to the dramatic evolution, the turning point, and the happy (sad) end. What is the lesson learned?
3. Tell your story starting from the beginning. Build an atmosphere of curiosity. Tell the surprising moment of your story with a dramatic voice. Observe your listeners.
4. If indicated, relate your story to the topic discussed.

How to go about it (as a listener/interviewer)?

1. Contribute to a good climate in the group. Show your interest. Give the storyteller an adequate reason to tell.
2. Be a great audience. Listen closely, be receptive and fully comprehending.
3. Do not resist the story. Hear it out and then come back with additional questions.
4. Observe an implicit contract of trust unless you feel the teller is not telling the truth.

Source: Swiss Agency for Development and Cooperation (SDC) 2009. "Knowledge Management Toolkit." Berne: SDC. Available online at http://www.daretoshare.ch/en/Dare_To_Share/Knowledge_Management_Toolkit (accessed October 17, 2010).

BOX 9.2
Stories and Tacit Knowledge

Version A	Version B
In our evaluation of a project in Bangladesh we noted a wide variance in the competence of individual villages to develop sustainable and effective solutions to problems encountered, for example in replacing broken parts or developing low cost products such as new latrines. The lessons to be learned from this evaluation are that we should: • work against over-dependence on donors; • note and encourage entrepreneurial approaches to problems; • identify existing and repeatable good practices; and • build and strengthen communication between villages to assist cross-fertilization of ideas at the grassroots level.	Bangladesh is a really impressive place, in a positive sense. I was in a village last year working in water and sanitation. We were trying to promote the use of improved latrines, but could not produce concrete slabs and rings locally for a low cost. Somebody told me to visit the latrines of a lady in the village, so I went along and said, "Can I see your latrines?" She had made a latrine out of a clay pot with the bottom cut off. Then with a potter from the area she developed a small local production of bottomless pots, and they became the latrines. Ingenious. A few weeks later I was in another village and saw a hand pump; it was broken, just a small piece missing. So I said to the villagers, "Why don't you repair your pump?" And they said, "Oh, we just wait for another donor to bring a new pump." So I said, "Why don't you visit the lady in the village over there? She finds ways of getting things done for herself."

Source: The Swiss Agency for Development and Cooperation (SDC). 2006. Available online at http://opentraining.unesco-ci.org/cgi-bin/page.cgi?g=Detailed/22906.html;d=1 (accessed on March 8, 2011).

Resources

1. Denning, S. 2002. *The Springboard: How Storytelling Ignites Action in Knowledge-Era Organisations*. London: Butterworth Heinemann.
2. Swiss Agency for Development and Cooperation. 2009. *Knowledge Management Toolkit*. Berne: SDC. Also Available at (http://www.daretoshare.ch/en/Dare_To_Share/Knowledge_Management_Toolkit/Story_Telling).

3. Swiss Agency for Development and Cooperation. 2007. *Story Guide—Building Bridges Using Narrative Techniques.* Berne: SDC. Also available online at (http://www.km4dev.org/forum/topics/story-guide-building-bridges and http://www.nelh.nhs.uk/knowledge_management/km2/storytelling_toolkit.asp
4. Weblink : http://en.wikipedia.org/wiki/Storytelling

THEATRE AND SONG

In many communities around the world, the prevailing oral culture renders popular means of entertainment as powerful sources of education and social engagement. Theatre, drama, and song are such tools that can assist in influencing attitudes, behaviour, and policies. Performance can allow young people, marginalized communities, and remote populations to assert their right to equality in personal and public relationships and thereby contribute social change, including the formulation and implementation of policies.

BOX 9.3

Using Theatre to Influence Policy, Politics, Practice, and People

The Equity Gauge concept combines *(a)* public participation, *(b)* advocacy, and *(c)* measurement. It harnesses the comparative advantages of all possible stakeholders of a health system—researchers (academics), health workers, health managers, policy makers, legislators, and the general public (communities). The Zambia chapter (EGZ)'s aim was "to provide equity of access to cost-effective health care services as close to the family as possible" starting with four contrasting districts: Lusaka (the urban capital), Chama (poor and remote rural), Chingola (industrial and mining), and Choma (wide rural with some commercial farming).

EGZ stakeholder Chapters were formed in each district, with one male and one female from the following categories: political parties with MPs, human rights groups, women's groups, youth groups, church leaders, traditional leaders (chiefs), civil servants, and any other influential social groups locally identified. The Chapters were tasked with defining "equity or inequity" in local languages and to brainstorm how they could inform health workers, health managers and policy makers what this would look or feel like in real-life health care provision.

(Box 9.3 contd.)

(Box 9.3 contd.)

Stakeholders identified theatre, songs, poems, and religious sermons as approaches to get their messages across. Local communities, co-ordinated by District committees, designed their separate messages for their target audiences.

Using theatre, they acted out their experiences in seeking health care, the transport difficulties, the level of responsiveness and compassion from health workers, the processes of fees and waiting times, attitudes to vulnerable groups, and the quality of care expected and received. Drama competitions were held, and the best in each district was invited to a national competition—watched by health officials from the Ministry, parliamentary committee, districts, and others.

Politically, the KT techniques used catalysed the debate of user fees in parliament and front-paged newspapers which resulted in the immediate reduction of some user fees and, with time, complete abolishment of others.

Practically, health worker sensitization sessions were added to annual action plans and health-workers brought equity issues to their planning sessions. In addition, they reflected more welcoming behaviour with clients.

Equity became embedded as "a serious national issue." The theatre and drama events were video taped and available on a DVD available at www.research-matters.net

Source: Extracted from submission by T.J. Ngulube, Equity Gauge Zambia and from the Equity Gauge video available online at http://blip.tv/file/891299 (accessed October 17, 2010).

Resources

1. Muiruri, J. 2005. *Child Participation in Awareness Raising through Theatre.* African Medical and Research Foundation (AMREF). AMREF shares the successes of the Dagoretti Children in Need project which aims to improve the physical and psychological health, living conditions, and skills of children and adolescents in vulnerable circumstances. The report focuses on the project's use of theatre for rehabilitation, outlining AMREF's "theatre-like-home" approach and the impact this approach has had. Available online at http://www.amref.org/silo/files/child-participation-in-awareness-raising-through-theatre.pdf (accessed October 17, 2010).
2. InterACT!—Ghana, Malawi. This is a Theatre for a Change programme in Ghana and Malawi that works to promote the rights of individuals, groups, and communities to make decisions and influence policies that affect their sexual and reproductive health. Available online at http://www.tfacafrica.com/ (accessed October 17, 2010).

3. Tubiyage—Burundi. The Tubiyage project works to encourage national reconciliation and contribute to social change in Burundi. It does this by raising awareness and educating the population about forgiveness and reconciliation, human rights, democracy, and good governance, all using interactive theatre, which includes theatre of the oppressed and playback theatre techniques. Available online at http://www.comminit.com/en/node/123555/304 (accessed October 17, 2010).

REFERENCES

1. Denning, S. 2004. "Where to Use Storytelling—Practical Uses of Ancient Art—Business Uses of Storytelling." Available online at www.stevendenning.com (accessed October 17, 2010).
2. Prusak, L. "Storytelling in Organisations: The Attributes of a Good Story." *Storytelling: Passport to the 21st Century*. Available online at www.creatingthe21stcentury.org (accessed October 17, 2010).
3. Canadian International Development Agency (CIDA). 2003. *Knowledge Sharing: Methods, Meetings and Tools*. Ottawa, Canada: CIDA.

SECTION

V

The Toolbox

Examples, Templates, and Guides

10

Strategy Checklist

COMMUNICATION STRATEGY TEMPLATE

As highlighted in chapter 6, the following enumerates the essential elements of communication organizations must address:

1. **Review:** How have you been communicating in the past?
2. **Objectives:** What do you want communication to achieve? Are the objectives SMART?
3. **Audience:** Who is the audience? What information (and inspiration) do they need to act on your work?
4. **Message:** What is the message? Do you have one message for multiple audiences or multiple messages for one or more audiences?
5. **Basket:** What kinds of communication "products" will best capture the messages?
6. **Channels:** How will you promote and deliver the products?
7. **Resources:** What is the available budget? Will this change in the future? What communication hardware and skills do you have?
8. **Timing:** What is your timeline? Would a staged strategy be most appropriate? What special events or opportunities might arise? Does the work of like-minded organizations present ideas and opportunities?

9. **Brand:** Is all your communication "on brand?" How can you ensure that we are broadcasting the right message—consistently?
10. **Feedback:** Did your communication influence your audiences? How can you measure your performance and identify cause-effect clues between methods and results?

Examples of a Communication Strategy

Best practice examples not only act as mentors; they can be copied.

Resources

1. The International Monetary Fund. 2007. "The IMF's Communication Strategy." Available online at https://www.imf.org/external/np/pp/2007/eng/052907.pdf (accessed October 14, 2010). This example shows how communication can help an organization achieve its core goals.
2. The Medical Research Council. 2007 (update). "Communication Strategy 2005–2010." Available online at http://www.mrc.co.za/about/commstrat2007.pdf (accessed October 14, 2010). MRC lays out its strategy and imperatives. It understands its niche and audiences well.
3. Africa Drive Programme. 2006. "Communication Strategy and Plan." Available online at http://www.adp.org.za/Trust_Meeting_Documents/ADP_Trust_Meeting_07_09_06/Documents/ADP_ComStrat_V0_1.doc (accessed October 14, 2010). This document has a breakdown of the communication requirements and several tables that demonstrate how to develop and pitch key messages.

11

The Two-pager: Writing a Policy Brief

This prominent KT tool boils down the findings and argument into brief, compelling, and easily understood points. It does not tell the audience everything they need to know—just enough to ensure they will want to know more. It is a teaser, an appetizer. Crafted in the right, audience-informed language, the two-pager will leave its readers wanting more.

This section focuses on practical tips and tools for writing a policy brief, a document designed for an audience that has some control over how research evidence might ultimately be converted into policy. Every audience has its own story and language needs, its own reading and absorption abilities. The details the media want are different from those a decision-maker may need, which are different still from those another researcher may require. The trick is in identifying the audience, assessing its needs and preferences, and tailoring the message accordingly.

WRITING A POLICY BRIEF

A policy brief is a message from researchers to policy makers, delivered with "brevity and clarity." The structure is to frame a potential and/or problem, show possible remedies in context, and make specific recommendations (sometimes with associated costs of each). The first section outlines the problem. The last section has the policies. And the middle section bridges the two, with persuasion in two pages. (There can be versions in 1:3:25 page formats as well.)

The style is plain (no frills) and professional—clear presentation of facts in a logical sequence. Adjectives, especially, will raise suspicion of emotion, bias, and salesmanship so they should be used sparingly or not at all. Whenever one appears in a draft script, if it is essential, consider downgrading it, and if it is not essential, then delete it.

BOX 11.1
Types of Two-pagers

The target audience defines different types of two-pagers:

Press Releases – stories in simple language highlighting the significance of the research and the corresponding need for action. Like newspaper articles, they can involve direct, quoted interviews with researchers. These can also be used for other promotional purposes—a webpage, for instance. See Chapter Seven for more.

Briefing Notes – more in depth and scientific examination of the issue, typically for an audience that already understands the science. Like an extended abstract.

Policy Briefs – outlines in simple terms the problem, the potential remedies, and a discussion of how to bridge the two.

To envision the *process*, imagine researchers are asked by the Ministry of Health for a simple document to help the Minister and others understand the science (in context) around male circumcision (MC) as an HIV-prevention intervention, particularly given the immense amount of attention to the issue as published in *The Lancet*. The process starts by reviewing recent evidence, which in this case shows through several authoritative scientific studies (random-controlled trials) that circumcision can be a very effective HIV-prevention intervention. There are no studies with contrary findings, but there is much that remains unknown. How might governments operationalize MC as a policy? How does it fit into existing HIV-prevention strategies? Should governments make the procedure free?

Or subsidize it? Should they mandate it? And if so, how might certain segments of the population react?

Problems* ←——— *Possibilities* ———→ *Policies

This is the niche for a policy brief. There is a *problem*—should male circumcision be implemented as an HIV reduction tool, and, if so, how? There are *possibilities*—all kinds of debate on how MC might be operationalized. And there are *policies*—with several starkly different choices available.

Though the following policy brief is on an issue (MC), *The Lancet* article will be the source of the content in this example. However, as illustrated by the Burkina Faso example in Chapter Seven, a strong policy brief will be informed by multiple research results or a synthesis.

The audience's tone and language needs are already known. S/he needs a summary of both the science *and* the context. The brief must not only deliver the salient scientific facts in a non-academic form, but also explain their implications. Clearly the brief will need to do more than simply translate scientific findings/papers into "plain-speak."

The brief needs to make the evidence *understandable*, explain why the evidence is *significant*, and setout evidence-informed policy *options*. As you break down the argument into its essential components, it helps to devise statements that will be the "hooks" for an introductory paragraph. If these are clear, then the story—with a little "filler" here and there—almost writes itself.

Introduction

1. The evidence can be made succinct and compelling by reducing it to a single sentence, i.e., *male circumcision leads to a (dramatic) drop in HIV infection in men, and this has (strong) implications for policy and implementation.* Everything that follows is driven by that statement, and what the audience needs to know about it.

2. How sure is the science? The brief needs to cover this immediately, so that the fact around which everything else revolves is securely anchored. For example: *Authoritative scientific research in South Africa, Kenya, and Uganda indicates a reduction of at least 50 percent.*
3. What are the implications? If decision-makers can be convinced that action is cost-effective, or will even save government money, then these action options draw a much greater chance of being implemented. For example: *Male circumcision (MC) could become a powerful tool in the fight against HIV, producing a greater effect by involving lower cost than other strategies.*

Discussion

If the first part of the brief is the evidence, and the third part is the policy, then in the discussion the audience must be shown how to connect the first with the third.

1. In a two-pager, that does not mean providing answers to all the problems; it means guiding the audience to the right questions. *While the evidence is indisputable, there are a number of issues that need to be taken into account to optimize the policy imperative.*
2. A three-point approach could group the issues into three broad subjects: Impact on Health Systems; Cultural Responses; and Safety and Education. *Implementing male circumcision will have a number of effects on the health system, challenge some cultural practices, and require safety measures and public-awareness campaigns.*

What will those effects/challenges/measures be, and why? The extent to which these need to be amplified is a case-by-case value and space judgment, based on the level of audience need/understanding and the context.

1. **Health system:** The brief needs to recognize that any intervention occurs within a broader system, and raise the possibility that increased attention to one intervention may negatively affect other preventative or curative strategies—as concerns, for instance, HIV/AIDS, antenatal care, malaria control, or nutrition, as well as introduce financial and human resources uncertainties. *Any new intervention will affect the human and financial resources of health systems and raise questions of cost such as who pays, who will deliver the intervention (public or private, what level of training and equipment, etc.), and the degree of resource priority. The probable cost of MC is $10 per person. The operation and post-care is simpler for children, more complex for adults.*
2. **Culture:** Context mapping may well identify other research or knowledge that might inform understanding. Is there, for instance, research examining the socio-cultural incidence and impact of male circumcision? This may have been conducted by an anthropologist or sociologist, and have nothing to do with HIV but yet be entirely relevant to the inquiry. MC in general carries significant stigma, both positive and negative, and any successful policy must take this into account. In parts of East Africa, MC can be a "rite of passage" among certain cultures, and thus any policy that affects this tradition will certainly provoke a strong response that must be considered at the policy level. If, for instance, the government were to mandate MC as a "clinical practice," then it would need to have a plan for addressing affected communities. *Male circumcision carries major religious, social, and cultural meanings for large segments of the population. Further research is needed to quantify and map these factors.*
3. **Safety and education:** While circumcision does provide certain medical benefits, it is not without risks. For instance, if freshly circumcised men engage in sexual behaviour, their risks of acquiring HIV soar. Similarly, undergoing

circumcision does not make one "immune" to the disease and thus it must be situated within the broader context of HIV-prevention strategies. *Any surgical procedure is not without risks, so policy must determine standards; MC does not offer immunity so there must also be public education and continuation of other strategies.*

Within the first page, the Minister has been reassured of the certainty of the facts, advised that the potential is great, and alerted to what the details and difficulties might be. Of course there is a vast amount more to know in all these respects; the policy brief question is not whether every point has been covered, but whether enough has been said—as a first attempt—to pre-empt fundamental mistakes, capture interest, and engage on-going consultation.

Policy Options (Recommendations Optional)

What is the next step? The policy brief answers with options (possibilities) that logically flow from the first page, and may take the opportunity to advocate.

1. *Public pressure could be intense, for the immediate introduction of free MC for all. That is what the pure science and many members of the public call for. However, in context such a measure could be very costly, overstretch resources, and trigger opposition groups.* An extreme option has been offered, the evidence and public interest has been recognized, the importance of context has been stressed, and reasons not to take such action have been given as a neutral observation.
2. The predictable (and hoped-for) rejection of such action becomes the Minister's own decision. *An alternative measure, which would be immediate and inexpensive, could/would be to form a multi-stakeholder task force to discuss and map the context of MC both culturally and scientifically. This would be compatible with both policy and public interests.* Scope for

amplification can add guidance and independent credibility: *The Task Force could/should include community members, religious leaders, researchers, Ministry staff, and any other concerned groups. An urgent deadline is advised. Time costs would be high, but financial costs low.*

3. More importantly, hunger for a more realistic and phased approach has been created; the appeal of other options has been increased, ready for uptake. *In parallel, commission multi-disciplinary research into the socio-cultural contexts, finance options, clinical/competency standards, and potential delivery mechanisms. A comprehensive plan for its implementation is essential. Multi-disciplinary research would fill knowledge gaps and enable the most responsible decision. Time costs could be up to two years, and financial costs would depend on the study method selected.*
4. In order to ensure that the options are considered it is often possible to push the boundaries of the debate, and make the more realistic options seem less frightening. *Make male circumcision free and immediately available to all.* This is a radical suggestion made knowing full well that the government is unlikely to take such a course. The pitfalls to such an approach are numerous, given that the context is largely unknown, the financial implications would be enormous, and capacities of the health system would likely be severely strained.

Finally, a consolidated recommendation (*in context*!): *With high public interest in MC-HIV results, but a clear need for thorough planning, a combination of the task force and multi-disciplinary research will enable government to respond immediately while assembling robust evidence on which to base further action.*

Remember, the objective is not to cram as much information as possible into two pages. It is to express, elegantly and concisely, what the problem is, what the considerations are, and what the policy options might be. The two-pager is an appetizer—you should always have more information on hand.

Keep the choice of font simple and conventional, so as not to jar the audience with something unexpected or aesthetically suspect. Suggested fonts include Garamond, Times New Roman, Optima, Century, Arial, and Helvetica.

THE COMPLETED POLICY BRIEF

The complete brief, with sub-headings to punctuate the narrative and reflect the logic, a brief heading to reveal the core issue, and a footnote on contact and further information, thus reads:

BOX 11.2
The Completed Policy Brief

Male Circumcision and HIV Resistance;
What are the Policy Issues and Options?

Male circumcision leads to a (dramatic) drop in HIV infection in men, and this has (strong) implications for policy and implementation. Authoritative scientific research in South Africa, Kenya, and Uganda indicates a reduction of at least 50 percent. Male circumcision (MC) could become a powerful tool in the fight against HIV with greater effect and lower cost than other strategies.

While the evidence is indisputable, there are a number of issues that need to be taken into account to optimize the policy imperative. Implementing male circumcision affects the health system, challenge some cultural practices, and require safety measures and public-awareness campaigns.

Any new intervention will affect the human and financial resources of health systems and raise questions of cost such as who pays, who will deliver the intervention (public or private, what level of training and equipment, etc.), and the degree of resource priority. The probable cost of MC is $10 per person. The operation and post-care is simpler for children, more complex for adults.

Male circumcision carries major religious, social, and cultural meanings for large segments of the population. Further research is needed to quantify and map these factors—in the context of a policy which might universally recommend MC as a medical intervention, perhaps with clinical standards as opposed to traditional practices.

(Box 11.2 contd.)

(Box 11.2 contd.)

Any surgical procedure is not without risks, so policy must determine standards; MC does not offer immunity so there must also be public education and continuation of other interventions.

Policy Options

Public pressure could be intense for the immediate introduction of a policy that dictates free MC for all. That is what the pure science and many members of the public call for. However, in context such a measure could be very costly, overstretch resources, and trigger opposition groups.

An alternative measure, which would be immediate and inexpensive, would be to form a multi-stakeholder task force to discuss and map the context of MC both culturally and scientifically. This would be compatible with both policy and public interests. The Task Force should include community members, religious leaders, researchers, Ministry staff, and any other concerned groups. An urgent deadline is advised. Time costs would be high, but financial costs low.

In parallel, commission multi-disciplinary research into the socio-cultural contexts, finance options, clinical/competency standards, and potential delivery mechanisms. A comprehensive plan for its implementation is essential. Multi-disciplinary research would fill knowledge gaps and enable the most responsible decision. Time costs could be up to two years, and financial costs would depend on the study method selected.

With such high public interest in MC-HIV results but a clear need for thorough planning, a combination of the task force and multi-disciplinary research will enable government to respond immediately while assembling robust evidence on which to base further positive action.

For more information on this, see the article at <www....> or directly contact <name> at <phone number> and <email>

SUPPORTING A POLICY BRIEF

A policy brief is an effective tool but not a stand-alone cure-all. It should be used in conjunction with any and often many other KT strategies and techniques.

As seen in the earlier Burkina Faso example, convening meetings and policy dialogues is one useful accompaniment or framework for both the creation and the discussion of a policy brief. As a policy brief is itself a synthesis, the best tend to be focused on an issue (e.g., malaria treatment) as opposed to a particular set of findings (e.g., a research project studying a new malaria treatment regime). That is not to say that a brief on a particular paper or findings has limited value—merely that policies on issues as large and contested as malaria treatment tend not to be changed by one study alone. A research team's role in KT is to contextualize the research results, work within the broader field, and then to bring the weight of that field to bear in any policy influence it might have.

As a policy brief is just one tool in the KT arsenal, it can be supported with several others. Lavis et al. suggest that a policy brief be framed within the 1:3:25 graded entry format, where:[1]

- 1 = a one-pager of clear and concise take-home messages for skimming or time-pressed decision-makers;
- 3 = a three-pager executive summary (such as a policy brief) with more details and resources for interested decision-makers and practitioners; and
- 25 = a 25-pager scientific paper or synthesis for administrators or implementers.

Some key advantages to the 1:3:25 approach are:

- The shorter formats increase the chances of being read. They also build capacity among researchers to express themselves with brevity.
- The multiple formats respect the different story and language needs of the different audiences. A one-size-fits-all approach may not adequately address an audience's needs.
- Placing take-home messages up front respects how decision-makers tend to read research reports—reading the abstract first and the conclusions second.

The following guidelines on developing an MC Policy Brief were authored by Dr John Lavis and piloted at a June 2007 workshop at the REACH-Policy headquarters in Arusha, Tanzania. Research groups from Uganda, Kenya, and Tanzania worked for a week on developing strategies for writing a policy brief on MC, guided by these considerations. Research Matters acted as a co-facilitator at this workshop; an earlier draft of the Toolkit chapter on "The Two-pager: Writing a Policy Brief" was given to all participants.

Guidelines for Country Groups[2]

1. **Possible Working Title:** "Male circumcision: whether and how to support its inclusion as part of a comprehensive HIV prevention strategy."
2. **Authors:** List the proposed authors and their affiliations.
3. **Policy Issues:** The discussion highlights the range of different issues that may or may not be applicable to specific East African contexts. Groups could:
4. **State the focus of the policy brief:** Governance, financial or delivery arrangements or to program and service coverage, provision or reimbursement:
   - *Service coverage, provision or reimbursement:* Should MC be included as part of a comprehensive HIV prevention strategy and, if so, to which groups?
   - *Delivery arrangements:* Who should provide the service, when, and how?
   - *Financial arrangements:* Who should pay for the service, and how?

Describe *how the policy issue has been framed* in different ways in East African health systems (and, if instructive, in other health systems):

- MC should be widely offered as an HIV-prevention strategy (i.e., a widely implemented "vertical" program).
- MC should be included as part of a country's comprehensive HIV prevention strategy (i.e., a widely implemented "horizontal" program).

- MC should be supported as part of a country's comprehensive HIV prevention strategy, with the initial focus being on ethno-cultural groups with high rates of HIV infection, low rates of male circumcision, and high or potentially high rates of acceptability (i.e., a targeted "horizontal" program that supports both traditional male circumcision and "medical" circumcision that is delivered and financed in part as a government program).

Describe the *magnitude of the problems or challenges* linked to the policy issue within East Africa health systems (e.g., demographic data, healthcare utilization data, expenditure data), how the problems or challenges have changed over time, and how the problems or challenges have affected particular groups or jurisdictions:

- Prevalence of HIV infection by ethno-cultural groups.
- Benefits (to both men and women and for both HIV infection and other sexual and reproductive health outcomes) and harms (to both men and women and for both complications and behavioural responses) of male circumcision (as identified by three randomized trials and the meta-analysis of these trials, as well as by a synthesis of observational studies, the latter of which can help in explaining how and why the intervention is thought to work).
- Benefits and harms of alternative ways of "delivering" male circumcision (i.e., who should provide it, to what age group, and using what procedure and safety precautions).
- Benefits and harms of alternative ways of "financing" male circumcision (as identified by Lagarde's synthesis).
- Rates of male circumcision by group (and within group by age and by medical versus traditional circumcision, and within medical circumcision by delivery and financial arrangements), as well as before and after media coverage of trial results.
- Rates of acceptability of male circumcision by group and profile of factors that increase or decrease acceptability (as identified by Westercamp's synthesis).

- Profile of ethno-cultural perspectives on male circumcision.
- Profile of human resources (and related training) and financing capacity by group.
- Benefits and harms of alternative ways of bringing about change, including the design of public-awareness campaigns and provider-focused behaviour change strategies.

Describe how the policy issue has been framed for the purposes of the policy brief: *MC should be supported as part of a country's comprehensive HIV prevention strategy, with the initial focus being on ethno-cultural groups with high rates of HIV infection, low rates of male circumcision, and high or potentially high rates of acceptability (i.e., a targeted horizontal programme).*

Resources

1. The SURE guides provide guidelines and resources for preparing and using policy briefs http://www.evipnet.org/local/SURE%20Website/guides.htm
2. Mills, E., C. Cooper, A. Anema and G. Guyatt. "Male Circumcision for Prevention of Heterosexually Acquired HIV Infection: A Meta-analysis." (Manuscript under review).
3. Siegfried, N., M. Muller, J. Deeks, J. Volmink, M. Egger, N. Low, S. Walker and P. Williamson. 2005. "HIV and Male Crcumcision—A Systematic Review with Assessment of the Quality of Studies." *The Lancet Infectious Diseases*. 5(3): 165–173. [Note that the full Cochrane review is also available.]
4. Westercamp, N. and C. Bailey. "Acceptability of Male Circumcision for Prevention of HIV/AIDS in sub-Saharan Africa: A Review." *AIDS Behav* published online 20 October 2006. Synthesis of the effects of financing mechanisms.
5. Lagarde, M. and N. Palmer. 2006. "Evidence From Systematic Reviews to Inform Decision Making Regarding Financing Mechanisms that Improve Access to Health Services for Poor People." Alliance for Health Policy and Systems Research 2006. Synthesis of the effects of ways to bring about change at the level of the general public and at the level of healthcare providers.
6. Auvert, B., D. Taljaard, E. Lagarde, J. Sobngwi-Tambekou, R. Sitta and A. Puren. 2005. "Randomized, Controlled Intervention Trial of Male Circumcision for Reduction of HIV Infection Risk: The ANRS 1265 trial," *PLoS Med* 2005. 2 (11): 1–11.
7. Bailey, R.C., S. Moses, C.B. Parker K. Agot, I. Maclean, J.N. Krieger, C.F. Williams, R.T. Campbell and J.O. Ndinya-Achola. "Male Circumcision for

HIV Prevention in Young Men in Kisumu, Kenya: A Randomised Controlled Trial," *The Lancet* 2007. 369(9562): 643–56.

8. Gray, R.H., G. Kigozi, D. Serwadda, F. Makumbi, S. Watya, F. Nalugoda, N. Kiwanuka, L.H. Moulton, M.A. Chaudhary, M.Z. Chen, N.K. Sewankambo, F. Wabwire-Mangen, M.C. Bacon, C.F. Williams, P. Opendi, S.J. Reynolds, O. Laeyendecker T.C. Quinn and M.J. Wawer. 2007. "Male Circumcision for HIV Prevention in Men in Rakai, Uganda: A Randomised Trial," *The Lancet* 2007. 369 (9562): 657–66.

LOCAL APPLICABILITY

Any research findings must be assessed for local applicability—any important differences between where the research was done, and where it will be used in policy making. Some examples to illustrate this point are:

- **Differences in governance:** Research on the effectiveness of bulk purchasing arrangements in lowering prices for prescription of drugs may have been done in countries with no political concentration in the ownership of pharmacies, whereas in some countries policy-makers may have a monopoly in pharmacy ownership.
- **Differences in constraints and practical realities:** Research on the effectiveness of a team-based approach to maternity care in reducing both maternal and child morbidity may have been done in countries with midwives and traditional birth attendants, whereas many policymakers may work in countries with neither type of health provider.
- **Differences in baseline conditions:** Research on the effectiveness of promoting HIV testing among pregnant women may have been done in countries where less than 10 percent of pregnant women were offered HIV testing, whereas many policymakers may work in countries where 85 percent or more of pregnant women are offered HIV testing.

- **Differences in perspectives and political challenges:** Research on the effectiveness (and safety) of Nurse Practitioners in providing routine medical care for children may have been done in countries with shortages of physicians and weak medical associations, whereas many policymakers may work in countries with a surplus of physicians and a very strong and vocal medical association.

ASSESSMENTS OF EQUITY

Disadvantages should be considered in relation to each of the following potentially relevant dimensions: Place of residence, Race (ethnic origin), Occupation, Gender, Religion, Education, Socioeconomic status, and Social network and capital (PROGRESS).

KT's test questions include:

- Are there differences in the effectiveness of the policy option in disadvantaged settings?
- Are there different baseline conditions which would make a problem more or less important in disadvantaged settings?
- Are there different baseline conditions within disadvantaged settings which would affect absolute effectiveness?
- Are there important considerations in implementing a policy to ensure inequities are not increased and that they are reduced?
- Would a policy option likely reduce or increase health inequities within the country, or would it result in no change?

SCALING UP

Pilot tests of research findings are not a result—they are indicators. Without the ability to scale up, successful pilots can be meaningless. KT "context" demands assessment of obstacles to scale-up, such as complexity, cost, capacity limits, regulation, human resources, systems compatibility, sustainability, or any other factor that might prevent the expansion of a beneficial policy towards universal access.

NOTES AND REFERENCES

1. Lavis, J., H. Davies, A. Oxman, J.L. Denis, K. Golden-Biddle and E. Ferlie. 2005. "Towards Systematic Reviews that Inform Health Care Management and Policy-making," *Journal of Health Services Research & Policy*. 10(1).
2. These guidelines have been reproduced here with the permission of Dr John Lavis.

12

The Conference 2.0

MAKING MOST OF CONFERENCES

ORAL PRESENTATIONS

Some golden rules for speech-making are: to rehearse thoroughly, preferably with a mock audience, to be completely familiar with the speech material, and to comply with time limits.

Rehearse

Once the 20-minute (maximum) "three-message speech" is ready; it is highly advisable to rehearse:

- **Video-tape yourself:** This helps judge pace, mannerisms, speech patterns, and appearance.
- **Pay attention to timing:** There should be no short-cuts during rehearsal; a 20-minute speech should take 20 minutes to rehearse. Timing is essential in the three-message speech to ensure that each message receives proper and balanced treatment.
- **Enlist an audience:** A "mock" audience can provide feedback on speaking style, and whether the ideas are clear.
- **Use real conditions:** If possible, rehearse the speech at the very podium in the room where the speech will be delivered. This

allows familiarization with the available technology, acoustics, sight-lines, and so on.

- **Get to know the presentation:** In rehearsing, catch any problems with visual aids (not loading properly, slides in the wrong order, spelling mistakes, etc.).

FIGURE 12.1
Pillow Talk

Source: www.phdcomics.com

The Big Moment

Some tips for the (frightful moment of) actual delivery:

- Unless the session chair offers an extensive introduction, it is always a good idea to introduce oneself properly, giving the relevant aspects of identity.
- Never quit, never get desperate or angry or rattled. Simply apologize (e.g., for a technical glitch) and continue.
- Start and end strong.
- "The right word may be effective, but no word was ever as effective as a rightly timed pause" (Samuel Clemens a.k.a. Mark Twain).[1]
- Stand up.
- Vary the pitch and tone of your voice. Enunciate.
- Face the audience: make eye contact.
- Do not read from a paper.

- Do not read the visual aids.
- Do "read" the audience, and respond to it—give it what it wants.
- Respect time limits.
- Add some flair: "Your audience wants to be wowed, not put to sleep."[2] Try for an unforgettable moment.

BOX 12.1
Avoiding Distractions

Talking clearly means not distracting your audience. Do you pace? Chain yourself to a chair. Do you say 'uh' between every sentence? Get therapy. Do you touch your nose or your chin all the time? Cut off your hand. All of these things can be distracting because when you are anxious, you will do them very fast.

Source: No author attributed. Available online at www.teacherweb.com/fl/pam/aoit/HowtoPresent.pdf (accessed October 14, 2010).

Answering follow-up questions (like appearing on a television interview) is a highly sophisticated process; a key skill in its own right with many dozens of techniques. If this is not your forte, it is worth seeking training on how to take and keep control, deliver honest credibility, deflect awkward questions without appearing evasive, stop talking when a concise answer is complete, limit duration, and so on.

Almost every person who does well in such situations has been trained.

The Follow-up

Questions are an essential part of any conference presentation, so budget for a question period. If there are no questions, briefly expand upon an earlier topic. If there are difficult or downright abrasive questions, say something like:

- "I'm going to come back to that later."
- "By all means let us you and I discuss that afterwards."[3]
- "That's an interesting perspective I had not thought of—could you elaborate on that for us?"

The Technology Supporting the Presentation

Oral presentations too often become subordinate to the PowerPoint. Technology subsumes substance. Use PowerPoint to give visual support to a presentation. Photographs, charts, and graphs can illustrate the main messages with color, flair, and emotion. Websites like "Death by PowerPoint" abound (http://www.slideshare.net/thecroaker/death-by-powerpoint), relating horror stories of how technology can "kill" even the best speech.

> *If the audience has never seen a PowerPoint presentation before, they will ooh and aah at the little graphical effects. If the audience has seen one before, they will groan at your attempt to look cool.*
>
> ***Everything: How to Give a Good PowerPoint Presentation.***
> **Available online at everything2.com/index.pl?node_id=1134342**

If you have 20 minutes for your speech, plan for a maximum of two minutes on each slide, hence keeping the total to ten slides: one for the introduction of the messages, eight for the details of the messages, and another to reinforce the main messages with some action points.

The "good" slide in Figure 12.2 uses font size 9. It shows a visual that has highly relevant information, and some humour. A laughing audience is one that is listening—humor is an outstanding attention-keeping device. This slide also shows the responsible use of bullets—the three points are "talking points" that the speaker can expand into greater detail. The slide does not tell the story: it suggests and supports one.

Other technology tips

1. Always be prepared for technology to crash or malfunction at the worst possible moment. Rehearse a contingency in case it all goes wrong.
2. Hold laser pointers steady (i.e., do not circle an object) or do not use them at all.
3. Bring backups on two or three different formats (e.g., memory card/flash disk, CD, stored on web mail, and be prepared to do the presentation without any visual aids at all).

FIGURE 12.2
Good Slide and Bad Slide

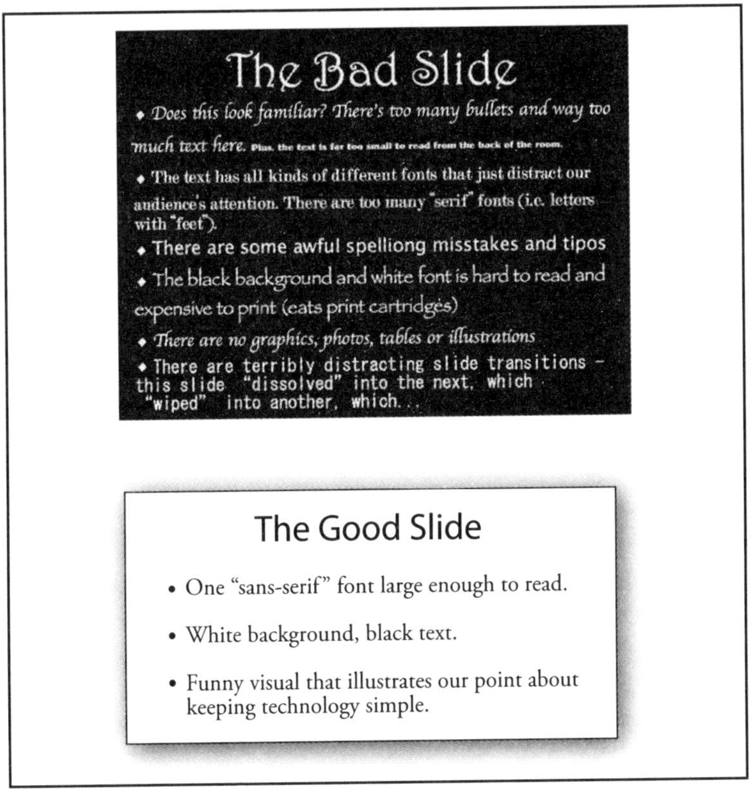
The Bad Slide
• Does this look familiar? There's too many bullets and way too much text here. Plus, the text is far too small to read from the back of the room.
• The text has all kinds of different fonts that just distract our audience's attention. There are too many "serif" fonts (i.e. letters with "feet").
• There are some awful spelliong misstakes and tipos
• The black background and white font is hard to read and expensive to print (eats print cartridges)
• There are no graphics, photos, tables or illustrations
• There are terribly distracting slide transitions – this slide "dissolved" into the next, which "wiped" into another, which...
The Good Slide
• One "sans-serif" font large enough to read.
• White background, black text.
• Funny visual that illustrates our point about keeping technology simple.

FIGURE 12.3
Preparation

SO, ARE YOU READY FOR YOUR TALK?
I THINK SO. I GOT MY LAP-TOP, MY LASER POINTER...
I GOT BACKUPS OF MY MULTIMEDIA PRESENTATION ON CD-ROM AND USB MEMORY STICK
AND I GOT A HARD COPY TRANSPARENCY VERSION JUST IN CASE...
YES, BUT ARE YOU READY FOR YOUR TALK?
I DON'T THINK SO. EVEN THE BUTTERFLIES IN MY STOMACH ARE THROWING UP...
JORGE CHAM © 2004
www.phdcomics.com

Source: www.phdcomics.com

4. On the presenting computer, make sure that all auto-update features (e.g., virus check, software update) are turned off. Turn off the screen saver. Turn off any instant messaging. Quit any other open programs (e.g., email, internet browser, etc.) that may interrupt or distract you.
5. Keep any illustrations simple and minimize PowerPoint's built-in animation features.
6. Less is more. "Simplicity is the best aesthetic."[4]

POSTER PRESENTATIONS

The Structure of a Poster

The structure of the poster will depend on the instructions that came with the acceptance letter from the conference organizers. This will determine the amount of space available. In order to ensure it looks professional, there will likely be a cost associated with producing the poster. This will depend on whether there is in-house capacity and skill to design it, or whether outsourcing will be required. Finally, transportation of the poster in a protective file or tube needs to be considered.

The Design

- **Fonts:** Keep them simple and large enough (18–24 point) to be read at a distance.
- **White space:** Not every space needs to be covered in order to ensure that readers are able to follow the logic.
- **Graphics:** Self-explanatory photos, tables, and other graphics are preferable to tabular material (e.g., pie charts rather than spreadsheets).
- **Text:** Carter and Nilsson succinctly advise: "Start with your conclusions. Use less and larger text. Emphasize figures and illustrations."[5]

- **Extraneous material:** Anything remotely "extra" should be eliminated.
- **Reading direction:** The main focal point should be obvious (typically the top center) and the flow of the narrative should be logical and easy to flow (usually left to right and top to bottom).
- **Handouts:** The poster is an excellent opportunity to disseminate work, and if the poster-as-appetizer works, supporting material may be needed to satisfy the audience's hunger for more.

FIGURE 12.4
Poster Examples

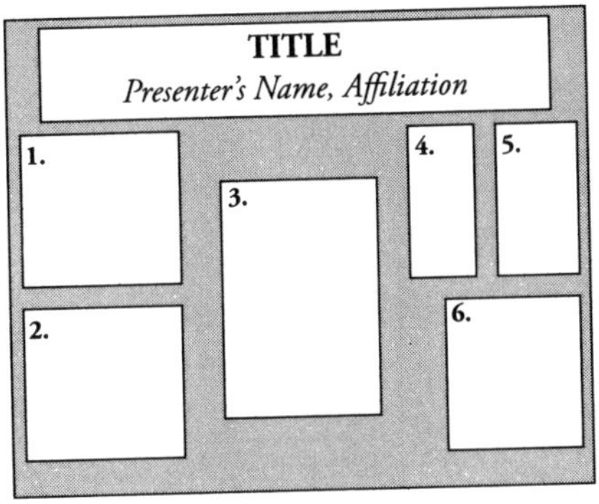

Poster #1
This poster guides the reader through its content by using numbered boxes. There is plenty of white space here, and the layout is balanced, simple and pleasing to the eye.

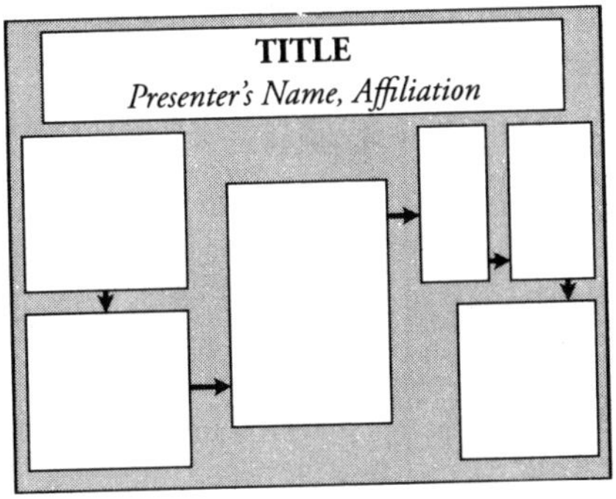

Poster #2
This poster guides the reader through its content with the use of arrows (which provide a little more excitement than numbers).

(Figure 12.4 contd.)

(Figure 12.4 contd.)

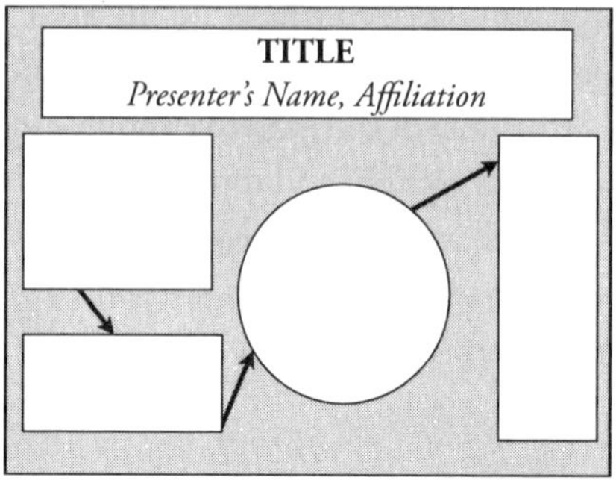

Poster #3
Key to this poster is the circle in the middle: here could be an arresting graphic or photo as the poster's centrepiece.

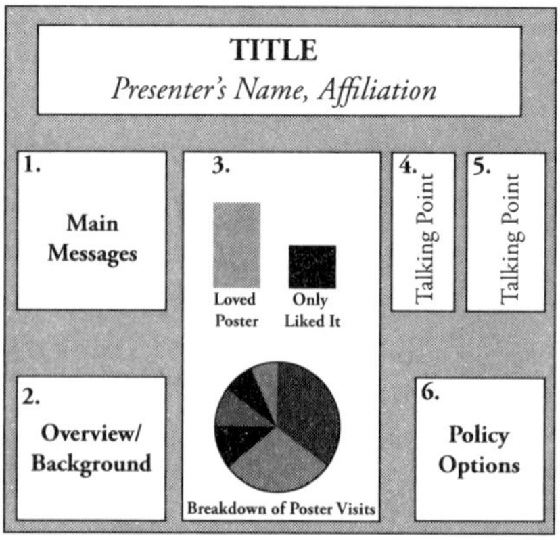

Poster #4
A slight variation on the others, this emphasizes the main messages and the policy options. Graphics in the centre add colour and simple explanations for what can be complex concepts.

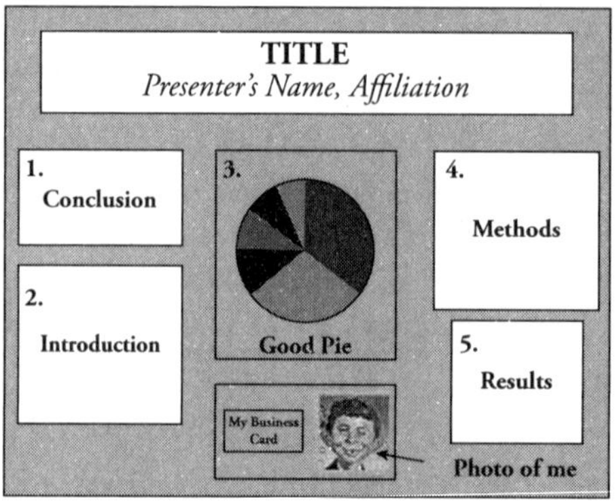

Poster #5
This poster has the key additions of a business card and a photograph of the presenter–so that, if we're not present, people can find us later in the conference to discuss our ideas further.

NOTES AND REFERENCES

1. As quoted in Dahlin, M. 2006. “Giving a Conference Talk.” Austin: University of Texas. Available online at www.cs.utexas.edu/users/dahlin/professional/goodTalk.pdf (accessed October 14, 2010).
2. Gallo, C. 2008. “Deliver a Presentation Like Steve Jobs,” *Business Week*. January 25. Available online at http://www.businessweek.com/smallbiz/content/jan2008/sb20080125_269732.htm (accessed October 14, 2010).
3. Adapted from Hayes, K.G. “Effective Research Presentations: A Guide for Graduate Students.” Oklahoma State University. Available online at www.gradcollege.okstate.edu/download/pdf/EffResePres.pdf (accessed October 14, 2010).
4. Shewchuk, J. “Giving an Academic Talk”. Available online at www.cs.berkeley.edu/~jrs/speaking.html (accessed October 14, 2010).
   Note that the *New Yorker* cartoons throughout this chapter were originally found in this article.
5. Carter, N. and K. Nilsson 1999. “Tips for a Readable Poster”. Available online at http://edu.medsci.uu.se/occmed/poster/default.htm (accessed October 14, 2010).

13

Tapping Technology

Netiquette, Browsers, and Distribution Lists

Failure to use a computer—fully and well—would be as nonsensical as failing to use the ballpoint pen or the telephone. In a world of attachments, blogs, and viral videos, it really is *compute* or *kaput*!

EMAIL

Everyone uses email. Not everyone uses it well. Observing some golden rules in "netiquette" can help:

- Keep messages short and to the point. Get a key "hook" in the first sentence to avoiding joining spam messages in the trash.
- One email, one subject. If there are lots of issues, use a numbered list.
- All conventional rules pertaining to good grammar, spelling, and punctuation apply.
- Never write in CAPITAL letters. It is like "shouting" at the reader.
- Never send a message without proofreading it first.
- Always check the "To", "Cc" and "Bcc" fields before sending, especially if it contains sensitive information.
- Answer emails promptly, even if just to acknowledge receipt.

- Never assume that any message will be kept private.
- Write something meaningful in the subject line.
- Use the "Reply to all" option sparingly.
- Use plain text. Keep it simple.
- Limit attachments to 1MB unless you know the recipient has high speed connection. Otherwise forewarn.
- Do not "attach" what could be a simple cut-and-paste.
- Do not overuse the "Priority" function.
- If an email is time-sensitive, say so in the subject line.

BOX 13.1

Who Needs to Receive Your Message?

'To': This field is for the direct audience; those from whom an action or response is expected.

'Cc' (or *Courtesy Copy*): is for indirect audience, those who need to be "in the know". Only copy "upwards"—many people are offended if correspondence to them is copied to their subordinates.

'Bcc' (or *Blind Courtesy Copy*): allows an additional list of addresses to be hidden. In parallel, an email apparently sent to you might have been sent as a 'Bcc' to others.

Resources

1. "Email Etiquette Rules for Effective Email Replies." Available online at www.emailreplies.com/ (accessed October 14, 2010).
2. I Will Follow Services website. 1997. "Email Etiquette." Available online at www.iwillfollow.com/emailetiquette.html (accessed October 14, 2010).
3. Thorton, S. 1998. "Rules and Regulations: Email Etiquette." Available online at www.lse.ac.uk/Depts/ITS/rules/email.htm (accessed October 14, 2010).
4. Kuntze, M., S. Rottmann and J. Symons. 2002. "Communications Strategies for World Bank- and IMF-Watchers: New Tools for Networking and Collaboration." Available online at http://www.brettonwoodsproject.org/strategy/Commsreport.doc (accessed October 14, 2010).

The Gilbert Email Manifesto (GEM)

Michael Gilbert's Email Manifesto[1] says email is an absolutely vital strategic tool that *must come first*. Before developing a website or podcasts or any other electronic communications strategy, understanding email and following Gilbert's three golden rules: can significantly increase your online presence and influence:

- **Rule 1:** Resources spent on email strategies are much more valuable than the same resources spent on web strategies.
- **Rule 2:** A website built around an email strategy is much more valuable than a website that is built around itself.
- **Rule 3:** Email-oriented thinking will yield better strategic thinking overall.

BOX 13.2

Failing at Email

- Not collecting email addresses;
- Buying email addresses (as spammers do);
- Investing more in websites than in email;
- Not having an email strategy at all;
- Not responding to email;
- Communicating without a human voice (genuine language is what connects people);
- Not converting people to online communication;
- No email newsletter;
- Not testing;
- More concerned with content than the relationship.

Source: Adapted from Gilbert, M. 2003. "Twelve Ways to Fail at Email" at http://news.gilbert.org/12Ways

Creating an Electronic Distribution List

Most computers and mail software now automatically record and retrieve email contacts.[2] It is worth augmenting these with other contact details as a "contacts database" or an electronic address book. It saves time, and can be useful for setting up "distribution lists" (Listservs) as a means of sending the same message to multiple recipients.[3]

BOX 13.3
Alternative Browsers

Thunderbird: Developed by Mozilla, Thunderbird offers an alternative to proprietary and potentially expensive email software such as Outlook, Eudora, or Entourage. It is a freely available and open source email program, and can be downloaded at www.mozilla.com.

Any bulk mailing must give recipients an "unsubscribe" option—up front! Emailing something like a newsletter needs a brief introductory note. The "subject" line of the email is thus very important—"URGENT" or "Hello" will likely be caught by spam or junk-mail filters.

THE INTERNET

Though there are many different ways to access the Internet, "browsers" Internet Explorer, and Mozilla Firefox are perhaps the most common.

BOX 13.4
Some Basic Definitions

Open Source: Software whose source code—the version of the software as originally written—is made available for anyone to study, inspect and use. Open source is the public sector of the computer world, and it's getting stronger by the day.

Freeware: "Software that is available at no monetary cost but for which the source code is not made freely available."[1]

Shareware: Software obtained free of charge, "accompanied by a request for payment"; "try before you buy".[2]

Public Domain: The body of knowledge "in relation to which no person or other legal entity can establish or maintain proprietary interests ... This body of information and creativity anyone may use or exploit, whether for commercial or non-commercial purposes."[3]

Sources: [1]Open Source Definition. The Linux Information Project, January 2007. Available at: http://www.linfo.org/open_source.html (accessed October 14, 2010).
[2,3]From http://www.wikipedia.org (accessed October 14, 2010).

It can take considerable time to install the programmes and become acquainted with them. Thunderbird or Open Office require above-basic computer knowledge (whereas everyone can easily—and beneficially—download and install Firefox).

- **Firefox:** The pre-eminent open source web browser, used now by over 10 percent of all web surfers. Available at: www.mozilla.com/firefox/.
- **Thunderbird:** Mozilla's open source email software. Available at: www.mozilla.com/thunderbird.
- **Open Office:** This huge open source project provides word processing, spreadsheets, and more. Available at www.openoffice.org.

BOX 13.5
Tabbed Browsing

Tabbed browsing allows us to open a link in a page we are viewing without having to close that initial page. We can keep open the "front page" of a news site, for instance, and open up all stories we want to read just behind it. This reduces clutter, improves our computer's performance, and saves valuable time.

NOTES AND REFERENCES

1. Gilbert, M. 2001. "The Gilbert Email Manifesto (GEM)." Available online at http://news.gilbert.org/features/featurereader 3608 (accessed October 14, 2010).
2. Most email programmes have a contact database option. Open source contact database software can also be downloaded. *See* http://civicrm.org/ for one example.
3. Useful information on creating electronic distribution lists is available online at www.dgroups.org; http://www.freeemailtutorials.com/mozillaThunderbird/thunderbirdAddressBook.cwd; and for Outlook at http://support.microsoft.com/kb/284292.

14

Word Processing

When it comes to word processing, most of us use this software for writing papers or taking notes. What few realize is that a word processor can also be used as an effective desktop publishing tool to create effective communications documents like brochures and newsletters.

CREATING A NEWSLETTER

There are a number of compelling reasons for any organization to have a newsletter. They highlight research findings; announce a special event, and work to keep an organization in the public eye with updated and useful information. They can be (though not always admittedly) inexpensive to make, print and disseminate, and they are a tool for distilling complex events into manageable bites.

As with any KT tool, newsletters require careful choices around design and content, and both must be tailored for a specific audience. Whatever its content or style, a newsletter must selectively inform: like an appetizer, a good newsletter must leave the reader wanting more. Here, we will keep things simple and focus on:

- determining the audience and the channels to reach them;
- deciding design, quality, and size;

- reviewing materials;
- performing some reverse engineering; and
- bringing it all together.

The Audience

Audience will dictate every element of the newsletter. Any attempt to satisfy multiple audiences (of different needs and comprehension) with a single product may well disappoint or alienate both.

The Design

If you know the audience, you know what they will want to read, and you will have an idea of how to present that content. For instance, a newsletter pitched at a highly scientific audience will use different graphics (e.g., complex charts and logs) than one aimed at community groups (e.g., using photographs).

- The logo and title (or masthead) must capture the audience's attention at a glance. Something clean, elegant, and professional that will stand out and intrigue. Logos are an essential part of any organization's identity—logos represent an organization's image, style, and quality.
- The text must be both easily legible and visually interesting. Columns, text boxes, and bullets can be used to break up slabs of text. White space (areas without any content) creates a clean, clear look, and avoids a "cramming" effect.
- Include different types of information. There may be results to highlight, future plans, and perhaps a report on a conference attended. There might be important future events to feature or a particular research project or researcher to profile and, certainly, links to further information, resources, and contact information.

- Include different types of media. Photos, graphs, charts, cartoons, text boxes, all give the eye a break from plain text.

If the audience is primarily local, and if dissemination will be chiefly electronic (email or internet), the issues of quality and size become extremely sensitive. Recipients may not be able to download large files (anything over 1MB). They will be less likely to print large or colorful files as they consume expensive ink—ideally, we want the recipients to print the newsletter. People tend to scan information on their computer screens, not reading it as intently as they do the hard-copy.

Any emailed newsletter should be around 500kb, and in .pdf format. Ideally there would be two versions of the newsletter—a high-quality one published professionally, and a low-quality, small file-size newsletter compressed for electronic dissemination.

Most, if not all, word processors include useful templates that have made these kinds of design decisions already. All we need to do is insert our content, without any layout worries. The newsletter example following this chapter was created entirely from an existing template.

MATERIAL REVIEW

Whatever the motivations behind the newsletter—whether for information or advocacy purposes—it is important to review the materials that will (i.e., text, photos, graphics) support the core messages.

As seen in this chapter's internet discussion, one can certainly cannibalize text written for other purposes. A small amount of editing can, for instance, turn an executive summary or the opening of an annual report into a punchy "article" for the newsletter. Photographs taken as part of a data collection stage might add the necessary illustration of a strong concept or finding.

REVERSE ENGINEERING

Other newsletters can be good "inspiration" and allow us to perform some reverse engineering, where we take a final product and then disassemble it step-by-step to see how all the small parts created the end result. An online search engine can return us with dozens of examples of good—and many bad—newsletters. These examples were taken from the www.research-matters.net website.

THE IMPORTANCE OF TRIAL AND ERROR

Keep trying, experimenting and testing. And keep saving our work. Use the "Save As" feature to keep multiple versions of the document (e.g., Newsletter-v1.doc, Newsletter-v2.doc, Newsletter-v3.doc) in case you are not quite sure of the changes and want to check them (and even undo them) after more experimenting.

Knowing that the content and design depend upon the audience and the available materials (including who will do it), some simple suggestions for a newsletter include:

- a brief overview of the organization;
- a brief description of a new project (and what makes it so cutting-edge);
- a brief biography of an involved researcher;
- an acknowledgement of any involved donor;
- the titles of any previous projects, including links to more information;
- a mention of any past publications;
- an advertisement for open positions or calls; and
- all contact information; from street to email to website addresses.

FIGURE 14.1
The Completed Newsletter

NATIONAL HEALTH = NATIONAL DEVELOPMENT

NH=ND

NH=ND is a research organization in M—— dedicated to studying the governance, equity and health impacts on vulnerable populations. ***Our knowledge works to change national policy.***

A Quarterly Newsletter | **Issue N° 17 —Fall 2008**

The Paper

Look for quality without ostentation. Ordinary bond can be cheap. Gloss Art perhaps too showy. 90 grams per metre (gsm) is perhaps enough to prevent unsightly "see through". More than 120 gsm can be too expensive and cumbersome.

The Title

Even a newsletter needs a name! "News" or "newsletter" can be the masthead - but every issue can have an original title, perhaps by theme.
Page 2

The Style

Our "house style," makes our work instantly recognizable and consistent. Best of all, we don't have to decide with every new newsletter which fonts, margins, and print areas to use - this is already done.
Page 2

Headlines

Be consistent with our choice of colour and font.
Page 2

Body Type

Again, let's use only one type of font throughout. That keeps things easy for us and easy on the eye of our viewers. Also, is our type justified?
Page 3

Columns

How many columns is too many? Is 6 too much?
Page 4

Changing Malaria Control?

The pages of our newsletter may contain several different items, but this newsletter has a fairly standard format: above we have "links" to the content inside, and in this section we have our most important content, our major or lead article. It is topped by a catchy headline and has several supporting photographs.

Pictures, diagrams and charts showing our programming in action are incredibly useful. They capture immediate interest and add colour to complex research processes. They help people understand what we do. From a design perspective, they also give the eye a needed "break" from straight text. Every good newsletter has plenty of "white space" - areas with no content whatsoever.

This woman declares, "They used DDT in North America and Europe to eradicate malaria. Why can't we use it here?"

Smart Flourishes

Recalling the communications strategy for NH=ND in Chapter Six of this Toolkit, NH=ND identified women's groups as a primary target for its messages. Notice how each picture addresses that core demographic? Notice as well how each picture has remarkably similar colours? We have not altered these photos in any way - save a crop and zoom in the above photo to eliminate unnecessary background - but out of our stock of hundreds of photos we chose those that reflected our demographic (women and children) and our design and colour scheme. We even extended that colour scheme to our headlines...

Fun Fact: *The structure of this newsletter was entirely created using a word processor template. All the hard work was done for us!*

Smart Flourishes Part 2

Let's never get carried away with our flourishes. **Less is more and consistency is essential.** Used skillfully, these types of flourishes can add a professional touch; used liberally, flourishes scream amateurism. Perhaps it's best to test both the content and the "look and feel" of our newsletter with a small focus group before disseminating (especially the first time).

Using knowledge to change policy 1

INTEGRATION

A newsletter is one of those communications products that every organization—large, small or shoestring—should have. It summarizes essential information and leaves audiences up-to-date and wanting more. Even more, it becomes a core communications product for dissemination using the different tools discussed in this chapter. One might:

- email the newsletter directly to chosen recipients;
- send it to the organization's lists;
- post it to the organization's website (either as a .pdf document or by cutting and pasting relevant pieces of the newsletter's text onto the various pages of our site);
- post it to the organization's blog (as today's entry and as a "permalink" that can be easily seen and accessed in days to come);
- via the organization's online social networking, alert "friends" that the newsletter is ready to read.
- use the email function in the organization's social networking website to disseminate the newsletter; and
- encourage the organization's social networking "friends" to comment on the newsletter, and to send it on to others who may want to see it.

Email, the internet, and desktop publishing are intensely connected applications. When used well, all three can bring new attention, new publicity, new relevance, and perhaps even new funding. They are tools that we can bring together as the foundation for an online communications strategy.

Beyond any doubt, the past decade has seen online possibilities mushroom—from a technical, a substantive, and an access point of view. With computers now widespread, internet connectivity steadily improving around the globe, and easy-to-use and free tools readily available, there has never been a better time to take advantage of online opportunities. Such an approach remains only one of many, but the more you understand the online world, the more you can use it to achieve your goals.

15

Monitoring and Evaluation

FREQUENTLY ASKED QUESTIONS

WHAT IS THE DIFFERENCE BETWEEN "MONITORING" AND "EVALUATION"?

Monitoring is on-going "observation," simply measuring performance against pre-set levels. It is usually carried out internally.[1]

Evaluation is a more systematic and deeper assessment typically carried out at the end of a project cycle.[2] They examine not only what happened, but also how and why it happened that way, and what might be done to improve performance.[3] As Patton[4] and others stress, the best evaluations are action-oriented.

WHAT ARE THE USUAL STEPS IN CARRYING OUT AN EVALUATION?

The seven major steps are:[5]

1. Define the purpose and parameters of the evaluation.
2. Identify key stakeholders.
3. Define the evaluation questions.
4. Select appropriate methods.

5. Collect data.
6. Analyze and interpret data.
7. Use and communicate results.

These are similar to those in research design and protocols. Note that steps 5 and 6 need to be repeated often as monitoring requirements of a project. They are covered in more detail in chapter 3's discussion of Evaluative Thinking. Step 7 is also explored in further detail in chapters 6 and 7.

Step One: Purpose and Parameters

The purpose of evaluation should always be an action—one which the evaluation makes possible. According to Chelimsky and Shadish, the benefits of evaluation can be divided into three key areas: evaluation for *accountability*; evaluation for *development*; and evaluation for *knowledge*.[6] According to Mcguire everything else is just a subcategory.[7]

- **Accountability:** To demonstrate that a project has made efficient use of its resources.[8] There may be other horizontal or vertical accountability needs beyond those of a project's funders.
- **Development:** To gather lessons learned—or an understanding of successes and failures—that will then be used for improvement, replication of success, and avoidance of mistakes.
- **Knowledge:** To enhance knowledge on a particular subject.[9] What works? What does not? And how do these lessons and experiences contribute to our knowledge on Topic X?

Step Two: Stakeholders

Successful evaluations serve their *primary users*. In many cases that will be the research team itself, while a funding agency may be a *secondary user*. The distinction is part of context mapping discussed in chapter 4 and Communication Strategies in chapter 6.

Step Three: Questions

Knowing the users' information needs determines what questions should guide the evaluation. Any question must be framed so it can be answered on the basis of empirical evidence.[10] You should be able to use measurable outcomes to arrive at your answers. For Patton, "the starting point of any evaluation should be *intended use by intended users*."[11]

Resources

1. IDRC Evaluation Unit. 2004. "Identifying the Intended User(s) of an Evaluation." *Evaluation Guidelines 7*. Ottawa: IDRC. Available at: http://www.idrc.ca/en/ev-32492-201-1-DO_TOPIC.html (accessed October 18, 2010).
2. Patton, M.Q. 2002. "Utilization-Focused Evaluation (UFE) Checklist". *Evaluation Checklist Project*. Available online at http://www.wmich.edu/evalctr/checklists (accessed October 18, 2010).

BOX 15.1
Five Key Evaluation Questions

What?	Did we do what we said we would do?
Why?	What did we learn about what worked and what did not work?
So What?	What difference did it make that we did this work?
Now what?	What could we do differently?
Then what?	How do we plan to use evaluation findings for continuous learning?

Source: Population Health Directorate. 1996. *Guide to Project Evaluation: A Participatory Approach*, Population Health Directorate, Health Canada, August. The approach is based on work done by Ron Labonte and Joan Feather of the Prairie Region Health Promotion Research Center.

Steps Four and Five: Methods and Collection

Evaluations should always be based on empirical evidence and follow a systematic procedure for gathering and analyzing data—whether it is quantitative or qualitative—to maximize credibility and reduce possible bias;[12] include the selection of: data collection methods; data collection instruments; units of analysis; sampling techniques; and timing, frequency, and cost of data collection. Methods of data collection include:

- **Performance indicators.**
- **Formal surveys.**
- **Rapid appraisal methods,** which include key informant interviews, focus groups, community group interviews, direct observations, and mini-surveys.

The ideal design for evaluation is often limited by what Bamberger calls "real world constraints."[13] These typically include time, *budget*, *human resources*, *political*, and *data hindrances*. Plans that consider limitations avoid surprises or disappointments. These constraints need to be mentioned in the design as well as in the reports.

Step Six: Analyze and Interpret Data

Raw data must become "usable, accessible summaries, and reports that add to the body of knowledge about project success and promote change in attitudes, skills and behaviour."[14] Analysis of quantitative data is often straightforward—figures that can be analyzed through averages, ranges, percentages, and proportions.[15] Today, computer programmes greatly assist. Qualitative data—perceptions, ideas, and events—are more difficult to analyze. Descriptive analysis, thematic coding and content analysis offer the solution.[16]

Step Seven: Use and Communication of Results

There are many different—and often more appropriate, audience- specific—ways to package and deliver findings other than a

BOX 15.2
Words versus Numbers

"All research ultimately has a qualitative grounding."

- Donald Campbell

"There's no such thing as qualitative data. Everything is one or zero."

- Fred Kerlinger

For years now, proponents of qualitative and quantitative data have locked horns, with each side arguing superiority.

Most distinctively, qualitative data are expressed words, while quantitative data take the form of numbers. More specifically, while quantitative data can be "measured," qualitative data can only be "described." While the former is "inductive"—no hypothesis is required before data collection is carried out—the latter is "deductive." Qualitative data provides us with rich description and takes the context or environment into account. Quantitative data can be analyzed using rigorous statistical methods that then allow results to be generalized to a larger population group.

In recent years, scholars and researchers have begun to realize that neither is unconditionally better, and that the two are not mutually exclusive. As Patton (1999) observes, "Quantitative data give us the large patterns and points to areas where we need more detailed information and understanding; qualitative in-depth thinking then help us to get additional indicators to understand the big picture and to generate surveys to look at generalizable patterns. "The value of combining both quantitative and qualitative methods is no longer in dispute. The challenge now is to find the right balance on a case-by-case basis."

Note: For more information on this topic, see:

- *The Qualitative-Quantitative Debate,* Research Methods Knowledge Base. Available at: www.socialresearchmethods.net/kb/qualdeb.php
- The Qualitative versus Quantitative Debate. Writing Guides, Generalizability & Transferability. Colorado State University. Available at: http://writing.colostate.edu/guides/research/gentrans/pop2f.cfm
- Patton, M.Q. 1999. "Utilization-Focused Evaluation in Africa." Evaluation Training lectures delivered to the Inaugural Conference of the African Evaluation Association, 13-17 September 1999, Nairobi Kenya. Available at: www.preval.org/documentos/00552.pdf

conventional evaluation report. As with any print tool, an evaluation report is only as good as the channel that can distribute it.

A typical evaluation report structure looks like this:

- **Executive summary:** No longer than three pages, summarizing the findings, conclusions, and recommendations. Constraints can be noted here or in the next section.
- **Introduction and background information:** the purpose of the evaluation, the questions it asked, and the main findings.
- **Description of the evaluated intervention:** A brief overview of the "purpose, logic, history, organization and stakeholders" of the project under study.[17]
- **Findings:** The data collected and their analysis, structured around the evaluation questions.
- **Conclusions and recommendations:** Findings placed in context and the applicability of the results to other situations. Finally, recommendations to inform policy, or to improve future projects.
- **Annexes:** Some alternative ways of communicating results include: "meetings, seminars, workshops, conferences, media presentations"[18] as well as press releases, audio-visual materials (e.g., video or radio spots), websites, policy briefs, networks, and more. A mix of strategies ensures maximum impact and uptake.

WHAT IS EVALUATION CRITERIA?

How do we know what "good" or "bad" is? How do we recognize "success"?[19] The bigger question is "exactly what is it we are evaluating? What do we want to find out? Against what criteria should we assess our project? How do we determine whether resources have been properly used?" The OECD's Development Assistance Committee has agreed upon five international criteria used to evaluate development assistance: *effectiveness*, *impact*, *relevance*, *sustainability*, and *efficiency*. For each criterion used, or combination, there should be a list of questions that reveal the extent to which the objectives are being met.

BOX 15.3
Five Evaluation Criteria

Effectiveness: The extent to which a development intervention has achieved its objectives, taking their relative importance into account.

Impact: The totality of the effects of a [project], positive and negative, intended and unintended.

Relevance: The extent to which a [project] conforms to the needs and priorities of target groups and the policies of recipient countries and donors.

Sustainability: The continuation or longevity of benefits from a [project] after the cessation of development assistance.

Efficiency: The extent to which the costs of a [project] can be justified by its results, taking alternatives into account (in other words a comparison of inputs against outputs).

Source: Molund, S. and G. Schill 2004. *Looking Back Moving Forward: Sida Evaluation Manual.* Stockholm: Sida.

SOME TYPICAL QUESTIONS[20]

Effectiveness

- To what extent have the agreed objectives been met?
- Are the achieved activities sufficient to realize agreed outputs?
- To what extent is the identified outcome the result of the intervention rather than external factors?
- What are the reasons for the achievement or non-achievement of outputs or outcomes?
- What could be done to make the intervention more effective?

Impact

- How has the intervention affected the well-being of different groups of stakeholders?
- What would have happened without the intervention?

- What are the positive and negative effects? Do the former outweigh the latter?
- What do the beneficiaries and other stakeholders perceive to be the effects of the intervention on themselves?

Relevance

- Is the intervention in line with the livelihood strategies and cultural conditions of the beneficiaries?
- Is the design of the intervention relevant to the context?
- Is the timing of the intervention relevant from the beneficiaries' point of view?
- Do the proposed interventions have potential for replication?

Sustainability

- To what extent does the positive impact justify continued investments?
- Are the stakeholders willing and able to continue activities on their own?
- Is there local ownership?
- Did local stakeholders participate in the planning and implementation of the intervention to ensure local engagement from the start?
- Is the technology used in the intervention appropriate to the prevailing economic, social, and cultural conditions?

Efficiency

- What measures have been taken during the planning and implementation phase to ensure that resources are efficiently used?
- Could the intervention have been done better, more cheaply or more quickly?
- Could an altogether different type of intervention have solved the same problem at a lower cost?

WHAT IS A PARTICIPATORY EVALUATION?

In a participatory evaluation, the entire process—from planning to implementation—involves all the project's stakeholders and the use of a facilitator.[21] Participatory evaluations "seek to be practical, useful, formative, and empowering: practical in that they respond to the needs, interests, and concerns of their primary users; useful because findings are disseminated in ways in which primary users can use them; and formative because they seek to improve programme outcomes."[22]

BOX 15.4
Characteristics of Participatory Evaluations

Focus and ownership: These evaluations are primarily oriented to the information needs of *stakeholders* (and not, for instance, a donor).

Scope: The range of participants and their roles in the process may vary. For example, some evaluations may target only programme providers or beneficiaries, while others may include the full array of stakeholders.

Participant negotiations: Participant groups meet to communicate, negotiate consensus on evaluation findings, solve problems, and make plans to improve performance.

Diversity of views: Views of all participants are sought and recognized. More powerful stakeholders allow participation of the less powerful.

Learning process: The process is a learning experience for participants.

Flexible design: Design issues are decided (as much as possible) in the participatory process. Generally, evaluation questions, data collection and analysis methods are determined by the participants, not by outside evaluators.

Empirical orientation: Good participatory evaluations are based on empirical data. Typically, rapid appraisal techniques are used to determine what happened and why.

Use of facilitators: While participants actually conduct the evaluation, one or more outside experts serve as facilitators.

Source: Adapted from USAID Center for Development Information and Evaluation. 1996. "Conducting a Participatory Evaluation," *Performance Monitoring and Evaluation TIPS,* Number 1.

WHAT IS THE DIFFERENCE BETWEEN A FORMATIVE AND A SUMMATIVE EVALUATION?

Formative (or interim) evaluations take place while activities are still underway. They can correct flaws or unintended consequences or capitalize on positive developments.[23] *Summative* evaluations occur when all activities have ended. They are carried out when it is too late to make changes. They assess whether or not initial goals have been met and to collect data about outcomes and strategies, and the activities leading to them.[24] As evaluation theorist Bob Stake explains, "When the cook tastes the soup, that's formative; When the guests taste the soup, that's summative."[25]

WHAT IS A PROCESS EVALUATION? PROGRESS EVALUATION? IMPACT EVALUATION?

A *process evaluation* focuses on the ways in which activities have been planned and carried out in addition to studying outputs and other relevant results.[26] It does not assess the effects of a project, but rather examines the process leading to those effects.[27]

A *progress evaluation* assesses the extent to which a project is meeting its goals, measured against progress benchmarks.[28]

An *impact evaluation* examines a project's total effects, including the positive and the negative, the intended and the unintended at the end of the project cycle. It can also assess long-term effects, "at the scale of societies, communities or systems."[29] As is a constant caution in many evaluations, the main challenge with measuring impact lies in the difficult task of attributing causality. How do we know that X created Y?

RESOURCES

1. DFID. 2005. *Guidance on Evaluation and Review for DFID Staff.* Evaluation Department. London: DFID.
2. Molund, S. and G. Schill G. 2004. *Looking Back Moving Forward: Sida Evaluation Manual.* Stockholm: SIDA.
3. OECD. 1991. "The DAC Principles for the Evaluation of Development Assistance."

WHAT IS BASELINE DATA?

Effectiveness and impact assessments are only possible if there are pre-determined benchmarks against which change and progress can be measured. A baseline study provides a "portrait" of a situation before the implementation of any activities or interventions.[30]

HOW CAN WE DETERMINE CAUSALITY?

Recording change is one thing. Attributing cause is another. Did the project itself cause the observed changes? Or were there other factors, none, some, or a bit of both? The difficulty lies in determining whether the changes would have taken place if the project had never existed.

To navigate these tricky questions, we can use a *counterfactual*—a hypothetical example against which we can compare those actual, real-world changes. A non-exposed control group can give an idea of how the target group might have fared without the intervention.[31] In many cases, it will not be possible to determine whether deliberative activities were *solely* responsible for changes.

WHICH EVALUATION APPROACH IS RIGHT FOR MY PROJECT?

Each project, programme, and organization needs to select the approach best suited to its own context. There is no set rule. The best choices are made by those with strong knowledge of all the options. Further, different evaluation methods can complement each other.

WHAT IS A LOGICAL FRAMEWORK APPROACH?

A Logical Framework Approach (often called a logframe) is an application of Results-Based Monitoring (RBM). Logframes assess the *causal relationship*—the links between cause and effect—between inputs, processes, outputs, outcomes, and impacts. Such frameworks are usually developed by project planners to clarify objectives and guide implementation. Evaluators use logframes to understand a project's assumptions and assess achievements against performance indicators.[32] The logframe method can be particularly useful when

TABLE 15.1
Logframe Outline

	Narrative Summary	*Indicators*	*Means of Verification (M&E)*	*Assumptions*
Goal – overall goal project contributes towards	Descriptive statements	Measurable changes: quantity, quality, timing.	Tools to determine if changes have occurred– MSC, AI, AARs, etc.	Other events/ conditions that help activities lead to outputs to purposes to goals.
Purpose – observable changes in behaviour		May relate to processes, products and impacts		
Output (1) – tangible goods and services to achieve Purpose				
Output (2)				
Output (3)				
Activities – what project does to produce outputs		Inputs – all HR, financial, technical re-sources needed to do Activities		

Source: Adapted from Hovland, I. 2007. "Making a Difference: M&E of Policy Research." London: Overseas Development Institute Working paper 281. Available online at www.odi.org.uk/rapid/Publications/Documents/WP281.pdf (accessed October 18, 2010).

carrying out a formative evaluation and/or a progress evaluation, especially in rectifying shortcomings.

Logframes are prone to linear relationships between inputs and outcomes and therefore attribute causality without taking into consideration other external factors. Despite routine and long-standing criticism, logframes remain a favoured M&E approach among many international funders.[33]

A logframe approach should involve: a problem analysis; an objectives tree; an objectives hierarchy; a stakeholder analysis; and a preferred strategy that includes all activities and outputs. Once these steps have been taken, project designers can proceed to the Logframe Matrix, which is essentially a tabular summary of the preceding steps, and shows what the project intends to do, what its key assumptions are, and a plan for conducting M&E.[34]

Resources

1. BOND Guidance Notes. "Beginner's Guide to a Logical Framework Analysis." Series 1. Available online at http://www.ngosupport.net/graphics/NGO/documents/english/273_BOND_Series_1.doc. (accessed October 18, 2010).
2. Hovland, I. 2007. *Making a Difference: M&E of Policy Research.* London: Overseas Development Institute Working paper 281. Available at www.odi.org.uk/rapid/Publications/Documents/WP281.pdf (accessed October 18, 2010).
3. Örtengren, K. 2003. *The Logical Framework Approach: A Summary of the Theory Behind the LFA Method.* Available online at http://www.sida.se/shared/jsp/download.jsp?f=SIDA1489en_web.pdf&a=2379 (accessed October 18, 2010).
4. Programme on Disability and HealthCare Technology. 2004. *Constructing a Logical Framework. Knowledge and Research.* Available online at http://www.kar-dht.org/logframe.html (accessed October 18, 2010).

WHAT ARE MODULAR MATRICES?

This self-assessment tool designed by Rick Davies gives at-a-glance simplicity, and sometimes reveals glaring juxtaposition, between elements that should or should not be aligned. These matrices help evaluators judge "to what extent their *outputs* (past, current or planned) contributed to their desired *impacts*; to what extent their outputs were geared towards their target *audiences*; and to what extent their outputs were aligned with *significant events* (e.g., policy events or key meetings)".[35] The project may then be redesigned accordingly.

Hovland explains: "For each output, crosses are distributed across the output row depending on where the output's *desired* impact lies. The matrix can then be compared to the project's *actual* distribution of effort across different groups of actors, in order to assess whether any resources need to be reallocated."[36]

TABLE 15.2
Example of a Modular Matrix (Outputs x Impacts)

Impacts / Outputs	Strengthen local research capacity on topic	Increase awareness about topic among policymakers and in media	Build relationships between research partners and civil society organisations	Influence change towards more propoor policy
Project launch		XXX		X
Website	X	X		X
One-on-one meetings with policymakers		XXX		XX
Public meeting series	X	X	XXX	X
Network building	XX	X	XXX	X
Research reports	XXX		X	
Policy briefs	XX	XXX	X	XX

Source: Reproduced from Hovland, I. 2007. "Making a Difference: M&E of Policy Research." London: Overseas Development Institute Working paper 281. Available online at www.odi.org.uk/rapid/Publications/Documents/WP281.pdf (accessed October 18, 2010).

Resource

1. Davies, R. 2005. "Moving from Logical to Network Frameworks: A Modular Matrix Approach to Representing and Evaluating Complex Programs." Available online at www.mande.co.uk/docs/MMA.htm (accessed October 18, 2010).

WHAT IS A RAPID OUTCOME ASSESSMENT (ROA)?

Developed by the Overseas Development Institute's Research & Policy in Development (RAPID) program, ROA draws on elements from three M&E methodologies:

- Episode studies of specific policy changes—tracking back from policy changes to identify key actors, events, and influences—assessing their relative importance.
- Case study analysis of specific research projects—tracking forward from specific research and related activities to assess their impact.
- Outcome Mapping approaches (see question 13 later)—identifying changes in behaviour of key actors and analyzing what influenced these changes.

The ROA was designed as a *learning methodology* to assess the contribution of a project's actions and research on a particular change in policy or the policy environment. The ROA cannot be used to capture economic impact of research through policy change.

Resource

1. ILRI and ODI website: "Process and Partnership for Pro-Poor Policy Change Project." Available online at http://www.pppppc.org/Project/Methodology.asp (accessed October 18, 2010).

WHAT IS OUTCOME MAPPING?

Outcome Mapping (OM) was developed by the International Development Research Center's (IDRC) Evaluation Unit as an alternative approach to evaluation. The rationale was recognition that causality and impact for any project are extremely difficult to assess. How can we isolate for x when all of x, y, and z influenced various parts of a, b, and c over a five-year period? Overwhelmingly, long-term impacts—such as improvements in the livelihoods of local populations—are *not* due to a single project, but to a number of inputs over a significant amount of time. So OM examines only one particular category of results: *outcomes*. Here, outcomes are defined as "changes in the behaviour, relationships, activities, or actions of the people, groups, and organizations with whom a programme works directly."[37]

FIGURE 15.1
Three Stages of Outcome Mapping

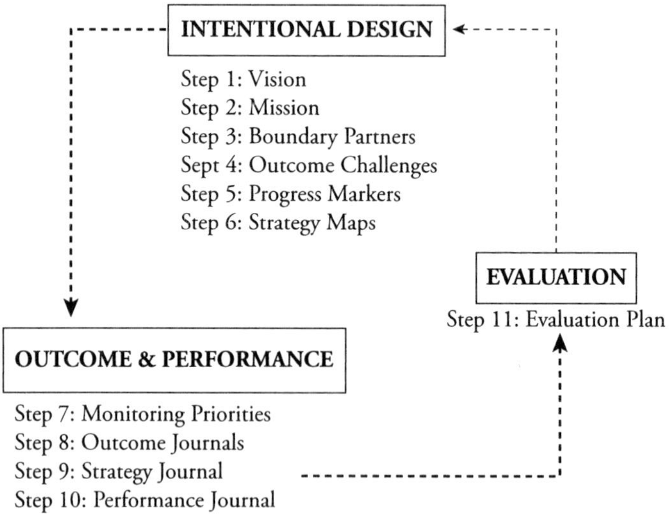

Source: Earl, S., F. Carden and T. Smutylo. 2001. "Outcome Mapping: Building Learning and Reflection into Development Programs." Ottawa: IDRC. Available online at http://www.idrc.ca/en/ev-9330-201-1-DO_TOPIC.html (accessed October 18, 2010).

OM is typically divided into three different stages. The *Intentional Design* stage is especially strong at helping projects and programmes reach consensus on the macro-level changes they would like to contribute to. This stage typically answers four questions: Why (overall, "in a perfect world" vision statement)?; How (mission, strategy maps, organizational practices)?; Who (the "boundary partners" the project/programme seeks to influence)?; and What (outcome challenges and progress markers)? For some projects, the *Intentional Design* stage represents their only significant use of OM, with other tools providing further monitoring and evaluation.

The second stage, *Outcome and Performance Monitoring* outlines the means by which a project/program will monitor its actions, especially in support of boundary partners, and the identified outcomes. The last stage, *Evaluation Planning* helps to determine evaluation priorities to better align resources with end-use.

When used in its entirety, OM is meant to be "an integrated planning, monitoring, and evaluation approach that is best used at the beginning of a programme once the main focus of the programme has been decided."[38] It is possible to use some of its elements and tools in isolation and in combination with others.

Resource

1. The Outcome Mapping Learning Community. Available online at www.outcomemapping.ca (accessed October 18, 2010). This is an excellent online resource—a virtual hub created by users of OM from around the world.

HOW CAN I BLEND OUTCOME MAPPING AND A LOGICAL FRAMEWORK APPROACH?

Note: the answer to this question has been adapted from the IDRC Evaluation Unit publication, "Draft Version: Outcome Mapping Highlights. Can OM and LFA share a space?"[39]

There is no formula for how best to create a shared "space" for both, as any M&E approach depends upon the nature and complexity of the work to be undertaken, the reporting obligations to donors, and other required uses of the monitoring and evaluation data, as well as a project's M&E resources.

The rational approach is to understand what kinds of information and uses each have, their advantages and disadvantages, and to find ways for them to add value to each other.

Bearing in mind the increased cost of using two systems, on what variables can we blend them?

BOX 15.5
Differences between LFA and OM

What questions does an LFA ask?	*What questions does OM ask?*
Goal: What is the ideal situation that will serve as our reference point for guiding the programme?	What is our ideal world? How will we ideally contribute to it?
Inputs: What ingredients do we need to create the desired changes?	Whom can we influence? What are the attitudes, activities and relationships that will best contribute to the vision?
Activities: What is the project doing with its inputs/ingredients?	What is the transformative story that will best describe the change we want?
Outputs: What are the results directly related to our activities? What are the immediate changes we can see?	How will we support that change?
Outcomes: What are the changes that flow from our outputs?	What do we need to do to remain healthy and best contribute to change?
Impact: How has the big picture been affected by our contributions?	As impact is complex and difficult to measure, how can progress markers show us what we are really contributing to?

Source: Ambrose, K. "Outcome Mapping and Logical Framework Approach: Can They Share a Space?" Available online at http://www.outcomemapping.ca/forum/files/OM-LFA_DRAFT_165.pdf (accessed October 18, 2010).

BOX 15.6
Blending Maps and Logs

Enabling participation and social learning	Using the LFA and/or the Intentional Design as a visual aid and tool for discussion, learning and consensus among stakeholders, to inspire and guide the actions of the program and partners. Building in multiple logic integration and equitable collaboration into the planning, monitoring and evaluation process.
Recognizing and systematizing complexity	Drawing on the LFA to guide stakeholder understanding about the sequence of changes to which the program expects to contribute to through its influence on the boundary partners. Focusing not just on the end development results, but also on an understanding of the processes that leads to them.
Prioritizing learning and multiple accountabilities	Planning structured and systematic learning process, which the stakeholders can use to guide their decisions and actions. Modifying the LFA based on analysis and changing circumstances. Shifting from attribution to contribution, inviting the constant reconstruction and analysis of what is taking place in the programme's sphere of influence. Offering donors an opportunity to learn more about how results were – or were not – achieved.
Improving organizational learning	Strengthening the capacity of the program team for reflection and adapting to changing conditions to maintain relevance. Readying the program to be an agent of change and subject to change.

(Box 15.6 contd.)

(Box 15.6 contd.)

Promoting evaluative thinking and utilization-focused evaluation	Advocating greater understanding by implementing organizations and boundary partners about the links between the program actions, the boundary partners' actions and development changes. Interpreting and using the data obtained on the indicators.

Source: Ambrose, K. "Outcome Mapping and Logical Framework Approach: Can They Share a Space?" Available online at http://www.outcomemapping.ca/forum/files/OM-LFA_DRAFT_165.pdf (accessed October 18, 2010).

WHERE CAN I GET MORE INFORMATION ON M&E?

There are many different authors and information sources on M&E. A select list includes:

Resources

1. Aubel, J. 1999. *Participatory Program Evaluation: A Manual for Involving Program Stakeholders in the Evaluation Process.* Catholic Relief Services. Available online at: http://www.childsurvival.com/documents/PEManual.pdf (accessed October 18, 2010).
2. Earl, S., F. Carden and T. Smutylo 2001. *Outcome Mapping: Building Learning and Reflection into Development Programs.* Available online at: http://www.idrc.ca/en/ev-9330-201-1-DO_TOPIC.html (accessed October 18, 2010).
3. Hovland, I. 2007. "Making a differenceDifference: M&E of Policy Research". *ODI Working Paper 281.* Available online at www.odi.org.uk/rapid/Publications/Documents/WP281.pdf (accessed October 18, 2010).
4. Patton, M.Q. 1999. "Utilization-Focused Evaluation in Africa". Evaluation Training lectures delivered to the Inaugural Conference of the African Evaluation Association, 13–17 September 1999, Nairobi Kenya. Available online at www.preval.org/documentos/00552.pdf (accessed October 18, 2010). Also *see* Patton, M.Q. 1997. *Utilization-Focused Evaluation.* Sage PressPublications Inc.: Thousand Oaks, CA.
5. Performance Monitoring and Evaluation: TIPS Series. 1996. USAID. Available online at: http://www.usaid.gov/pubs/usaid_eval/ (accessed October 18, 2010).

6. The Global Social Change Research Project. Free Resources for Methods in Program Evaluation and Social Research. Available online at http://gsociology.icaap.org/methods (accessed October 18, 2010). This site lists links to free online books, manuals, guides and 'how-to' information about all methods relating to evaluation, such as surveys, observations, statistics, how to present results, free software, and more.
7. W.K. Kellogg Foundation Evaluation Handbook. 1998. Available online at http://www.wkkf.org/knowledge-center/resources/2010/W-K-Kellogg-Foundation-Evaluation-Handbook.aspx (accessed January 24, 2011).

NOTES AND REFERENCES

1. Molund, S. and G. Schill. 2004. *Looking Back Moving Forward: Sida Evaluation Manual.* Stockholm: Sida.
2. Adapted from OECD/DAC. 2002. *Development Assistance Manual.* Paris.
3. USAID Center for Development Information and Evaluation. 1997. "The Role of Evaluation in USAID," *Performance Monitoring and Evaluation TIPS,* Number 11. Available online at http://pdf.usaid.gov/pdf_docs/PNABY239.pdf (accessed October 18, 2010).
4. See Patton, M.Q. 2002. "Utilization-Focused Evaluation (U-FE) Checklist." *Evaluation Checklists Project.* Available online at http://www.wmich.edu/evalctr/checklists. Also *see* Westat, J.F. 2002. *The 2002 User Friendly Handbook for Project Evaluation.* National Science Foundation.
5. Adapted from *Guide to Project Evaluation: A Participatory Approach.* 1996. Population Health Directorate, Health Canada; and Westat, The 2002 User Friendly Handbook.
6. Chelimsky, E. and W. Shadish 1997. *Evaluation for the 21st Century: A Handbook.* Thousand Oaks, CA: Sage Publications.
7. McGuire, M. 2002. *Literature Review on the Benefits, Outputs, Processes, and Knowledge Elements of Evaluation.* Canadian Evaluation Society Project in Support of Advocacy and Professional Development. Toronto: Zorzi and Associates.
8. *Guidance on Evaluation and Review for DFID Staff.* 2005. Evaluation Department. London: DFID.
9. Chelimsky and Shadish, *Evaluation for the 21st Century.*
10. USAID Center for Development Information and Evaluation, Performance Monitoring and Evaluation TIPS, Number 11.
11. Patton, "Utilization-Focused Evaluation (U-FE) Checklist."
12. Patton, "Utilization-Focused Evaluation (U-FE) Checklist."
13. Bamberger, M. J. Rugh, and L. Mabry 2006. *Real World Evaluation—Working Under Budget, Time, Data, and Political Constraints.* Sage Publications Inc.: Thousand Oaks, CA.

14. *Guide to Project Evaluation: A Participatory Approach.* 1996. Population Health Directorate, Health Canada.
15. *Guide to Project Evaluation: A Participatory Approach.* 1996. Population Health Directorate, Health Canada.
16. Westat, *The 2002 User Friendly Handbook.*
17. Molund and Schill, *Looking Back Moving Forward.*
18. Molund and Schill, *Looking Back Moving Forward.*
19. Scriven, M.\ 2007. "The Logic and Methodology of Checklists". Available online at http://www.wmich.edu/evalctr/archive_checklists/papers/logic&methodology_dec07.pdf (accessed January 24, 2011).
20. These have been adapted from *Guidance on Evaluation and Review for DFID Staff.* 2005. Evaluation Department. London: DFID.
21. USAID Center for Development Information and Evaluation. 1996. "Conducting a Participatory Evaluation," *Performance Monitoring and Evaluation TIPS,* Number 1. Available online at http://pdf.usaid.gov/pdf_docs/PNABS539.pdf (accessed January 24, 2011).
22. Bradley, J.E., M.V. Mayfield, M.P. Mehta and A. Rukonge 2002. 'Participatory Evaluation of Reproductive Health Care Quality in Developing Countries'. *Social Science & Medicine.* 55 (2): 269–282.
23. Westat, The 2002 *User Friendly Handbook.*
24. Westat, The 2002 *User Friendly Handbook.*
25. Quoted in Westat, *The 2002 User Friendly Handbook.*
26. Molund and Schill, *Looking Back Moving Forward.*
27. Westat, *The 2002 User Friendly Handbook.*
28. Westat, *The 2002 User Friendly Handbook.*
29. Molund and Schill, *Looking Back Moving Forward.*
30. Molund and Schill, *Looking Back Moving Forward.*
31. Molund and Schill, *Looking Back Moving Forward.*
32. *Guidance on Evaluation and Review for DFID Staff.* 2005. Evaluation Department. London: DFID.
33. Hovland, I. 2007. *Making a Difference: M&E of Policy Research.* London: Overseas Development Institute Working paper 281.
34. Hovland, *Making a Difference.*
35. Hovland, *Making a Difference.*
36. Hovland, *Making a Difference.*
37. Earl, S. F. Carden and T. Smutylo. 2001. *Outcome Mapping: Building Learning and Reflection into Development Programs.* Ottawa: International Development Research Center.
38. Earl et al., *Outcome Mapping: Building Learning and Reflection.*
39. For further information, *see* www.outcomemapping.ca. (accessed October 18, 2010).

Index

About the Editors

Gavin Bennett is a journalist, author, and strategic communication consultant. Born in Kenya and educated in Uganda, Kenya, South Africa, and UK, he has 40 years' experience in writing and editing, mass media, professional journals, and other print and video productions in Africa, Europe, and the Americas. He has won a number of national and global awards for his strategic advice and project implementation for multinational corporations, government parastatals, NGOs, academic institutions, and projects of his own initiative.

Nasreen Jessani is currently a part of the Knowledge Translation and Policy Task Force of WHO's Food-borne Diseases Epidemiology Reference Group. She was a Program Officer with the Governance, Equity and Health Program of Canada's International Development Research Centre (IDRC), where she spearheaded the IDRC/SDC Research Matters initiative. She has worked with Constella Futures Group International, Family Health International, the World Health Organization, the Bangladesh Rural Advancement Commission (BRAC), and the International Labour Organization. She has a background in global public health policy and management and has previously served on WHO EVIPNet's Global Steering Group.